LOSING
OUR WAY

ALSO BY BOB HERBERT

Promises Betrayed: Waking Up
from the American Dream

LOSING
OUR WAY

· · ·

An Intimate Portrait of a

TROUBLED AMERICA

Bob Herbert

DOUBLEDAY

New York · London · Toronto · Sydney · Auckland

All rights reserved. Published in the United States by Doubleday,
a division of Random House LLC, New York, and in Canada by
Random House of Canada Limited, Toronto, Penguin Random
House companies.

www.doubleday.com

Jacket design by John Fontana
Jacket photograph by Hiroshi Watanabe/Gallery Stock

Library of Congress Cataloging-in-Publication Data
Herbert, Bob, 1945–
Losing our way : an intimate portrait of a troubled America /
Bob Herbert.—First edition.
pages cm
ISBN 978-0-385-52823-8 (hardback)   ISBN 978-0-385-53589-2 (eBook)
1. United States—Social conditions—21st century.
2. United States—Economic conditions—21st century.
3. Middle class—United States.   4. United States
Politics and government—1989–   I. Title.
HN59.2.H467 2014
305.5'50973—dc23   2014022729

MANUFACTURED IN THE UNITED STATES OF AMERICA

1 3 5 7 9 10 8 6 4 2

First Edition

For my wife, Deborah
And to the memory of my parents,
Adelaide and Chester

CONTENTS

LOSING
OUR WAY

The moment came unexpectedly, which is how denial is often pierced. Guntars Lakis, an architect in Bridgeport, Connecticut, had been watching his small kids at soccer practice. They came running toward him when practice was over, sweating, giggling, and clamoring for Italian ices. That was when he realized how far he had fallen. In a lush, beautifully landscaped suburban park, on a late afternoon in summer, he felt ashamed. "They wanted an Italian ice after practice," he told me, "and I didn't have four dollars in my wallet to buy it for them. I didn't have any money at all."

The twenty-first century has not been kind to the middle class in America. The economic nightmare that descended on the Lakis family was part of an epic change in the lives of individuals and families across the country. Millions of hardworking men and women who had believed they were solidly anchored economically found themselves cast into a financial abyss, struggling with joblessness, home foreclosures, and personal bankruptcy. Some were astonished to find themselves turning to food banks and homeless shelters. The hard times would eventually spread like a blight across the country, wiping out savings, crushing home values, and upending carefully nurtured career plans. For much of the population, the very notion of economic security evaporated.

Spirits sank along with bank balances. The Great Recession and its dismal aftermath showed unmistakably that a great change had come over the country. The years that had been unkind to the middle class were positively brutal to the working class and the poor. The United States was no longer a place of widely shared prosperity and limitless optimism. It was a country that had lost its way. By 2012 the net worth of American families had fallen back to the levels of the early 1990s. Poverty was expanding, and the middle class had entered a protracted period of decline. Signs of distress were everywhere. There were not nearly enough jobs for all who wanted and needed to work. Middle-aged professionals were being forced into early, unwanted retirement. Low-wage, contingent work—without benefits and with no retirement security—was increasingly becoming the norm. Even young graduates with impressive credentials from world-class colleges and universities were finding it difficult to put together a decent standard of living. For millions of Americans, there was no work at all.

As I traveled the country doing research for this book, I couldn't help but notice that something fundamental in the very character of the United States had shifted. There was a sense of powerlessness and resignation among ordinary people that I hadn't been used to seeing. The country seemed demoralized. I remembered the United States as a far more confident and boisterous place in the days when I was growing up in suburban New Jersey in the 1950s and '60s. Kids, grown-ups, everybody had their dreams and were unabashedly flexing their muscles, ready to make them come true. The bigger the dream, the better. Each day was the dawn of new possibilities. All you needed was energy and a willingness to work hard.

That bold confidence in the future now seemed as old-fashioned as typewriters and telephone booths. There was still plenty to admire about the United States, and crowds could be heard from time to time chanting "U.S.A.! U.S.A.!" at rallies and ball games. But what I was seeing in my travels was a deeply wounded society, with a majority of respondents in poll after poll saying the U.S. was in a state of decline. The symptoms were numerous, varied, and scary. The economy seemed to work only for the very wealthy. By 2013 the richest 1 percent in America was hauling in nearly a quarter of the nation's entire annual income and owned 40 percent of its wealth. The bottom 80 percent of Americans, 250 million people, were struggling to hold on to just 7 percent of the nation's wealth. No wonder people were demoralized.

The high rollers continued to thrive despite the recession and its widespread suffering. The head of Goldman Sachs, Lloyd Blankfein, was compensated to the tune of $13.2 million in 2010 as salaries and bonuses on Wall Street roared back from the economic debacle set in motion by the recklessness of those very same Wall Street bankers and their acolytes in government. By 2013 the stock markets were setting record highs, and banks that were once thought too big to fail were growing bigger still.

The incomes of the über-rich came to mind one winter morning as I was reading a desperate letter written by a woman in her mid-fifties to Senator Bernie Sanders of Vermont. The woman and her husband were unemployed and about to lose their home to foreclosure. "I pray to God," she wrote, "that we do not have to resort to living in the car which is unimaginable in the middle of January in zero degree temperatures with no gas money to run the engine to keep warm."

For ordinary Americans, the story of the past several years has too often been about job cuts, falling wages, vanishing pensions, and diminished expectations. Birthrates plummeted in the wake of the recession as couples put off having children for financial reasons. The lowest birthrates ever recorded in the U.S. were in 2011 and 2012. By then, nearly one in every four American children was poor. For black children, it was one in three. The decline in births came as studies were showing alarming increases in mortality rates for some segments of the population. From 1990 to 2008 the life expectancy for the poorest, least well-educated white Americans fell by a stunning four years. For white women without a high school diploma, it fell by five years.

One night, after I'd moderated a program on Afghanistan at the Kennedy Presidential Library in Boston, a World War II veteran came up to me and asked plaintively, "What happened to us?" His tone and weathered face conveyed a sense of real loss. He'd known a different America, having worked as an engineer and raised a family in the Midwest in the post–World War II period when the United States showed every sign that it was really getting its act together, becoming in actual fact a more perfect union. As we talked, I thought back to that era, which in many ways was a golden time. By the mid-1960s the warm glow of success was spreading like the summer sun to most of the country. The first of the baby boomers had put aside their Davy Crockett hats and *Mickey Mouse Club* ears and were entering college. Television was moving from black and white to color. Unemployment was low, wages and profits were high, and the nation's wealth, compared to today, was distributed in a much more equitable fashion.

America was on a roll during those Eisenhower-Kennedy-Johnson years. Economic, social, and cultural doors were being flung open one after another. There was a buoyancy to the American experience that was extraordinary.

The nation was far from perfect, and I would be the last person to suggest otherwise. There was plenty of conflict, small-mindedness, and bigotry. Vietnam would prove an unmitigated disaster. Blacks and women had to mobilize to fend off treatment that was hideously and often criminally unjust. But there was also an openness to new ideas and a willingness to extend a collective hand to those who were struggling. It was a time in which the Supreme Court struck down one racist statute after another; a time that gave us Medicare and Medicaid, the Peace Corps, and the space program. The middle class, America's proudest creation, was thriving, and it was not yet a mortal sin for someone running for public office to mention the poor.

In those heady, sun-washed days, described by the writer Nelson Lichtenstein as "the high noon of American capitalism," everything embodied in the great promise of the United States—freedom, equality, opportunity, and widely shared prosperity—appeared to be coming to fruition. Doris Kearns Goodwin wrote of the mid-1960s that "steadily increasing affluence seemed an enduring and irreversible reality of American life." The Temptations of Motown, who helped power the era's soundtrack, sang of momentary setbacks in love but felt compelled to add the sociological aside "There's plenty of work and the bosses are paying."

Half a century later the plaintive question of the elderly World War II veteran hung in the air: "What happened?" How did this proud and triumphant nation, a dynamic and robust country that served as the economic and cultural model for much of the world, end up in such deep trouble, so deeply wounded? How did we reach a state of affairs in which the outlook had grown so dim? Why was there so much suffering in the United States—families crushed in the economic downturn, thousands upon thousands of GIs struggling with terrible physical and psychic wounds inflicted in the wars in Iraq and Afghanistan, and millions of children whose futures were being foreclosed by poverty and shrinking opportunities?

The most direct answer to the veteran's question was that as a society we had behaved irresponsibly, self-destructively, for decades. We lost sight of the effort and sacrifice required to build and maintain a great nation. We refused to fend off the destructive excesses of free-market zealots and casino capitalists. Greed was not only tolerated but encouraged, and that led to catastrophic imbalances in wealth, income, and political power. Over time the great American ideals of fairness and justice for all, and the great American values of thrift and civic engagement, began to lose their hold on us. We embraced shopping. We behaved as if the acquisition of material goods, from sneakers and gold chains to vast seaside estates, was the greatest good of all.

The devastating wounds that have caused Americans such pain were self-inflicted. We fought wars that should never have been fought. We allowed giant banks and predatory corporations to plunder the nation's wealth and resources without regard for the damage done to the economy, the environment, or the people. We neglected the nation's physical infrastructure to the point where bridges were collapsing, water systems were failing, and the historic city of New Orleans was submerged in a catastrophic flood that shocked not just the nation but the world.

After so much neglect and so many bad policy decisions, we ended up with a government and an economy incapable of meeting the human needs of a complex and diverse nation of more than 300 million people.

The abiding premise of this book is that things do not have to be this way. There is no reason to sit still for an intolerable status quo. Democracy is still alive, if not particularly healthy, in America. Ordinary citizens can still roll up their sleeves and—with enough effort, commitment, and willingness to sacrifice—reclaim their nation's lost promise. The dream can still be revived. Wounds can heal. A fresh start can be made. But only if citizens overcome their reluctance to engage in collective civic action on an organized and sustained basis. In other words, only if ordinary citizens choose to intervene aggressively and courageously in their own fate.

My goal in this book is to get beyond the din of clueless politicians and nonstop talking heads and show what really happened, how we got into such a deep fix, and how we can get out of it. Like a print in an old-fashioned darkroom, a clearer portrait of America will emerge. We'll see the great challenges facing the nation from the perspective of the ordinary individuals and families who are directly affected by them: a young army captain who was badly wounded in Afghanistan, a woman who was driving across the Interstate 35 bridge in Minneapolis when it collapsed into the Mississippi River, young people trying to cope with staggering amounts of student debt in the worst economic environment since the Great Depression. I've focused most intently on four specific areas: the employment crisis, which was badly underestimated and poorly understood; the need to rebuild and modernize the nation's infrastructure and the relationship of that vast project to employment; the critical task of revitalizing the public schools in a way that meets the profound educational imperatives of the twenty-first century; and the essential obligation that we have as rational and civilized beings to stop fighting pointless and profoundly debilitating wars.

There will be subtexts that weave their way through these interrelated themes, especially the poisonous effects of wealth and income inequality. And I'll trace the relevant history that brought us to the present troubled moment. But there won't be any suggestion that there are neat and tidy solutions to the crises facing America. We don't need another ten- or twelve-point plan. There are good ideas all over the place, even great ideas. But none of them have a prayer of working if the citizenry is not somehow aroused to reclaim America from the powerful moneyed interests—the "malefactors of great wealth," as Teddy Roosevelt so memorably called them—who have been the ones most responsible for driving the nation into such a wretched state of affairs. The historian Howard Zinn once told me, "If there is going to be change, real change, it will have to work its way from the bottom up, from the people themselves. That's how change happens."

All of the great movements in America—from abolition and civil rights, to the labor and women's movements and the fight for gay rights—all were led by citizens fed up with an intolerable status quo. That is how societies change. That is how America can, should, and—with the proper commitment and cooperative spirit—will change.

1 *Falling Apart*

I am not going to die today.

—MERCEDES GORDEN

Mercedes Gorden glanced out at the highway, which she could see from her third-floor office on the sprawling campus of the Best Buy corporate headquarters in Richfield, Minnesota. It was after five, rush hour, but the traffic wasn't too bad. She didn't really care. She'd recently been promoted by her company, Accenture, which did employee relations work for Best Buy, and her raise had kicked in that day.

"I wasn't in any hurry," she would later recall. "I was in a great mood. I thought about picking up a bottle of wine on my way home and maybe celebrating my raise with my fiancé. There was nothing out of the ordinary about the day."

Nothing at all. August 1, 2007. Newspapers were reporting that the Italian movie director Michelangelo Antonioni had died. Presidential candidate Barack Obama, a long shot for the Democratic nomination, was meeting in Washington with members of the 9/11 Commission. A pair of senators, Chris Dodd of Connecticut and Chuck Hagel of Nebraska, had scheduled a press conference to discuss the sorry state of the nation's infrastructure, but few reporters were interested, and the press conference was a bust.

It was around 5:30 when Mercedes collected her keys, smiled at a couple of co-workers who teased her about her promotion, and headed for the parking garage.

Mercedes was thirty-one years old, dark-haired, athletic, and known for her quick smile and contagious laugh. She had a gift for making friends easily. She loved to dance and was in love with Jake Rudh, who was trying to make it locally as a disc jockey. Marriage was a given, and the additional income from her raise would help. They hadn't set a date, but Mercedes had already purchased her wedding dress. "I was ready," she laughed.

She climbed into the black four-door Ford Escort and buckled up. As she pulled out of the campus parking lot and headed toward the highway entrance, there was no way to know that she was on her way to what would seem like a glitch in the universe.

"It was very hot," she would say afterward. "Ninety degrees. But it wasn't that humid, so when I got onto the highway I put the windows down. It felt great. I had the jazz station on and I was just cruising."

The ride home to Minneapolis at rush hour usually took twenty-five to thirty minutes. That particular stretch of Interstate 35 West was given a small taste of fame in the movie *Fargo,* when a pair of characters come around a mild curve and watch the Twin Cities skyline slide dramatically into view.

"The sun was off to my left," Mercedes said. "The traffic was moving okay for a while, but then construction work on the highway slowed it down."

Four lanes of highway had been reduced to two, and traffic slowed to ten miles per hour. Mercedes passed the Metrodome stadium on her left, an architectural eyesore that was home to the Twins and the Vikings. It looked like a giant piece of furniture that had been wrapped in a sheet by departing tenants.

For drivers heading north, there were no real visual clues that the highway was becoming a bridge that crossed the Mississippi River some eighty feet below. But Mercedes knew very well that the river with its muddy, treacherous currents was down there.

As she approached the bridge, she could see the construction crew hard at work in the intense heat as the two lanes of traffic inched past. "I'll tell you the truth," she said, "I never felt that safe on the bridge, you know, with all the construction work going on. They were always jackhammering or something, and it looked like tons of equipment were piled up on the bridge. I hated driving over that bridge."

There is an exit just before the bridge that leads to an alternate route, and Mercedes considered it. A mental roll of the dice. As she remembered, "I thought about it, but in a split second or however long it was, I just said, 'Screw it, I'm taking the bridge.' So there I was in all that traffic. I got over probably the first half just fine, maybe a little more than halfway. And then all of a sudden I saw the pavement ripple like a wave. It looked like an ocean wave almost, like a tide coming in. It was just up and down. I thought, 'What the hell is this?'

"I saw a look of panic on a construction worker in front of me. It almost seemed like he was bracing himself, trying to get his balance, because the bridge had started to sway back and forth and I could feel my car doing that."

And then, in a horrifying burst of clarity, Mercedes realized—with the traffic still moving slowly, helplessly forward—that the bridge was going down.

"I thought, 'Oh my God, you're kidding me!' I was in disbelief and instantly pissed off. Fear was not my first emotion. I'm like, *'You're fucking kidding me! This thing is coming down and I'm on it?'* I'm thinking, *'What are the freaking odds?* Impossible, right?'

"So I thought, 'Okay, if this thing's coming down, I'm going for a ride, and it's going to suck. It's going to be bad, bad, bad, and it's going to hurt. But, you know, I am not going to die today. I am not going to die.' I'm thinking all these things in a matter of seconds because the bridge was opening up in front of me. Two pieces of concrete that were connected opened up, and I could tell that I was going to go flying through that opening."

For a split second she thought she might get a reprieve.

"I was hoping I could get past the opening as the concrete was pulling apart because the car in front of me made it over, but I didn't know whether I should step on the gas or the brake or whatever. And then all of a sudden my car was plummeting through the opening.

"It was really bizarre and surreal. I just held on to my steering wheel and gripped it really tightly and just said, 'Here we go.' And, you know, I think I made my anger and my stubbornness work for me because I had decided this wasn't going to kill me, no matter how horrible it turned out.

"I plummeted I think around six or seven stories. I had this feeling of weightlessness for a moment, and even though it was a bright, sunny day, everything went dark, I think because of all the dust and debris of the bridge falling apart. On the way down, everything got dark. I don't know, I guess my eyes were closed part of the time. It was dark, and I could feel the descent. And I had no idea where I was going, where I was headed. It was just this abyss. And I just thought, 'Jesus, what's going to happen?' I just prayed that things weren't going to smash me to bits. There was so much concrete falling apart and so much steel bending, and there were cars flying everywhere."

Because she had driven more than halfway across the bridge, Mercedes's Escort came down on the far side of the water. With a tremendous crash it pitched head-on into a concrete retaining wall and landed right side up on the riverbank. A minivan immediately crashed upside down onto the trunk of the Escort.

"I didn't feel the slamming into the wall so much," Mercedes said. "What I remember feeling were my tires finally landing on the ground and I felt quite a bounce. I had no idea I had broken my back at that point because, you know, I went right into shock. I remember the minivan crashing on my trunk. A couple of more feet and it probably would have killed me."

When the I-35W bridge broke apart high above the river and came down in a stunning explosion of concrete, steel, and rock-pitted debris, it was more than a horrific real-life tragedy. It was a metaphor for the widespread deterioration of American society. The bridge collapse came two years after the submersion of New Orleans and four months before the start of the Great Recession. As the eight lanes of the forty-year-old steel truss bridge began to ripple and sway on that steamy August evening, it was almost as if something related to the solidity of the society itself was giving way. There were signs everywhere that the American center was not holding, from the wretched job market to the deplorable state of the government's finances to the increasingly prohibitive cost of a college education to the steady decline of the middle class. As I moved about the country, covering one disaster after another, I couldn't help but think that there was a great deal of denial about how bad things had become. America was hurting, and an area in which the evidence was both stark and deeply symbolic was the nation's once-gleaming but now increasingly decrepit physical plant—its roads, bridges, drinking water systems, electrical grid, ports and levees, and so on. Large portions of those vast and complex systems, some dating back to the nineteenth century, had reached the end of their useful lives. Buried in those strained systems were important answers to the major dilemmas facing the country. Neglect, underinvestment, and denial had all contributed to the increasingly dire state of the nation's physical plant, and that echoed what was going on in other important sectors of the United States.

There had always been a link between the state of the infrastructure and the social and economic health of the society. Time and again an economic boom has followed periods of sustained infrastructure improvement. It is impossible to calculate all of the benefits from (to mention just a few examples) the Erie Canal, which connected the Great Lakes to the Atlantic Ocean and helped make New York America's premier city; the rural electrification program and other capital improvements of the New Deal; the railroad and aviation systems that helped knit the nation together; the schools, colleges, and libraries that are so crucially important to the life and culture of the people; the interstate highway network launched by the Eisenhower administration; and the space program. But in recent decades, the challenge of maintaining the nation's physical plant has joined the many other challenges that the U.S. has been unable or unwilling to meet. The human toll has often been profound, as the tragedies in New Orleans and Minnesota have demonstrated. But the social and economic costs—the lost prosperity, the forfeiture of discoveries and innovations that would have come with modernization, the myriad employment and other opportunities that never materialized—have also been enormous. Those losses have damaged the nation as surely as the I-35 bridge collapse damaged the victims and their families.

Mercedes remembered being very calm as she sat in her smashed car on the bank of the river with the van still upside down on her trunk. "I was kind of debating," she said. "Am I alive? Am I not alive? When I figured out that I probably was alive, I took an inventory of my body. Was I impaled anywhere? Was I bleeding? I didn't see anything. My clothes had a little bit of debris on them. I was wearing a white blouse that day. And black slacks. I was like, 'Is that it?' There was an inner sense that there was something wrong with my legs, but I couldn't quite place it because there was no pain. Little did I know that my legs were completely mangled beneath the dashboard."

Time seemed to cease as Mercedes sat in her car. Then came the sudden thought: "I need to get the hell out of here." She began struggling to get out. She could move from the waist up but couldn't extricate herself. "I was trapped. My legs were completely pinned.

"My next concern was that there was this hose hanging above me—I assumed it was a deicer hose—and it was dripping deicer fluid on my neck. It was burning me. So I grabbed my bag and held it up to block the fluid. Then I saw little puffs of smoke coming up from the hood of my car, and I thought, 'Jesus, is this thing going to catch fire? Is my car going to explode?' So I had all these thoughts about being pinned in the car and dying in a fire.

"It was eerily quiet at that point. And I'm looking around, having no idea where I'm at."

Remnants of the wrecked bridge were hanging overhead. Mercedes had been traveling in the northbound lane. When she looked to her left, she could see what was left of the southbound lane dangling from the highway. "I could see some other vehicles that had fallen from the bridge. I remember seeing a truck, but that's about it. I knew a bunch of people must have died."

Mercedes's mind slowly cleared and she began screaming for

help. Behind her car and the flipped van on the trunk was another
vehicle, also upside down, with a family of four inside. Mercedes
couldn't turn around far enough to see it, but she could hear what
sounded like a teenage girl screaming for help for her mother, who
apparently was unconscious.

People began showing up on the riverbank, first staring in disbelief, then trying to help. Mercedes would later remember that
she didn't own a cell phone at the time. "I was still holding out,
trying to be the last person in the country to get one. But a Good
Samaritan let me use her phone. I called Jake. I told him I'd been in
a horrific accident, but he had no idea it was me because apparently
my voice was strained and really high, just very different. Once
he figured out it was me, he said, 'What are you talking about?'
Rather than explain it, I told him to turn on the TV. By that time
I could hear the helicopters above me, and I'm like, 'I know this is
already on television. There is no way it's not.' So he turned on the
TV and he sees it instantly and he's like, 'Oh my God, are you in
that? What can I do? Can I come get you?' But I said, 'No, I have
no idea where I'm at. I'm sure somebody will call you from the
hospital, if I don't myself."

The girl whose screams had echoed Mercedes's was seventeen-
year-old Brandi Coulter. She and her father, Brad, her mother,
Paula, and her eighteen-year-old sister, Brianna, had been two
vehicles behind Mercedes on the bridge. Brad was at the wheel
of the Honda minivan with Brianna next to him in the front passenger seat. Paula and Brandi were in the back. Paula was dozing.
The Coulters were planning to meet up with relatives for a family
celebration at a restaurant in Roseville. They had inched across the
midpoint of the bridge when the roadway began to shake. Brad
looked around and saw the construction workers scurrying about.
And then the bridge gave way. After a sixty- or seventy-foot free
fall, the pale gold minivan crashed upside down on the riverbank,
leaving all four members of the family dangling wrong side up,
held in place by their seat belts. Three were dazed and profoundly
disoriented. Paula was unconscious. She would later explain details
to me that had been told to her again and again in the aftermath of
the accident. There was a period of stunned silence that was broken

first by Mercedes's screams, which seemed to come out of nowhere, and then Brandi's. Frightened and in pain, Brad (who suffered from claustrophobia) and the two girls struggled to climb through shattered windows and get out of the van. Brandi was unnerved by the periodic groans that came from her mother, who was bleeding and still trapped in her seat. Brad could see that his wife was badly hurt and was afraid that trying to pull her from the vehicle would only worsen her injuries. He could barely stay upright himself. Five of his vertebrae had been fractured. He would later recall looking up and seeing a portion of the bridge that hadn't fallen hanging precariously above them. He worried that the rest of the structure would suddenly come down and crush his entire family.

The warm evening air began to carry the sound of people calling for help. Wrecked cars were scattered in the water. With Brianna weeping and Brandi nearly hysterical, Brad waited what seemed to him an interminable time until rescue workers arrived. They managed to get Paula out of the van but not before dropping her one time, which horrified everyone. Paula does not remember the accident, but she told me about a brief moment described to her by Brad and the girls. Brandi, nearly overwhelmed by the sight of her helpless mother, could not stop crying. "She was so upset," Paula said. "And apparently, even though I don't remember it, I had a brief moment of consciousness after they got me out of the van. And I said, 'Honey, it's okay. Brandi, we'll be fine. I love you. We'll be fine.' " Brandi, still sobbing, managed to calm down. The rescue workers placed Paula on a plywood plank and carried her to a tri- age center.

Thirteen people were killed in the collapse of the I-35W bridge, and nearly 150 were injured. It was remarkable, almost miraculous, that the death toll was not much higher. Dozens of cars and trucks fell from the bridge, and others were wrecked on the roadway. Some burst into flames. Truck driver Paul Eickstadt died while still at the wheel of his tractor trailer. Seventeen or eighteen construction workers who were about to begin their night shift fell into the river.

There is a tendency to recoil from a tragedy of such dimensions, to categorize it as an aberration, something so rare that there is no real reason to worry much about it happening again. Find out what went wrong and fix it, sure. Help the survivors and their families, by all means. Then move on. The problem is that disasters related to infrastructure are not rare. New Orleans was the poster child. There had been warnings for years that the city was vulnerable to a powerful hurricane, that the levees and flood walls would give way if the onslaught was fierce enough. Then came Katrina. The death toll, never precisely documented, was extraordinarily high, and untold thousands were left homeless and destitute. When the floodwaters receded, the city's Lower Ninth Ward looked as if it had been hit by a nuclear bomb. Much of that devastation and loss of life could have been avoided if the warnings about the levees had been heeded. As the historian Douglas Brinkley reminded us in *The Great Deluge*, his book about the flooding that followed Katrina, the submersion of New Orleans "was a man-made debacle, resulting from poorly designed levees and floodwalls."

Physically, the United States is not just falling apart. It's rotting, rusting, decaying. It's blowing up. An estimated ten thousand people are killed on the nation's roadways each year in accidents caused, at least in part, by infrastructure failures related to design flaws, inadequate maintenance, structural deficiencies, and aging. The near misses would make your hair stand on end. Just eight months after the collapse of the I-35 bridge, a young structural engineer in Philadelphia named Peter Kim made a stunning discovery after stopping for lunch at a neighborhood delicatessen. A heavily traveled elevated section of Interstate 95, which runs the entire length of the East Coast, was nearby. "I was with a colleague," he told me, "and we had just finished our sandwiches and were on our way back to work when I spotted the crack." Then he corrected himself. "It was more than a crack." What he had spotted through the window of his car was a terrible fracture in one of the concrete columns holding up the highway. The two men climbed from the car and walked over to the column for a closer look. As they stared, openmouthed, they could hear the cars and trucks roaring by just over their heads. Kim could not believe the extent to which the column had deteriorated. The men took photos with a cell phone and forwarded them with an urgent message to the Pennsylvania Department of Transportation. There was little time to lose. A two-mile stretch of the highway traversed by 190,000 vehicles every day was immediately closed. Crews spent the next two weeks making emergency repairs. Ed Rendell, who was governor at the time, told me that if the pillar had failed, if it had crumbled, the result would most likely have been catastrophic. "It's just hard to imagine how bad it would have been," he said.

There are endless infrastructure nightmares in America. On a quiet Thursday evening in September 2010, a natural gas pipeline exploded in a residential neighborhood of San Bruno, California, about twelve miles south of San Francisco. The blast was thunderously loud, and the ground shook, as in an earthquake. An enormous fireball, thirty to forty stories high, roared through the neighborhood. Whipped by winds coming off San Francisco Bay, the towering flames became a firestorm that spread with shocking speed, destroying well-kept suburban homes by the dozens. Trees went up in flames. Cars, trucks, and station wagons burned. Streets and sidewalks buckled and melted in the tremendous heat. Captain Charlie Barringer of the San Bruno Fire Department told the *Los Angeles Times,* "I thought a 747 had landed on us."

Eight people were killed in the fire that followed the explosion. The pipeline that erupted had been installed in the 1950s, when Dwight Eisenhower was president, and had not been properly monitored for safety. This is a chronic problem. Hundreds of natural gas pipelines have exploded in the United States over just the past few years, taking the lives of at least eighty people. Hundreds have been injured. Five months after the San Bruno disaster, a similar sudden eruption rocked a residential neighborhood in Allentown, Pennsylvania. That one occurred a few minutes before 11:00 p.m. Once again it was an old and deteriorating natural gas pipeline that blew. As one resident described it, "You just heard this big bang, then all this cracking and banging and booming, like a war was going on."

Dorothy Yanett and her husband, Bill, owned two houses in the neighborhood. Bill described what it was like to stand outside in the dark and the cold, watching the awful destruction: "We were like, 'There goes Bea's house. There goes Ed's house. There goes Don's house.' Then it was, 'Oh no! There's my house! And my other house! There's Tony's house.' They're all gone."

Bea was seventy-four-year-old Beatrice Hall, who, along with her husband, William, seventy-nine, was killed in the fire. A horrified neighbor could see Bea through a window as she was caught in the flames. Five people died, including Matthew Cruz, four months old.

On a cold morning in March 2014 an explosion on Park Avenue near 116th Street in Manhattan destroyed two five-story apartment buildings. Eight people were killed, several were badly injured, and dozens of families in the East Harlem neighborhood were left homeless. A natural gas leak, which investigators attributed to a defective pipeline that was most likely built in the nineteenth century, caused the explosion.

"Infrastructure" may be the least sexy word in the English language. But to get a sense of its profound importance, think of it as the circulatory system of American society, an infinitely complex network that weaves its way through virtually every aspect of our daily lives. Turn on the faucet and clean drinking water comes out. Flick a switch and the lights come on. Boot up your computer and high-speed broadband will take you to the Internet. The crumbling roads, structurally deficient bridges, and faulty natural gas pipelines are all part of this vital system that keeps the blood flowing and the nation's metaphorical heart beating. It moves people, power, water, energy, finances, communications, and goods of all kinds throughout the society. It cools us in the summer and warms us in the winter. It takes us to work and brings us home again. When it's in good shape, the country tends to be in good shape. But right now it's not in good shape. Nearly all aspects of this vital but aging network are breaking down to some extent. An analysis of federal data by the *New York Times* found that a significant water line bursts somewhere in the United States every two minutes. The Gerald Desmond Bridge in the Port of Long Beach, California, which is traversed by about 15 percent of all goods coming into the United States, was in such terrible shape it had to be rigged with nylon "diapers" to catch falling chunks of concrete.

America once had the finest infrastructure in the world, and that magnificent system of public works went hand in hand with a remarkably robust economy. But now that infrastructure is in sad shape, and it's no coincidence that the economy is as well.

After speaking with her fiancé, Mercedes passed the cell phone back to the Good Samaritan, whose name was Meagan O'Brien. Time was moving slowly, and Mercedes still had no idea about the extent of her injuries. All she knew was that she couldn't free herself. She began to feel groggy. Meagan opened the door on the passenger's side and climbed into the car. She took Mercedes by the hand and told her she had to stay conscious. Mercedes shuddered and groaned as she began to feel pain of a kind she had never felt before. As it increased, her fear intensified. Meagan talked and talked, trying to take Mercedes's mind off her increasing distress. She squeezed Mercedes's hand. She told jokes. She quoted poetry.

2 *Falling Apart II*

A bridge in America just shouldn't fall down.

—U.S. SENATOR AMY KLOBUCHAR

Most people viewing the ruins of the I-35 bridge had to work their way through a sense of disbelief. The idea that a major interstate highway bridge could suddenly break apart and collapse into the mighty Mississippi River seemed incomprehensible. When the bridge gave way, cars, trucks, and the people inside them hurtled toward the river like toys thrown from a window by a petulant child. Twenty-two-year-old Alicia Babatz, her tailbone broken, had to crawl through her smashed driver's side window and swim to safety after her car plunged into the water and began to sink. Fifty-year-old Vera Peck and her twenty-year-old son, Richard Chit, drowned in their car, which was crushed beneath concrete slabs and the wreckage of other cars. Brad and Paula Coulter and their teenage daughters, Brianna and Brandi, were all seriously injured when their minivan plunged seven or eight stories and landed upside down on the riverbank. Paula, forty-three, was hurt the worst. She suffered severe brain injuries that required multiple surgeries, and a shattered vertebra.

Mercedes Gorden had to fight off the thought that she would die trapped in her wrecked Escort. Her back was broken, both of her legs were shattered below the knees, and her ankles were broken. As the pain enveloped her body and she drifted along the edges of consciousness, she could do nothing but cling to the hand of the stranger beside her.

The rescue operation was enormously complex and difficult. The first people on the scene were passersby, many of whom rushed to help. Cars and trucks were on fire. Panicked motorists and construction workers were stranded on the precariously angled portions of the bridge that did not fall into the river. A school bus with fifty-two students, several adults, and the driver came to a stop at the very edge of a fractured section of the roadway. The only thing between the bus and the abyss was the parking brake. The driver, a woman whose own two children were on the bus, had a broken back. As one young passenger recounted, "We were riding over the bridge and the bridge collapsed, and we were right on the part where it went down—where it curved down."

Medical personnel receiving training at a Red Cross building nearby rushed to the scene, as did students and staffers from the University of Minnesota, which also had buildings within sprinting distance of the bridge. Some civilians plunged unhesitatingly into the river to try to rescue people trapped in vehicles. Motorists who had managed to extricate themselves from partially submerged cars and trucks were swimming for their lives.

Within five or ten minutes rescue workers began arriving from the Minneapolis Police and Fire Departments, the Hennepin County Sheriff's Office, local hospitals, and other public safety agencies. They loaded the injured by the dozens into whatever vehicles were at hand—cars, trucks, ambulances, even a flatbed truck. It took rescuers about a half hour to reach Mercedes. When it became clear that the Jaws of Life would have to be used to hack away at the car, Mercedes asked that they be gentle in pulling her from the wreck. One of the workers said they would try, but he noted that sections of the ruined bridge were still dangling high above them. Thousands of pounds of concrete and steel, not to mention additional vehicles, might come crashing down at any moment. Mercedes would have to be extricated as quickly as possible, he said, and it was bound to hurt. "It did," Mercedes told me. "It hurt like nothing I had ever felt before."

When they got her out of the car, they strapped her to a board and lifted her into a civilian's pickup truck for the bumpy, jolting ride to the Fairview University Medical Center.

Officials knew for many years that the Interstate 35W bridge was in bad shape. A long series of official reports showed that it had been poorly maintained and was steadily deteriorating. In 1990, twenty-three years after it opened, the bridge was declared structurally deficient by inspectors. That was not incentive enough for state officials to take the corrective steps necessary to restore a rating of satisfactory. As Barry B. LePatner wrote in *Too Big to Fall*, a book about the deterioration of the nation's bridge and highway infrastructure, "While accepting federal funding for ongoing repairs during the sixteen years until its collapse on August 1, 2007, the state never managed to improve the bridge's rating of poor. Despite repeated warnings from outside consultants from 2001 to 2006 that this fracture-critical bridge needed strengthening to avoid collapse if even one structural member failed, [state transportation] officials continued to treat the bridge as one that was safe for the over 160,000 vehicles that traveled across it every day."

Fracture critical is a type of bridge design that lacks redundancy—fail-safe mechanisms—if any crucial structural component of the bridge breaks down. Thus, the failure of any one of those components—the bridge's structural "members," as they are referred to by engineers—could cause the entire bridge to fall. Many fracture-critical bridges were built in the early post–World War II era. They were lighter, cheaper, and easier to design and construct. But because of their built-in potential for disaster, the federal government in the 1980s called for subsequent bridges to incorporate redundancies that would make a complete collapse much less likely.

The heightened danger of a catastrophic collapse means that fracture-critical bridges require even more careful monitoring than is usually the case. Timely maintenance and repair become that much more important. But critical work that should have been done on the I-35W bridge was postponed again and again, even as increasing traffic and structural modifications (including the addition of two lanes and a concrete median) added tremendously to the weight and other stresses on the bridge.

LePatner noted that at the time of the collapse, the Minnesota Department of Transportation had been working for eight years with teams of experts from a pair of consulting firms on what should be done to bring the bridge back into reasonably decent shape. But after detailed studies by the University of Minnesota and the consulting companies, the net result, according to LePatner, "was a tentative plan to address the serious issues presented by the consultants" at some time in the future. The state proceeded with a paving project that was merely cosmetic, LePatner said, adding, "Any action to add critical redundancy was either deferred or rejected."

Despite the bridge's poor condition and its egregious maintenance history, the National Transportation Safety Board, in its official report on the collapse, essentially let Minnesota officials off the hook. The board isolated a single factor as the probable cause of the disaster—a design flaw that led to the bridge being built with gusset plates that were too thin. The plates, large steel sheets used to connect several girders on the bridge, were a half inch thick. They should have been an inch thick. In the view of the NTSB, the collapse was caused by the following fatal combination: the undersized gusset plates, the additional weight loads that the bridge was required to carry as the years passed, and, on the day of the collapse, the added weight of nearly 600,000 pounds of sand, gravel, and equipment loaded onto the bridge by construction workers doing a repaving job. The many other problems known to have plagued the I-35W bridge were not considered by the board to be factors that contributed to its collapse.

Whatever the merits of the NTSB report with regard to the causes of the collapse, onlookers who began showing up at the scene, staring in horror, often through eyes filled with tears, tended to feel that the disaster was inexplicable. The question they asked again and again was, "How could something like this have happened?" They were not thinking in terms of government reports or schedules of maintenance and repair. They had something simpler in mind. The commonly held view was that of Amy Klobuchar, a U.S. senator from Minnesota, who said, as she stared at the terrible wreckage, "A bridge in America just shouldn't fall down." But

the sad reality is that there is nothing new about bridges collapsing
in the United States. On December 15, 1967, the same year that
the I-35 bridge opened in Minneapolis, the Silver Bridge connect-
ing Point Pleasant, West Virginia, and Kanauga, Ohio, collapsed
into the Ohio River. Forty-six people were killed. The bridge came
down during the evening rush hour at the height of the Christmas
shopping season. Survivors told harrowing stories that were virtually the same as those told by motorists who plunged from the I-35
bridge four decades later. A driver, whose truck sank to the bottom
of the Ohio River, described how he'd smashed the window of his
cab and then struggled through the icy, muddy water to the surface.
He'd been unable to save his co-worker, who, strapped in his seat,
perished.

The Mianus River Bridge on Interstate 95 in the Cos Cob section
of Greenwich, Connecticut, went down on June 28, 1983. Three
people were killed. Many more would have died if the collapse
had not occurred at 1:30 in the morning. I-95, which stretches all
the way from Florida to Maine, is one of the most heavily traveled
highways in the nation.

The Schoharie Creek Bridge on the New York State Thruway,
near the town of Amsterdam, collapsed on April 5, 1987, killing
ten people. The bridge swayed, as if in an earthquake, then broke
apart and plunged into floodwaters fed by a torrential spring rain
and melting snow. Among those killed were a mother and daughter on their way to a baby shower, a truck driver who had traveled
from Green Bay, Wisconsin, and an elderly married couple from
New Hampshire who were heading to Texas to visit relatives.

No matter how often these tragedies occur, we hear the same
explanations again and again. The collapses were caused by one or
more of the following: design flaws, bridges built on the cheap, poor
maintenance and lousy upkeep, repairs put off until another day.
The simple truth is that bridges fall down because of an unwillingness to spend the money that is necessary to build them properly
and keep them in good repair.

A tiny stress fracture that resulted from corrosion in a steel
component of the Silver Bridge was identified as the cause of the
catastrophic 1967 collapse. The Silver Bridge had been poorly

maintained, but in a finding similar to the official explanation of the I-35W disaster, investigators said it was a design flaw that enabled the stress fracture to trigger a complete collapse. It wasn't, in their view, the lousy maintenance that brought the bridge down. As LePatner wrote, "A West Virginia court found clear evidence of shoddy inspection procedures but declined to find the state (which owned the bridge) guilty of negligence."

Investigators said the Mianus River Bridge came down because of a buildup of rust, a design flaw, faulty inspections, and other problems. The rust buildup began a decade earlier when storm drains were paved over by a road crew. Instead of running off, rainwater collected at various key points on the bridge. Devastating amounts of rust and corrosion were the inevitable results. According to federal investigators, the failure of a pair of rusted pin bearings was the primary cause of the collapse.

Poor construction and lousy maintenance were the reasons given for the collapse of the Schoharie Creek Bridge. Built in 1954, the bridge was supported by four concrete piers. Two were buried in the creek bed, and inspectors said they had never been properly anchored. The dire implications of the problem were not recognized, because a poor inspection and maintenance regimen never detected the erosion of sand, gravel, and other elements of the soil that were supposed to hold the foundations of those piers in place. When one of the piers gave way as the floodwaters were roaring by, the center of the bridge caved in.

The *New York Times,* in its coverage of the Schoharie collapse, pointedly noted, "The bridge is believed to have been built with unusual speed so that it could be opened before then-Gov. Thomas E. Dewey left office."

America once led the world in its ability to plan, build, and maintain a vast nationwide network of safe and reliable bridges. But over the last several decades we've lost our edge. Today nearly a quarter of the nation's 600,000 bridges have been designated "structurally deficient" or "functionally obsolete." Public officials insist that those designations do not mean a bridge is unsafe to travel across. But common sense strongly suggests that a structurally deficient or functionally obsolete bridge is not a good thing. In its voluminous report on the I-35 bridge, which was rated "structurally deficient" way back in 1990, the NTSB said the following:

According to the FHWA [Federal Highway Administration], a status of structurally deficient does not indicate that a bridge is unsafe but only that the structure is in need of maintenance, repair, or eventual rehabilitation. If required to remain open to traffic, a structurally deficient bridge can be posted to restrict the gross weight of vehicles permitted to use it. If unsafe conditions are identified during a physical inspection, the bridge will be closed. According to FHWA data (December 2007), about 72,500, or 12 percent, of the 600,000 bridges in the National Bridge Inventory are currently rated structurally deficient. Bridges so rated were located in every state and U.S. territory, with no state having fewer than 20 and three states having more than 5,000 each.

A key point to keep in mind is that many structurally deficient bridges are not inspected as regularly and thoroughly as they are supposed to be, making it much easier for serious safety problems to develop and worsen.

Functionally obsolete bridges are those that were built to standards that are no longer adequate for today's traffic conditions. They may, for example, have lanes that are too narrow or clearances that are too low, or they may be excessively vulnerable to flooding. Such bridges are often avoided by emergency vehicles and school bus operators. Some bridges are both structurally deficient and functionally obsolete.

Taken collectively, America's bridges are at best mediocre. Thousands upon thousands are literally falling apart. One year after the I-35 collapse (and just a few miles up the road), a twelve-hundred-pound chunk of concrete from a fifty-year-old bridge broke apart and fell in large pieces into the northbound lanes of Interstate 35 East in St. Paul. Two cars were damaged but no one was hurt. A state senator, Scott Dibble, was asked at a press conference if he thought Minnesota's bridges were safe. "I think they are," he said, "but stuff keeps happening. We see bridges closed. We see stuff falling off bridges."

Many of the nation's bridges are approaching, or have reached, the end of their useful lives. Most were expected to last about fifty years, and a tremendous number were built during the construction boom of the 1950s and '60s. Because so many were poorly maintained, they are in even worse shape than might be expected for bridges that have been around for a half century or more.

Samuel I. Schwartz spent twenty years as an engineer with the New York City Department of Transportation and was the chief engineer in the mid- to late 1980s. The city endured a series of fiscal crises during that period. Infrastructure maintenance and repair were dangerously neglected, to the point where the public was put at grave risk. Schwartz, a dedicated official who would eventually be called upon to turn matters around, reflected in an interview on the many bridge failures that occurred. On a sunny, breezy afternoon in the summer of 1981, a pair of six-hundred-foot cables on the Brooklyn Bridge snapped and began swinging wildly through the air. One of the cables slammed into a photographer who was taking pictures from a pedestrian footpath, fracturing his skull. The man died a week later. In 1989, a five-hundred-pound concrete slab fell from the elevated Franklin D. Roosevelt Drive on Manhattan's East Side. It smashed through the windshield of a car being driven by a dentist from Brooklyn. The dentist was killed, and the car careened out of control, crashing into parked cars and concrete pillars before finally coming to a stop.

In 1988, as chief engineer, Schwartz ordered the perennially busy Williamsburg Bridge over the East River to be closed following the discovery of potentially devastating corrosion-induced cracks. Schwartz knew that a disaster on the Williamsburg could cost the lives of hundreds, if not thousands, of motorists, bus passengers, and elevated-train riders. The bridge remained closed for two months.

"We never seem to learn," Schwartz told me. "Even after all these years."

There is no reason for so many bridges in the United States to be in the sorry shape that they are. We know how to fix them. We could afford to fix them. We just don't. In its 2013 report card, the American Society of Civil Engineers noted, "The health of our nation's bridges is directly tied to the nation's ability to compete in a global marketplace. Therefore, it is of growing concern that the bridges in our nation's metropolitan areas, which are an indispensable link for both millions of commuters and freight on a daily basis, are decaying more rapidly than our rural bridges. Approximately 210 million trips are taken daily across deficient bridges in the nation's 102 largest metropolitan regions."

As absurd as it has been for the United States to allow its bridges to fall into such a wretched state of disrepair, that is just one part of a vast infrastructure debacle that is threatening the vibrancy of the nation. America's increasingly dilapidated physical plant includes the following:

- Badly congested roads and highways that are often in such disrepair that they are hazardous to human life and a drag on economic activity.
- Wasteful, overburdened, and increasingly decrepit water and sewer systems that date back in some cases to the late nineteenth and early twentieth centuries.
- Aging, fragile, and poorly maintained dams and levees (think New Orleans) that are a perennial threat to public safety.
- A haphazard and often unreliable system of electrical power so hobbled by poor maintenance and excessive demand that it will require more than $1 trillion in investments (and perhaps as much as $2 trillion) to bring it up to twenty-first-century standards by 2030.
- An outdated air traffic control system that keeps passengers bogged down with costly and nerve-racking delays and that has experienced many harrowing near misses.

If you want a clear image of our national penchant for self-destruction, think of the magnificent physical infrastructure that blossomed in the United States in the twentieth century, and then think of the degree to which we are now letting it go to ruin.

In the summer of 1919, Dwight Eisenhower, then a twenty-eight-year-old lieutenant colonel in the army, was part of a truck and tank convoy that traveled from Washington, D.C., to San Francisco. "Primitive" would be a kind way of describing the roads that the eighty-one vehicles bounced, rumbled, slid, and sometimes had to be hauled across. Truck tires blew, axles broke, and drainage ditches lurked like traps hungry for motorized prey. "No one was killed," said Dan McNichol in his book *The Roads That Built America*, "but there were injuries. Trucks crashed through bridges and into rivers. They skidded off roads and rolled down mountainsides or just succumbed to the beating of rutted roads."

Nine trucks were declared unsalvageable and left behind. The 3,251-mile trip took sixty-one days.

Fast-forward less than forty years and Americans were already breezily traveling over the nationwide interstate highway system, which was conceived and guided into being by President Eisenhower (for whom it is now named). That is the kind of progress the U.S. was once capable of. We've fallen so far from that lofty standard that the American Society of Civil Engineers gave the nation's roads a pathetic grade of D in 2013. According to the society, nearly a third of America's roads were in poor or mediocre condition. An estimated $170 billion in capital investments *annually* would be required to bring about significant improvements.

One night in 2010, I set out from New York, intending to drive to Washington for a meeting the following day between President Obama and a group of journalists. I rounded a curve on a stretch of highway between the Lincoln Tunnel and the New Jersey Turnpike and slammed into an enormous pothole at about forty-five miles per hour. Three tires and three wheels on my car were destroyed. It was only good fortune that prevented a more serious accident from occurring. While there are no specific numbers available, it is known that deteriorating, poorly maintained roadways result in thousands of traffic fatalities and tens of thousands of injuries every year. The excess wear and tear on vehicles and the damage from accidents run into the billions.

Stephen Flynn, a senior fellow at the Council on Foreign Rela- tions who is an expert on infrastructure and its relationship to national security, told me, in a rueful tone, that "somehow, as a nation, we've come to see infrastructure as something we can't afford—as a cost rather than an investment." That made no sense, he said. "We're like a generation that was fortunate enough to inherit the family mansion but then decided not to do any of the upkeep. The plumbing's falling apart; the wiring's gone bad. But we won't do anything to fix it."

During a conference on infrastructure at Iona College in sub- urban New York, Flynn recalled the days when his parents and grandparents experienced a rush of national pride each time they saw one of America's great public works. He compared that to a series of devastating infrastructure-related events that made a com- pletely different impression on his young daughter. "At age eight," he said, "she saw the lights go out in the Northeast because we can't trim trees out in Ohio. And then, two years later, the city of New Orleans drowned because we can't maintain the flood control system." Finally, he said, at age twelve, she watched the coverage of the I-35 bridge after it collapsed "under everyday commuters."

Those who can't see the point of investing billions in roads and bridges, or in a new and improved electrical grid, or in expanded mass transit systems are also oblivious to the single biggest weapon America has against joblessness and a perennially weak economy. Study after study has shown that rebuilding the infrastructure is the quickest way to put large numbers of people to work and that the return for each dollar invested in infrastructure renewal is sig- nificantly greater than all other investments in the nation's econ- omy. With the nation's physical plant in such sad shape at a time when millions of Americans are in dire need of full-time work, it's criminal to neglect this biggest of all bangs for the national buck.

If you want to create millions of new jobs, rebuild the infra- structure. If you want to establish the economy on a sounder, more competitive footing, move the infrastructure from the nineteenth and twentieth centuries into the twenty-first.

This would be enormously expensive and sacrifices would have to be made. Taxes would have to be raised, including taxes on ordinary working people. Some of the most extreme excesses of wealth would have to be curbed. Some variation of a national infrastructure bank would have to be established to leverage (and monitor) the necessary capital and identify the worthiest projects. The public and private sectors would have to work closely together, as would labor and capital.

There have been many serious proposals—blueprints—for creating a full-bore infrastructure renewal project. The New America Foundation recommended a five-year $1.2 trillion investment program, saying, "It is estimated that every $1 billion of public infrastructure investment generates, by the most conservative estimates, 23,000 well-paying jobs."

The authors of the report said their recommendations, if fully implemented, would create 5.2 million jobs in each of the program's five years. "Beyond this," they said, "it is important to note that infrastructure investment has a healthy multiplier effect throughout the economy. The CBO [Congressional Budget Office] estimates that every dollar of infrastructure spending generates on average a $1.6 increase in GDP [gross domestic product]. Some critical transportation and energy projects have even larger multiplier effects."

The U.S. will not be able to get its economic act together without a major, long-term commitment to rebuild its physical plant.

When Jake Rudh got the call that his fiancée was being taken to the Fairview medical center, he ran to his car and began driving at speeds that under normal circumstances would have gotten him arrested. "I was flying down side streets with my horn blowing and hazard lights flashing," he said. "I tried to be as careful as possible going through intersections. When I got to the hospital, she was already in surgery."

He waited three hours before finally getting to spend a few minutes with Mercedes once the first surgery was completed. He was shocked at what he saw. His fiancée was a mess. Looking at her was heartbreaking. In addition to both legs being crushed from the knees down and her left foot mangled and a vertebra fractured, she seemed broken and bloodied in general. Much of her body was swollen. Her forehead and nose had been burned by the impact with the car's air bag. There was massive bruising on her neck, shoulders, and chest from the shoulder harness. Her lower lip had been punctured by her upper row of teeth, and her facial expression seemed contorted. She was barely conscious. Rudh leaned over, kissed her very gently, and whispered that he loved her. Then he began picking glass from her face and hair. A doctor told him that Mercedes had suffered the kinds of injuries you'd associate with a skydiver whose parachute failed to open. Rudh asked about her prognosis. The doctor told him to be prepared for a very long and difficult road.

The few minutes passed quickly. Mercedes was wheeled away to be prepared for more surgery. Rudh, his body shaking, placed his face in his hands and wept.

3 Jobs and the Middle Class

Of all the aspects of social misery nothing is
so heart-breaking as unemployment.

—JANE ADDAMS

We realized after a while that things were
never going to be the same again.

—LYNDA SWINDELL

There is an unreal quality to the words as they hang in the air, too devastating to be immediately absorbed: "We don't need you anymore." "We're letting you go." "We're moving in a different direction." "You're very talented. I'm sure you'll find something soon."

When people are fired, they are subject to an onslaught of unwelcome emotions, powerful feelings that can range from the distressing to the downright debilitating, from disappointment to depression. There is a corrosive, even life-threatening quality in the worst cases. Optimism dims. Self-esteem takes a big hit and stress can become a permanent, unnerving feature of daily life. Spouses snap at one another. Parents yell at their kids. There is a tendency to eat too much, to drink too much, to resume smoking. A middle-aged man in Memphis told me that when he lost his job he felt as if he'd been hit by a car and he wondered whether he would survive. "The pain seemed almost physical," he said. "I'd had so much invested in my work." Teresa Flowers, a project manager in suburban Atlanta, recalled feeling "just mortified" when she was told that she was being laid off. "I was in shock," she said. "All I could think was, 'I want to work. I'm a hard worker.' " Russ Meyer, an advertising copywriter in Portland, Oregon, who was out of work for more than two years, said, "I just assumed that I would be able to find a job that would at least pay me what I was making before. But I've come to realize that that's a fantasy."

Welcome to the new world of employment in America, where job insecurity is the norm, wages are depressed, benefits are few, and anyone can be thrown onto the jobless rolls at any moment and stay there for months or years at a time. The most terrible of all of America's wounds is its chronic, insidious unemployment. It's a wound that is vast, deep, festering, and tragically resistant to healing. And it's changing the very character of the nation.

On a remarkably warm day in February 2012—Groundhog Day—I watched as a large man with a fringe of white hair, a mustache, and a delicate goatee lumbered toward the entrance of the DoubleTree hotel in Roswell, Georgia. I was there to meet him and talk about his long struggle with unemployment. Over coffee Lamar Hayes explained how his standard of living, once middle-class, had been crushed in the collapse of the housing market. Hayes was fifty-two, a college-educated family man with a conservative political outlook. "My life was always about hard work and taking care of my wife and daughters," he said. "Everything else was peripheral to that."

Hayes built houses for a living, the worst industry to be in when the real estate bubble burst. He supervised construction sites in the greater Atlanta area, and while he never got rich, his family lived comfortably. They had a home in Woodstock, a suburb north of Atlanta, and lived what Hayes described as a "typical American life." Going to work, for Hayes, was as normal as breathing. He'd never even imagined being jobless until one quiet, sunny morning in May 2008 when he got a call from his district manager. "I probably should have seen it coming, but I didn't," Hayes told me. "The company had been laying off people, but those of us who were left kept saying, 'Well, they can't cut any more.' They were scraped so thin. I never thought it would get to me."

He had to drive forty-five minutes from a construction site to his district manager's office to get the bad news face-to-face. His boss tried to be as positive and encouraging as possible. Hayes's work, he said, had been outstanding. If the economy turned around, perhaps he would be called back. But the bottom line was, "You're fired."

"It was heartbreaking," Hayes said. "It's hard to explain how much I loved what I did. I really loved it. And in your gut you feel like you did something wrong. Like it was all your fault. I called my wife and told her. And then after that I couldn't help myself. I just cried in my truck on my way home."

Hayes's story was not simply the sad tale of a man caught in an industry going through a terrible slump. I heard variations on this devastating theme again and again, from men and women in myriad professions and occupations from coast to coast. I heard it from lawyers and car salesmen and teachers and factory workers and programmers. I heard it from office managers, architects, and dishwashers. And I would continue to hear it. It was the story of our time. The American economy was no longer creating enough jobs for a population that continued to grow and was desperately in need of work. The societal implications were profound. Among other things, the nation's proudest achievement since World War II, the creation of a vast and thriving middle class, was at risk. Like the movement of tectonic plates beneath the surface of the earth, something fundamental had shifted beneath the ground of American employment. Good jobs were destroyed on a scale that for much of the post–World War II era had seemed unfathomable. By the second decade of the twenty-first century, America's heralded middle class was faltering badly, and parts of it were disintegrating.

"The rent was due yesterday," Hayes said.

I couldn't quite hear him. He leaned forward. "The rent was due yesterday," he said. "Right now, I don't have it." He took a long sip of coffee.

Hayes and his wife had two daughters still living at home and very little in the way of savings when he lost his job. He'd had to get back to some kind of work in a hurry. Construction was out of the question, and no other good jobs were beckoning. "I looked," he said. "I looked hard, but there was nothing—nothing that paid anything." Still somewhat in a state of shock, he went to work as a customer service representative at a Walmart. It was part-time, paid ten dollars and sixty cents an hour, and took a toll on his self-esteem. "I was used to making about seventy-five thousand dollars a year, so that was a real comedown," he said. "One day I filled in for a door greeter who had gone on a break. That's when the whole thing really hit home, because I'm standing there smiling at everybody who comes in, and I'm saying over and over, 'Welcome to Walmart. Welcome to Walmart.' I thought to myself, 'God must really have a sense of humor to let this happen. I'm a greeter at Walmart.' "

Ten-sixty an hour was not nearly enough income, so Hayes took a second job as a waiter at a Chili's restaurant—two dollars and thirteen cents an hour, plus tips. His wife was also working part-time. Their combined incomes put food on the table but were not enough to save their home, which they lost to foreclosure.

"We just fell behind," Hayes said. He stopped and took a deep breath as he talked about the family's last day at the home they'd lived in for many years. "We'd already moved everything out, and we just went back for, like, a final walk-through. I remember it so clearly. A spring day. Nice day. It was very sad. We've got pictures of everybody sitting on the front porch one last time."

There has been a widespread tendency to retreat into denial about the severity of the jobs crisis, to close our eyes and pretend, year after year, that something approaching a normal employment environment is just around the corner, just past the next policy initiative. We keep telling ourselves that the landscape will change. We'll see a burst of economic growth and jobs will be plentiful again—just as they were back in the 1960s, or maybe the late '90s. But that's not so. In 2013 and 2014, I was still hearing the same sad stories from jobless men and women that I'd been hearing during the Great Recession and the years that immediately followed. The

sorrowful truth was that the era of limitless job growth that built
the American middle class was gone. The evidence, often tragic,
was everywhere, in plain sight. The U.S. had been stuck for years
in the worst employment environment since the 1930s, with millions of ordinary Americans being left far behind, their hopes and
dreams dwindling. The stark, cold reality was that men and women
of all ages, in all regions of the country, millions upon millions of
them, have for years been scrambling to meet their most basic daily
needs in the face of mass layoffs, reduced hours, wage stagnation,
and the collapse of any hope of economic security.

In late 2013, four and a half years after the formal, technical
ending of the Great Recession, employment conditions in the U.S.
remained in horrendous shape. According to official government
statistics, more than twenty million Americans were jobless or
underemployed. Millions more were working at jobs that paid the
minimum wage or just a little more than the minimum. In the
shadows were other millions who had dropped out of the labor
force entirely or were working sporadically and were not counted
in the official statistics. In a special edition of the *American Prospect*
magazine in the fall of 2013, titled "Work in the Age of Anxiety,"
Harold Meyerson wrote, "Today, the share of the nation's income
going to wages, which for decades was more than 50 percent, is at
a record low of 43 percent, while the share of the nation's income
going to corporate profits is at a record high . . . In 2013, America's
three largest private-sector employers are all low-wage retailers:
Wal-Mart, Yum! Brands (which owns Taco Bell, Pizza Hut, and
Kentucky Fried Chicken) and McDonald's. In 1960, the three largest employers were high-wage unionized manufacturers or utili-
ties: General Motors, AT&T, and Ford."

The upward mobility that once defined the American dream had
made a U-turn. With the great American jobs machine sputtering,
it became more and more difficult for people to work their way
into the middle class and a whole lot easier to fall out of it. The
toll in purely human terms has been brutal. Homes have been lost,
families have fallen apart, and the grand expectations of countless
young people have been stymied. Way back in the 1930s, Franklin
Roosevelt had spoken of the "forgotten man." Three-quarters of a

century later, in the age of Bush and Obama, millions of jobless and underemployed Americans were once again being shoved to society's sidelines.

What is important to understand is that it was no accident that so many Americans have had to struggle economically for so long. A vast and shameful array of deliberate policy choices, going back decades, shaped the U.S. economy in ways that ensured that the benefits of growth would go overwhelmingly to those who were already at or near the top of the nation's financial pyramid. The interests of those at the top are very different from those in the middle and at the bottom. Employment was always the essential element in the financial well-being of the vast majority of Americans. But job creation was never a priority of the nation's corporate, banking, and political elite. They argued, with nonstop vehemence, that everyone would benefit from industrial and financial deregulation, from the erosion of safety net support and the weakening of labor unions, from unchecked globalization and the wholesale replacement of live workers by machines, and from the rampant privatization of services originally designed to meet public needs. It was a philosophy that allowed the fortunate few to amass greater riches than anyone on the planet had ever previously dreamed of. Even before the Great Recession, in the years 2000 to 2007, the U.S. was mired in the most stagnant period of job creation since the Depression. But the severity of the employment crisis was masked by an epic housing bubble and stunning amounts of personal debt. In June 2006, a year and a half before the recession started, Jackson Lears of the *New York Times* was writing, "Americans are awash in red ink. Consumer indebtedness is soaring, the savings rate is down to zero and people are filing for bankruptcy at record rates."

Struggling families were trying to get their hands on a lifeline any way they could, from nonstop mortgage refinancing to payday loans at interest rates that loan sharks would have envied. Equity in family homes was drained. Credit card balances reached historic highs. Student loan debt soared off the charts.

From 2000 to 2012, no net new jobs were created in the United States—not one—even as the working-age population continued to grow. That's a recipe for societal breakdown. From 1999 to 2009, a stunning one-third of all American families experienced the loss of employment by a household head. The first ten years of the twenty-first century achieved the dubious distinction of being the only decade since the 1930s in which the nation's median household income actually declined.

The recession, which began in December 2007, turned an already dismal employment situation into a catastrophe. In the five years following the onset of the recession, more than half of the American workforce endured the loss of a job, a cut in pay, or an involuntary reduction to part-time employment. A 2011 McKinsey & Company survey of two thousand business executives found that 65 percent of their companies had taken steps to "improve productivity and reduce employment" over the prior three years. The impact of such a drastic reduction in employment was devastating. Millions of Americans found themselves trapped in the grim category of long-term joblessness, a remorselessly corrosive predicament that is disastrous to individuals, families, and the society at large. Nearly half of the unemployed in the years following the recession were jobless for six months or more, with several million out of work for a year or two or longer. It was the first time since the era of breadlines and Hoovervilles that extended periods of joblessness had been so pervasive. In New York City in 2012, less than half of all working-age blacks had jobs. Nationally, teenage employment, often the first step in establishing a work ethic and subsequent career, became increasingly rare.

Americans old enough to remember the early postwar decades could barely recognize the new, rubble-strewn employment landscape. Lawrence Summers, the former Treasury secretary and presidential adviser, sounded the following alarm in the fall of 2011: "In 1965, only one in 20 men ages 25 to 54 was not working; by the end of this decade, it is likely to be one in six, even if a full cyclical recovery is achieved."

For the middle class, the crisis was nothing short of existential. America had gone further than any rich nation in history in the distribution of its abundance. It had created the largest, most prosperous middle class ever known. Now those hard-won gains were being lost. An analysis by the Pew Research Center that looked at the years 2000 to 2010 found that America's middle class had endured its worst decade since the Great Depression. Its wages and living standards, its quality of life, were all sinking. Paul Taylor, a top executive at Pew, said, "The notion that we are a society with a large middle class with lots of economic and social mobility and a belief that each generation does better than the [last]—these are some of the core tenets of what it means to be an American. But that's not necessarily the case anymore."

Suburban Roswell, Georgia, population eighty-eight thousand, is about a half hour's drive north of Atlanta. It's a prosperous, well-established community with roots extending back to the 1830s. The annual median family income when I visited in the spring of 2012 was an impressive $103,000. Roswell has often been cited as one of the best places to live in America. I was there to get a glimpse of the toll that the employment crisis was taking on a solid, upscale community and the towns nearby. With the poor all but crushed by the recession, increasing signs of distress were appearing in higher-income communities previously thought to be immune to serious economic setbacks. Some of the examples were startling. Wealthy Hunterdon County in western New Jersey, known primarily for its horse farms and scenic rolling hillsides, had experienced a dramatic increase in families seeking federal food assistance during the recession and its aftermath. The director of a social service agency that found itself offering assistance to an entirely new constituency told *Bloomberg News,* "Sometimes people will come in a Mercedes. Sometimes they come in [wearing] Ralph Lauren. But you never know. That may be all they have."

During the brutally cold winter of 2013–2014, Mark Swann, head of an agency in Portland, Maine, that operates homeless shelters and food pantries, was asked if he was seeing more middle-class families seeking assistance. "Definitely yes," he said. "It's common now to look up in one of our facilities and see someone coming in, their eyes wide open—they're scared to death. They had no expectation they would ever be coming to us."

One of my first stops in Roswell was city hall. Pillared, classically domed, and brightly lit, it may have been the quietest public building I'd ever visited. Hardly anyone was walking the spotless corridors. It seemed as if someone had pressed a mute button. When I approached the receptionist in Mayor Jere Wood's office, I was inclined to whisper. But she greeted me in a normal tone, which made me chuckle. The sustained quiet, eerie and a little disconcerting to a noise-hardened New Yorker, was broken.

Waiting a few moments for the mayor, I went over my notes. Fifty-eight percent of Roswell residents over the age of twenty-five had a bachelor's or master's degree. That was much higher than the national average. Unemployment was below the national average. And while real estate sales had largely stalled during the recession, housing prices had not collapsed. Roswell was weathering the economic storm. And yet it had problems. Unemployment might have been below average, but it was high by Roswell standards. And long-term unemployment in Roswell and its vicinity was severe. Support groups for the unemployed had been flooded with upscale individuals seeking help. The participants at such meetings were well dressed and their demeanor generally low-key, but their desperation was palpable.

Though there was not much poverty in Roswell, its small low-income population was hurting badly. Social service agencies and local churches had trouble keeping up with the demand for food assistance and emergency shelter. More and more people were seeking subsidized housing. And the influx of well-heeled young families that for years had been moving into Roswell had stopped. The city was no longer growing. The economic rot that was eating away at American living standards was not quite as visible in Roswell, but it was there nevertheless.

My thoughts were interrupted by the receptionist. "Right this way," she said.

I shook hands with Jere Wood, a thoughtful man in his mid-sixties who favored bow ties and wore his full head of gray hair somewhat long. As he began talking about his city, he seemed torn between two realities. On the one hand, he was proud that Roswell had fended off disaster. "We were sort of a solid, wealthy, mature city," he said. "We weren't going through a housing boom; we were built up to begin with. We didn't have a lot of people who had just bought a house and were deep in debt. And the city was on a very strong financial footing."

On the other hand, he noted, a substantial number of families in Roswell were in serious financial distress. Wood didn't try to sugarcoat it. "I'm also a lawyer," he said, "and I've seen a lot of people in my practice who have gone broke. And the building industry is in a depression. A lot of my contemporaries who had a comfortable middle-class income and good jobs—well, now it takes them months if not years to find a stable job. They've got mortgages, kids in college. They never anticipated being in that position. These are people with college degrees and careers, successful people who suddenly find themselves unemployed. I've never really seen it happen like that before, on that scale. The unemployment always used to be on the fringe.

"The other thing I've noticed is that usually it's the tenants who would go broke in a bad economy. In this recession, it was the tenants, and then the landlords, and then the banks that went broke. It's not just those on the margin who were affected."

As the mayor moved methodically from one point to the next, he made no effort, in either his tone or his expression, to mask his concern. Our conversation took place nearly three years after the recession had officially ended. I asked if he thought the worst was over. Wood paused, as if reluctant to answer. "Well," he said, "I feel that the worst will be with us for a long time to come."

As with many others, the realization that something fundamental had changed in the economy had dawned slowly on Wood, even after the recession hit. "The first year, I thought, well, we're in a dip," he said. "We've got enough reserves to bridge this. The second year, I said, 'Wait a minute. This is a long-term thing. It's going to be here awhile.' Now it's a recognition that we've got to change everything, change our thinking. We've got to adjust to this new normal."

Much of the nation remained in denial about the new normal,

which, in its most fundamental sense, was this alarming new era of radically insufficient employment. Too many Americans were out of work, and too many of those with jobs were making too little money. Policy makers consistently misread the crisis, underestimated it. Soon after President Obama took office, his administration projected that its $787 billion stimulus package would keep unemployment from surging past 8 percent. Before the year was out, it had reached 10.2 percent.

The U.S. was not, as many seemed to think, going through a tough but temporary bout of economic hard times. The crisis brought into sharp relief by the Great Recession had been building for decades and carried within it the seeds of a national calamity. The American economy depends above all else on a vast and prospering consumer class that can purchase the goods and services that are being produced or are capable of being produced. For a long time that worked wonderfully well. As the former labor secretary Robert Reich noted, "The earnings of the great American middle class fueled the great American expansion for three decades after World War II." Consumer spending, for better or worse, is the defining characteristic of American life. It accounts for fully 70 percent of economic activity. Without it, everything else screeches to a halt. If Americans stopped buying gifts between Thanksgiving and Christmas, the workaday world would collapse and we'd plunge into the dark night of depression. It's the mass purchasing power of ordinary working people and the taxes they pay on their incomes that drive the public and private investment, the economic growth, and the creation of new businesses that, in a virtuous cycle, create new jobs that further expand the purchasing power of the masses. When that cycle is running smoothly, prosperity can be spread widely. But when you destroy jobs and constrict wages, you foul up that high-performance cycle. And that's what has been happening in the United States. Employment is the one absolutely essential binding element of American society. When Americans cannot find jobs at good wages, everything else falls apart.

While the jobs crisis was the single most critical issue facing the country, there was no concerted effort on the part of the government to deal with it in any sustained way. Attention bounced from the wars in Iraq and Afghanistan to the passage and troubled implementation of the Patient Protection and Affordable Care Act (Obamacare), to marathon fights over austerity and deficit reduction. Though voters were emphatic in poll after poll that employment was their top priority, job creation got short shrift. Three years into the so-called recovery I visited Rich Crane and his wife, Susan, a middle-aged couple in the suburban town of Hazlet, near the New Jersey shore. They told me about spending an entire summer with no gas or electric service in their home because they couldn't afford the monthly payments. Rich had lost his job with an auto parts distributorship, and Susan was recovering from breast cancer surgery. Their savings had long since been spent. With their son, Richard, sixteen, they struggled for months against the prospect of absolute destitution. With no electricity, the house, on a normal-looking suburban block, had seemed particularly strange at night, an eerie throwback to a time when candles were the primary defense against the dark. Crane did what he could. "I rigged up a generator and a couple of car batteries so that when it got dark we had enough juice to keep a little 25-watt fluorescent light going and we were able to watch a 19-inch TV. We cooked on a grill and used the generator to get a little hot water heater working. That way we could shower and have just enough warm water to do the dishes and keep our clothes clean. It was rough. But nobody was yelling or anything. We tried to be considerate."

Crane had worked for the same company for twenty-four years before being let go just as the recession was starting. He eventually landed a job at a home furnishings outlet, earning twelve dollars an hour. The family's middle-class lifestyle seemed a distant memory.

The Cranes were not outliers. Huge numbers of twenty-first-century American families were caught up in similar struggles. Rahn Harper, a thirty-two-year-old husband and father in Columbus, Ohio, told me how he'd all but hit rock bottom after he lost his job as a $64,000-a-year branch manager for a GE subsidiary. With no severance and nothing but odd jobs for more than a year, the family's once comfortable life fell apart piece by piece. "We were up against it," Harper said. With his savings gone and the bills piling ever higher, without even enough money to buy food, he came to the grim conclusion one afternoon that he had no choice but to drive into downtown Columbus and sell some of his blood plasma. "They give you fifty dollars each time you make a donation," he said. "So I did it. More than once. I'll tell you the truth, it seemed like a kind of madness. Sometimes you'd be in there and you'd get dizzy because normally you have to eat before you go. But there were times when I couldn't eat because we were short of food and my wife and especially my son would come first. So there were times when I would get dizzy afterward and I'd have to wait a little while to make sure I was fine to drive home."

More than two years would pass before Harper would find another full-time job.

The long, slow, and never more than feeble recovery from the recession was like a curtain rising on America's new normal. The heyday of mass employment had been undermined by laborsaving technological advances, the demise of unions, the unconscionable mistreatment of workers by corporate executives, and the entry via globalization of two billion new workers eager for employment at wages that, to Americans, were scandalously low. When President Obama asked Apple's Steve Jobs what would be required to have iPhones made in the United States rather than in China, Jobs was reported to have replied, "Those jobs aren't coming back."

Policy makers could have taken steps to counter the forces that were undermining the well-being of America's workers, but they chose not to do so. Three years into the recovery, nearly a third of all unemployed workers had been jobless for a soul-crushing year or longer. Matt Diersen, an upbeat corporate product manager from Atlanta who had ridden the good years of his three-decade career with the joy and enthusiasm of a cowboy at a rodeo, summed up what it was like to be upended by long-term joblessness: "I'll tell you the truth, I couldn't believe it had happened. For twenty-two months my wife and I were living off savings. When that was exhausted, we went into our 401(k). Our name's not Rockefeller. My wife is a schoolteacher, and she was working. But we had a mortgage and a son and daughter in college, so her income by itself wasn't nearly enough."

One afternoon, when Diersen and I were having lunch in a

hotel restaurant, I noticed that he seemed listless and wasn't eating his food. We'd been in touch with each other for almost a year. In a soft, almost unbearably weary voice he said it was becoming impossible for him and his wife to even pretend that they had a middle-class standard of living. "You crimp and you save," he said, "and you do everything humanly possible to cut costs to the point where you're barely surviving. The only thing that can save you is a job. So you keep looking. You always think you're going to find work. But there's no work. I'm fifty-two years old, you know? I'm baggage at this point. I see that more and more every day. My wife and I filed for bankruptcy in February."

Capitalism American-style had broken down, and pretending otherwise was not helpful. Not only were too few jobs being created, but most of the meager and sporadic employment gains over the past several years were in low-wage sectors of the economy—jobs in restaurants, hotels, retail trade outlets, and personal services industries like hairdressing and home health care. Many were part-time, temporary, or both. According to the federal government, part-time jobs were responsible for an astonishing 77 percent of all the job growth in the first half of 2013.

America was the originator, the architect, of the high-consumption society. But you can't maintain high consumption in extended periods of high unemployment and low wages. That seemed to be well understood in the early post–World War II decades. Workers, a large proportion of whom were represented by labor unions, were increasingly well compensated, and they used their wages to start families, to buy and furnish new homes, to take vacations, and so on. That increased spending fueled business investments and additional hiring. Poverty was on the run and the middle class seemed secure. But that buoyant state of affairs began to fade in the 1970s and '80s. America's leaders in both the public and private sectors began turning their backs on the idea that a robust economy required high levels of employment at high wages and that the benefits of economic growth needed to be shared with ordinary workers. It was the fateful, though barely noticed, beginning of our tragic era of tremendous inequality.

In his biography of the economist John Kenneth Galbraith,

Richard Parker detailed the poor performance of the U.S. economy in the Ronald Reagan–George H. W. Bush era and the distress imposed on the middle class and the poor as the benefits of the economy were disproportionately siphoned off by those who were already wealthy.

Parker noted that economic growth "had been slower in the 1980s than in the 1950s, 1960s, or even the troubled 1970s." Bush had denounced Reaganomics as "voodoo economics," but there was a method to the voodoo madness. It was aimed at reversing the progressive trends in the early postwar distribution of income and wealth, and it worked almost exactly as intended. While much of the middle class and the poor stagnated or suffered during the Reagan era, those at the top did exceedingly well. As Parker wrote,

> From Franklin Roosevelt's presidency through Lyndon Johnson's (three decades when, as Galbraith always pointed out, the size of government steadily grew and tax rates were far more progressive), the gap between America's rich and poor had first narrowed dramatically and then stabilized, with the country's middle class growing larger and more prosperous, and the number of America's poor diminishing. But starting slowly under Richard Nixon and then sharply accelerating throughout the Reagan years, American income and wealth distribution went in exactly the opposite direction. By the early 1990s the United States was the most inegalitarian of all the advanced industrialized countries. (Galbraith sardonically allowed that post-Communist Russia was more unequal.) Moreover, America's middle classes were working harder—in terms of both total hours worked and the number of workers per household—just to maintain their median incomes.

The squeeze on the middle class and the poor was not something that happened naturally, like a change in the weather. The ruling class, which increasingly meant the alliance between the corporate class and elected officials, was deliberately handing ordinary Americans the short end of the economic stick. The rules were changed, gradually at first and then more blatantly as the years passed, so that the elite would reap the vast bulk of the benefits from the good economic times and would be insulated from the sacrifices and suffering when times turned bad. Jobs were created in the Reagan years, but workers benefited very little. As Parker wrote,

> The net job growth, like GDP growth, was slower in the 1980s than in any other decade since World War II, and the new jobs routinely paid less, provided fewer benefits, and offered less job security than those they replaced. The profound disconnections Americans endured in the 1980s hadn't been equaled since the 1930s. By the end of the Reagan-Bush era, 75 percent of Americans were reporting that they or someone close to them had been laid off since Reagan first took office, and 30 percent were saying that they had taken on extra work just to maintain—not improve—their incomes.

The hard times for workers would grow increasingly painful, an untreated economic wound with disastrous, often crippling effects on the lives of millions of individuals and families. One Sunday morning in the summer of 2012, I logged on to the *New York Times* Web site and spotted the "quotation of the day," which was from a young man named Jordan Golson. He had sold three-quarters of a million dollars' worth of technological wizardry at the Apple Store in Salem, New Hampshire. "I was earning $11.25 an hour," he said. "Part of me was thinking, 'This is great. I'm an Apple fan, the store is doing really well.' But when you look at the amount of money the company is making and then you look at your paycheck, it's kind of tough."

Tough and unsustainable. Few companies have ever been as successful as Apple. Its retail stores at the time of Golson's comments were earning more money per square foot than any other retailer in America—nearly twice as much as the second-place company, Tiffany. Apple's top executives were lavishly compensated. But most of Apple's employees in the United States were members of the low-wage service economy, typically earning about $25,000 a year. Apple salespeople were dedicated, many were college educated, and they made tons of money for their employer. But they were not paid commissions for the astonishing volume of iPods, iPhones, and iPads that they sold. They got their less-than-impressive hourly wage, and that was that. They might have been working for the highest of the highfliers when it came to retail, but their own economic condition was hardly robust.

America was trapped in a Catch-22 of its own making: There was no way for the middle class to prosper (or even survive) in the absence of well-paying jobs. But a high-tech, globalized economy shaped according to the dictates of shortsighted, profit-obsessed Wall Street financiers and corporate CEOs would never create enough good jobs for the middle class to retrieve its past glory. Corporate profits rebounded to record levels after the Great Recession in large part because of the savings that management realized by savaging payrolls. The very idea of paying a decent and secure wage for ordinary workers had become anathema in the business world. Allen Sinai, the chief global economist at the research firm Decision Economics, bluntly explained the reality to the *New York Times:* "American business is about maximizing shareholder value. You basically don't want workers. You hire less and you try to find capital equipment to replace them." The dumping of workers had long preceded the recession. Way back in the spring of 1995, an article in the *Wall Street Journal* carried the headline "Amid Record Profits, Companies Continue to Lay Off Employees." That same year, a frustrated Eric Greenberg, an executive with the American Management Association, said, "What these companies have been doing since the mid-80s is firing their customers."

Corporate America, obsessed with stock prices and bonuses, wasn't listening. By the 1990s, employers had lost whatever inhibitions they might once have had about firing workers. With labor unions hobbled and public protests muted, the job destroyers felt few constraints. A remarkable array of euphemisms began spewing like sparks from the high-speed blades on employee chopping blocks. No one was "fired." Employers announced that their staffs had been right-sized as employees were laid off, downsized, dismissed, discontinued, involuntarily severed, or surplussed. Employees at AT&T actually talked about living in a "surplus universe." Companies issued formal announcements about special leaves, separations, rebalances, employee bumpings, and, in one of my favorite verbal dodges, cascade bumpings. I wrote in a column that cascade bumpings actually sounded like a joyful experience.

Executives argued that downsizing—getting rid of all those workers—was essential, a business imperative that resulted from increased global competition. But the truth is that employers had discovered a gold mine in downsizing. Workers came to be seen less and less as valuable, functioning human beings contributing to the success of an enterprise and more and more as impediments to profits. They were tossed aside as easily as used tissues. Louis Uchitelle of the *New York Times* titled his book about the consequences of mass layoffs *The Disposable American*. He wrote that in the two decades from 1984 to 2004, the Bureau of Labor Statistics "counted at least 30 million full-time workers who had been permanently separated from their jobs and their paychecks against their wishes." Millions more "had been forced into early retirement or had suffered some other form of disguised layoff, masking the magnitude of the problem."

Self-absorbed corporate tough guys like "Neutron Jack" Welch at GE and "Chainsaw Al" Dunlap of Scott Paper and Sunbeam seemed to glory in the brutal process of casting workers into the netherworld of unemployment. Welch sacked more than 100,000 GE workers in the 1980s and '90s. Dunlap, who also dispatched workers by the thousands, reveled in his reputation as a heartless cutthroat. "If you want to be liked," he said, "get a dog."

The employment debacle was especially poignant for older workers, men and women over fifty. While that group endured somewhat fewer layoffs during the recession, the ones who did lose their jobs—before, during, and after the downturn—found it harder than anyone else to get back to work. In most cases they had been employed for decades, often at one company. They had raised (or were still raising) families and, typically, enjoyed a middle-class or upper-middle-class standard of living. The shock of suddenly being dumped from the workforce like so much trash was profound. In his book *Working Scared (or Not at All)*, Carl Van Horn, director of the Heldrich Center for Workforce Development at Rutgers University, wrote, "A staggering number of the unemployed over-age-fifty group that we tracked from 2009 to 2011 had been jobless a very long time. Eighty percent had been searching for over a year, including almost half who had been job hunting almost two years."

In many cases, older workers who lost their jobs faced nothing short of ruin. Desperate to feed themselves and their families, they often scrambled for low-wage work that had once been the purview of high school dropouts—bagging or delivering groceries, for example. Even those jobs proved hard to come by. One of the workers interviewed by the Heldrich Center said, "Being unemployed is frustrating, demeaning, and, at this point, frightening. Articles in the paper say we 'baby boomers' will have to work for a few more years . . . Now, you tell me how I can work for a few more years if I can't even get a job interview." Another said, "I've always worked so this is very depressing. At age sixty, I never believed I would be unemployed unless I chose to be."

Most older workers who were pushed out of good jobs would never again find employment with comparable pay and benefits. With so many people chasing so few jobs, younger, cheaper applicants were favored overwhelmingly. "It's heartbreaking," said Nadya Fouad, a professor of educational psychology at the University of Wisconsin–Milwaukee. "The older workers in this new job market try to cobble together whatever pieces they can. Some may be working several part-time jobs, and it's up to them to figure out how to provide their own benefits. Economically, it's a huge hit."

For a considerable segment of older workers, the loss of a job meant not just a fall to much lower-paying work but an abrupt and crushing end to their work lives altogether. Slowly, as one jobless year bled into the next, these middle-aged men and women would come to the realization that they would never work again. A fifty-seven-year-old man who had worked for more than thirty years at a job on the East Side of Manhattan, eventually becoming a highly paid marketing executive, summed the matter up over cocktails at a restaurant on Long Island. "It's over," he told me.

"I've been looking for work for three years. Savings gone. House about to go. Three years I've been putting on a shirt and tie, trying to convince myself that somebody needed the talent I have to offer, that I could help them and they would pay me. It's not going to happen." There were tears in his eyes. "I'm an embarrassment to my family," he said.

The psychological impact of a job loss can be devastating for people of any age. "You're in a high state of anxiety all the time," said Russ Meyer, the advertising copywriter from Portland, Oregon, who spent more than two years trying to find steady work. "You don't know where your money is going to come from or what's going to be taken away from you—your home, your car. And if you look for a job for two years and can't find one, you really start to wonder what's wrong with you. There's no way to escape the guilt of not being able to provide for your family—in my case, for my wife and my son. All these dreadful feelings are with you twenty-four hours a day."

The dreadful feelings speak to the fundamental importance of work for most Americans. Study after study has shown that a job is much more than a paycheck. Take away a job and you weaken the pillars of most workers' emotional and psychological well-being. Professor David Blustein of Boston College was among a number of scholars who have demonstrated that in addition to providing the essential economic support for most individuals and families, employment plays a central role in the development and maintenance of a worker's psychic health.

Men and women work to survive, yes, but employment is also the soil from which the seeds of self-determination grow. Blustein, a psychologist and the author of the book *The Psychology of Working,* spent more than twenty years studying the ways in which work provides meaning and structure for people's lives. He noted that decent jobs give people an opportunity to make better choices about their lives. Employment can also swing open the doors to wider connections with others, both in the workplace and in the world at large. "It's a crucial source for gratifying fundamental human needs," said Blustein. "It promotes feelings of self-worth and gives people a sense that they are making a contribution to their community."

Blustein grew up in New York City and likes to tell students about his mother, who worked for several years in a department store that served a working-class clientele in the borough of Queens. "She was a clerk in the cosmetics department. She would say to me, 'You know, I may not have a fancy job, but I love going to work, and I know I'm helping people, helping the women feel more attractive, feel better about themselves.' So for my mom there was a sense that she was contributing, which was really important."

The absence of work for those who want and need it is toxic in every imaginable way. Anxiety, depression, and severe family problems are common occurrences linked to the economic losses and reduced self-esteem that come with enforced joblessness. Households are often devastated. Intimate personal relationships can crumble, as if hit by a wrecking ball. Child abuse, spousal abuse, and marital breakups all tend to rise in periods of high unemployment. Parental joblessness is especially harmful for children. "You try to hide it from them, shield the little ones, but they know what's going on," said a mother of three from Columbus, Ohio, who was fired from her job two weeks after her husband lost his. "The kids know more than parents think. When you're stressed, they're stressed."

The impact on children can be both short-term and long-term. A number of studies have found that children in families hit by unemployment often suffer psychological distress. There can be a heightened tendency to act out, to fight or otherwise misbehave. A study at the University of California, Davis, found that children in families where a head of household had lost a job had a 15 percent higher likelihood of having to repeat a grade in school.

Some of the long-term effects were spelled out by Peter Orszag when he was President Obama's budget director. "A range of studies," he noted, "have found that having a parent experience unemployment is significantly associated with whether you graduate from high school, whether you go to college, whether you get a job after college, and how much you get paid in that job." The hobbling effects of parental unemployment can last the better part of a lifetime. As Orszag pointed out, "The children of workers who were once laid off have lower average wages as adults, even decades later, than those whose parents never experienced such setbacks."

Not everyone who loses a job is devastated. And plenty of people rebound quickly from a rough employment experience. But overall the damage inflicted by chronic unemployment is vast, and its terrible, often tragic human toll does not get nearly enough attention. Till von Wachter, an economics professor at Columbia University, has intensively studied the effects of unemployment on workers who lost their jobs in mass layoffs, especially during recessions. In addition to finding that such workers seldom recovered fully from their financial reversals, von Wachter and a colleague, Daniel Sullivan, the director of research at the Federal Reserve Bank of Chicago, documented a chilling mortality effect. The death rates of the high-seniority male workers they studied had spiked significantly after they were laid off.

"Our estimates," von Wachter and Sullivan wrote, "suggest a 50 percent to 100 percent increase in the mortality hazard during the years immediately following job loss." They found that even twenty years after the job losses, the death rates for the workers were 10 percent to 15 percent higher than would otherwise have been expected.

"We knew that those men had had a very hard time recovering in the labor market, with very large earnings losses that looked like they were going to be persistent," von Wachter told me. "It turns out they had an increase in mortality rates as well that was particularly large in the immediate aftermath of the layoff. It probably wasn't that surprising that you would see heart attacks, drinking, and suicides in the short term. There is a short-term phase where your life is very chaotic. But we then found out that even twenty years later their mortality rate was higher than the mortality pattern of the control group, which suggests that long-term income decline leads to a long-term increase in the mortality rate."

The suicides mentioned by von Wachter emerged as an increasing problem in the United States over the past several years. As the economy lagged, suicide rates rose, especially among middle-aged men. Suicides typically surge in severe economic downturns, and the Great Recession and its aftermath were no exceptions. Rates were already rising in the years 1999 to 2007. When the recession hit, suicides accelerated. By 2009–2010 the number of Americans committing suicide was approaching forty thousand annually, more than the number being killed in motor vehicle accidents. Most vulnerable were men in their fifties. Their suicide rate surged nearly 50 percent from 2000 to 2012. Deciphering the causes of suicide is always difficult, but analysts left little doubt that the strains associated with joblessness were significant contributing factors in the most recent upsurge. The British medical journal the *Lancet,* using data from the Centers for Disease Control and the U.S. Department of Labor, found that each rise of 1 percent in the jobless rate corresponded to a 1 percent increase in the suicide rate. The percentage increases translated into an estimated fifteen hundred additional deaths from suicide each year.

Something fundamental had gone haywire, and the loss of sufficient employment was at the heart of it. The new normal meant the end of the good times for millions who had thought they were prosperous and secure and a worsening of the bad times for those at the bottom of the economic heap. The recession eventually eased but the economy never really rebounded. The suffering remained widespread. On one of my visits to Roswell, I met with the leaders of a job-networking ministry at the Roswell United Methodist Church. The program was run by volunteers who told endless stories about the recession-driven onslaught of mostly white-collar men and women in need. "We prayed a lot," said Geoff Wiggins, one of the ministry's key volunteers. "Stress levels were very high." Three years after the end of the recession, there was still a tone of amazement in Wiggins's voice as he talked about what had happened to his community. At one point, during a breakfast of waffles and sausage at a restaurant just off a busy highway, he gestured toward the window and used the analogy of an auto wreck to describe the hard times that continued to bedevil many families: "Your car can get totaled through no fault of your own. You're driving down the road and something terrible happens. Well, a lot of these guys and gals that come to us have had their jobs and their

careers totaled. This level of distress is new to our community. I'm
fifty-eight years old and I've never seen anything to compare with
it. My neighbors and I had to pitch in to help one family where the
sheriff was putting their furniture in the street. That just doesn't
happen in neighborhoods like ours."

Wiggins laughed when I asked how he'd become so committed
to helping the unemployed. "Been there," he said. "Way back in
November 1991, I was a young guy working for a Fortune 500 company—one of the fair-haired boys, youngest corporate director in
my division. When I got called into the president's office, I was so
dumb, fat, and happy I thought I was getting either a bonus or a
promotion. What I got was a wonderful letter of commendation
and a severance package. My boss said, 'Thanks for your fifteen
years of service, you're a great guy, we wish you well. There's a
security guard in your office, and we need you out of here in an
hour.' That was more than twenty years ago, and it's still with me.
So you can see the impact a job loss can have on a person."

What's different now, Wiggins said, is the vast scale of the joblessness and how tough it has been for people to get back on their
feet. "The jobs just aren't there," he said. "We recently had a guy
show up—he's fifty-three years old, he's been unemployed nine or
ten months, his home has been repossessed, and he's in the middle
of a divorce. He's a wreck. So we're plugging him into our counseling services. In another case, I've been meeting one-on-one with a
young man in his forties. This guy was making over 300,000 a year.
He loses his job, and suddenly that income's gone. He's sharing a
house with four other guys right now. His wife has divorced him.
He's just not in a good place. He's angry and he's grieving, just as
surely as if a loved one had died. This is what unemployment does
to people."

Jay Litton, one of the driving forces behind the ministry, noted
that the suffering went far beyond those who were officially clas-
sified as jobless. "A lot of people are not showing up in the unemployment statistics because they've strung together two or three
part-time jobs," he said. "But they're not making a good living.
I've got a dear friend who finally got work after several months of

unemployment. He's working at a retail store and he's also delivering pizzas. This is somebody who is fifty-eight years old. That's the kind of thing we're seeing."

I was struck by the contrast between the outward appearance of apparently thriving neighborhoods in some suburbs of Atlanta and the evidence of growing hardship that emerged with just the briefest glimpse behind the curtains. Steve Swindell lived in East Cobb, an affluent community just to the northeast of Roswell. He was working at what he thought was a secure position as a sales representative for Pfizer, earning $150,000 a year, when the job market collapsed in 2009. After seventeen and a half years Swindell was given a modest severance package and ushered out the door. Though he was aware that the recession was blowing away jobs by the millions, he assumed that he would find work comparable to his old position long before his severance ran out. He was forty-four years old, college educated, married, and the father of four children. He was a homeowner. In terms of talent, energy, and experience, he thought of himself as in his prime. "I thought I would get a job right away," he said. "I'd been one of the top performers at Pfizer, and I'd never had to look for a job in my life. Everything had come pretty easily. Before Pfizer, I'd worked at GE. My résumé was strong. There were no problems at all in my work history. How could I not find a job?"

Swindell would soon learn that security was the first casualty of the new normal. Much of America's once solid middle class was teetering, with millions falling into conditions of economic distress that they had never previously imagined. Between 2007 and 2010 the net worth of the typical American family fell by nearly $50,000, with the middle class suffering the largest percentage of losses. Once a good middle-class job was lost, the chances of finding another one just as good were very slim.

"I found that it didn't matter how many jobs I applied for or networking meetings that I attended, I could not find decent work," Swindell told me. "I had trouble believing it. I had been making enough for my wife to stay home with our children, and now we were up against it. I'd get an interview here or there, but nothing came of them. I saw my neighbors still working, going off to their jobs each day. I felt that there was something wrong with me. I began to feel like I was unemployable."

Swindell's severance ran out and he began receiving unemployment insurance, a step that further eroded his self-image. "I was never the one who needed help," he said. "People depended on me and now, suddenly, everything was upside down. It was worrisome. Eventually, I got a temporary job as a delivery driver. And I got a job running the Jumbotron at Atlanta Falcons games. But that wasn't much money, and they only have eight home games a year. I did some contract work for Home Depot, but that only lasted three months. Now I'm making $11.60 an hour at the Trader Joe's grocery chain."

He stopped for a moment, as if absorbing what he'd just said. "I was in a leadership role at Pfizer," he went on, "and this is what I'm doing now."

I asked Swindell how he'd felt emotionally during the lowest moments of his job search. "It affected me in a dramatic way," he said. "I went into a major depression. I wondered what my kids were thinking about me—you know: 'My dad can't get a job.' I was surprised at how much I thought about what other people thought—neighbors, family members." He noted wryly that some of his bosses at Trader Joe's were in their twenties, half his age.

"I was walking around with all this resentment," he said, "which was unlike me—resentment toward Pfizer, toward corporate America. And even though it didn't make sense, I felt resentment toward the people who didn't seem to be affected by this economic crisis. Even toward my own family members, people I loved, who were going on with their lives—taking vacations, buying new cars. My life seemed to be standing still. I eventually got over it, but it took a long time.

"Our lives are completely changed now. The kids are in the free-lunch program at school. You can tell they're embarrassed by it. My oldest worries all the time that we're going to lose our home. And my wife went to work. She took a job as a lunch lady in the Cobb County school system. It doesn't pay much, but she gets health insurance. COBRA was way too expensive for us. She makes about $11 an hour, too, so we don't have much coming in. Our mortgage is about 75 percent of our combined incomes. We live on that other 25 percent."

The Swindells had always been frugal, but they were not prepared for either the level of privation or the emotional upheaval that would follow Steve's job loss. As Steve's wife, Lynda, put it, "We realized after a while that things were never going to be the same again."

Lynda Swindell is an upbeat, friendly, chatty woman in her mid-forties who graduated in the 1980s from the University of Louisiana with a degree in business management. She worked for the federal government at the Interior Department and the Social Security Administration before deciding to stay at home full-time with the children. "It was an enormous shock when Steve lost his job," she said, "because he'd expected to stay with Pfizer until he retired. That was our plan. I mean we'd moved around so much for that company, living in all kinds of different places. I hate to use the term 'loyalty' because obviously they didn't have any toward us. But anyway, suddenly it was over. So it was a real shock. But Steve had always been an excellent breadwinner. I just thought, 'well, you know, he'll go to work for a different company.' I wasn't that worried in the beginning. We had savings and he had his severance. But then it kept going on and on, and all these doors were closed to him. I felt terrible for Steve, and, frankly, I was scared. I knew if somebody would just give him a chance—because he is the hardest-working man you will ever meet—but nobody would give him a chance. And here we had four kids, and I'm thinking, '*What are we going to do?*' "

So Lynda joined the great American job hunt herself. "My main thing was that we had to get health insurance coverage. With four kids, I was a stickler for that. Well, all of a sudden I realized there were lots of moms coming out and looking for jobs because their husbands didn't have steady work. Maybe the guys had a contract job here and there, or they were working in jobs with no benefits, or they didn't have any work at all. The moms were worried, like

I was, about health insurance. So they were looking for anything that would provide coverage. But they weren't finding anything at all—with or without insurance. I remember this one woman, she got turned down by Target. She couldn't believe it. But that was so common. People were getting turned down for jobs that they felt they were overqualified for. This friend of mine, she had two interviews at Starbucks. She's college educated, just like I am. And she's like, *'I didn't get it!'* She said, *'Oh my God, I can't even get a job serving coffee!'*

"The same kind of thing happened to me. I'll tell you, it was sobering. I'm thinking, 'Wow, I can't even get a job that kids going to college used to get. Or kids with a high school diploma.' "

The good life that the Swindells had led for the better part of two decades—fun vacations, company cars, casual trips to the mall—was drifting into the further reaches of memory. The present was increasingly rough. Lynda eventually landed the "lunch lady" job and found herself feeling grateful for the opportunity to prepare and serve food in an elementary school cafeteria. "You work 8:00 a.m. to 1:30, and you get benefits," she said. "But even that job I couldn't get right away. I had to sub for several months at different schools, and then I had a three-week trial period before I was hired full-time."

It was not a fun job. Lynda and the other cafeteria staffers rotated the various tasks—working three days as a cook, then three days serving entrées, then operating the cash register, and so on. "Today it was spaghetti and chicken nuggets," Lynda said with a self-deprecating laugh. "I also have to work in the dish room sometimes, my least favorite—especially when they start school in August and it's hotter than Hades in there with a dish machine that gets to almost two hundred degrees. That's difficult. But I've made my peace with it.

"In the beginning I was pretty amazed. I told Steve, 'Hey, I went to *college*!' But here I am. I have to wear a hairnet and a uniform—can you believe it? Black pants and a blue shirt with a 'School Nutrition Services' logo. And I have to wear black nonskid shoes because if you work in the dish room you have to wash down the floor every day. I'm capable of doing more than this, but I'm not trying to sound superior. There's nothing wrong with this kind of work. It's all I could find."

Across a broad front, the American way of life has changed just as surely as the Swindells' lives have changed. A report by the Pew Research Center, done in conjunction with the Gallup organization and released in April 2008, before the full weight of the recession had taken hold, was titled *Inside the Middle Class: Bad Times Hit the Good Life*. The findings were harsh. A majority of respondents said that over the previous five years either their economic situation had stagnated or they'd fallen backward. "Fewer Americans now than at any time in the past half century believe they are moving forward in life," the report said. The Pew researchers seemed taken aback. They wrote, "This is the most downbeat short-term assessment of personal progress in nearly half a century of polling by the Pew Research Center and Gallup organization."

Matters only got worse. A Pew report in the summer of 2012 was titled *The Lost Decade of the Middle Class: Fewer, Poorer, Gloomier*. It found that since 2000 the American middle class had shrunk in size and "fallen backward in income and wealth." The gloom referred to in the report's title was palpable. Only about one in ten of the middle-class respondents surveyed by Pew described themselves as very optimistic about the nation's economic future. Less than half were even somewhat optimistic.

Time magazine, in the fall of 2011, asked, "Whatever happened to upward mobility?" Less than a year later it was asserting, in a cover story, that "the American dream may be slipping away."

How did things go so wrong? How is it that so many millions were finding it so difficult to get ahead, to emerge from the terrible, demoralizing rut of joblessness and underemployment? In a country as rich as the United States, why were so many being left behind?

The biggest factor by far was the toxic alliance forged by government and America's megacorporations and giant banks. That alliance of elites, fueled by limitless greed and a near-pathological quest for power, reshaped the rules and regulations of the economy and the society at large to heavily favor the interests of those who were already well-to-do. In the process they trampled the best interests of ordinary Americans.

Jacob Hacker and Paul Pierson summed the matter up best in their book *Winner-Take-All Politics: How Washington Made the Rich Richer—and Turned Its Back on the Middle Class* when they wrote, "Step by step and debate by debate, America's public officials have rewritten the rules of American politics and the American economy in ways that have benefited the few at the expense of the many."

The corporations, banks, hedge funds, and other wealthy interests had powerful armies of special pleaders—lobbyists, lawyers, fund-raisers, public relations executives—fighting day and night to shape government policies to their liking. Those armies and the endless billions of dollars in campaign contributions and other favors so lavishly distributed by the elites have corrupted the democratic process to the extent that ordinary individuals have virtually no say in how the nation and its economy are run.

The relationship between the government and the highly organized big-money interests became so tight, so symbiotic, it was often difficult to distinguish between the two. Key players spun through the revolving door of government employment and fabulously high-paying private sector jobs at dizzying speeds. Robert Rubin, for example, was a veritable whirling dervish. He entered the revolving door, briefcase in hand, as a co-chairman of Goldman Sachs. Then he became Treasury secretary of the United States under Bill Clinton, where he helped deregulate the banking sector and pave the way for manic Wall Street speculation—arguing, among other things, against the regulation of derivatives. Soon he was back out the door and making staggering sums of money, millions on top of millions, at Citigroup, where his strategic advice called for ever more risk taking, ever more speculation. Then, even with the economy collapsing in a tragic, world-class recession—the worst since the Depression of the 1930s—Rubin was seeding the Obama administration with his acolytes and protégés: Timothy Geithner, Lawrence Summers, and others. Rubin's Citigroup col-

lapsed in the derivatives-driven economic meltdown and had to be
rescued by taxpayers.

One blisteringly hot morning, a few years after the economic crash,
I drove from New York to Bridgeport, Connecticut, to visit the family of Guntars Lakis, the architect who had lost his job designing
high-end homes. He'd been out of work for two years. Lakis and
his wife, Annabel (known to all as Abby), had five children. On
that particular morning the family was in extreme distress. The
air-conditioning in their home had broken down, and there was no
money to fix it. A car with brakes in dire need of repair was parked
in the driveway until further notice. The house was unbearably
hot. We sat in the kitchen, and I looked around, taking notes. Guntars was friendly and cooperative but he seemed haggard. His loose,
oversized T-shirt was damp with perspiration. Abby was nursing a
new baby. She seemed worried and distracted.

Eventually, I would get used to scenes like that, families thrown
into turmoil by the stress of long-term joblessness and looming
bankruptcy, by the fear of what the future might hold. These were
the families not seen and for the most part not cared about by the
high rollers. Another hair-raising year would pass before Guntars
would find a decent job. But while the Lakis family story was like
so many others, one of the things that stood out in my conversations with Guntars was the contrast he drew between what his life
had become and what it had been like growing up in New Rochelle,
an affluent Westchester County suburb of New York. What he
remembered most about that earlier life was the sense of security
it offered. His mother was an engineer and his father an architect.
The family lived in a stereotypically suburban neighborhood, with
front and rear lawns and wooded areas nearby and a brook that
wove its way through the neatly landscaped properties. Guntars
recalled always "feeling safe" in those years. His parents and an
older sister were with him for dinner each evening. Money was
not a problem. The jobs of both parents were secure. Bills were
always paid on time, and there was never any thought that the

family home might be lost. Guntars could come home from school, watch cartoons, do his homework, and all would be right with the world. "It didn't matter how bad your day might have been," he said. "When you came into that house, there was a feeling of security. You took it for granted. You felt like a million bucks. Maybe I was naive, childish, but that's the way America always seemed to me. America just seemed like a really safe place."

4 *War and Its Aftermath*

Every gun that is made, every warship
launched, every rocket fired signifies, in the
final sense, a theft from those who hunger
and are not fed, those who are cold and are
not clothed.

—DWIGHT D. EISENHOWER

The heat. Lieutenant Dan Berschinski was used to intense summer weather, having grown up in a suburb of Atlanta. But the August heat in southern Afghanistan was something else again. It came with blast-furnace intensity. Daytime highs climbed well into the hundreds. The heat was a relentless, throbbing, shimmering presence, and the flaming sky over the sparsely settled desert landscape only heightened the feeling among American troops that Afghanistan was some grim, alien, hostile universe. Patrolling in that kind of heat in full combat gear, eighty or a hundred pounds of it, was beyond miserable. It could make a GI's legs go weak. It could disorient you, defeat you as surely as the enemy could. One of Lieutenant Berschinski's long list of duties as an infantry platoon leader in the summer of 2009 was to protect his men from the heat.

Berschinski was new to combat. Just twenty-four years old and a recent graduate of West Point, he had not had time to acquire the cynicism that developed like a permanent case of indigestion in so many veterans of repeated tours in Afghanistan and Iraq. He was in the first month of his first tour, and there was an unmistakable earnestness about him, the talented rookie just called up to the majors.

The weather was on his mind on Tuesday, the eighteenth, as his unit was gearing up for a reconnaissance mission in the Arghandab River valley, a bleak rural area in Kandahar Province north of the Taliban stronghold in the city of Kandahar.

"Water consumption was a big problem," he would say later, during a period when he had to come to terms with what had happened that day. "You combine those extreme temperatures with the load that soldiers now carry, and you could only move about three or four kilometers before you were totally dry, completely out of water. Trucks would have to drive in a resupply before you could go any farther. So not only did you have to worry about bombs and bullets, but you had to monitor your soldiers because if a guy went down from heatstroke, that could be a huge problem—you know, getting him evacuated and all. Guys were literally just frying their brains in that heat."

The news coming out of Afghanistan when Berschinski arrived in Kandahar Province was all bad. Soldiers and marines were dying at a higher rate than at any previous time in the long war. Commanders were telling the new American president, Barack Obama, that they didn't have enough troops to successfully complete their mission and didn't know if the war could be won even if more troops were poured in. The chairman of the Joint Chiefs of Staff, Michael Mullen, when asked publicly to assess the situation, was blunt. "It is serious and it is deteriorating," he said. Polls showed that Americans, struggling with terrible economic conditions at home, were tired of the war and cared little about it. The big story in the United States was the death several weeks earlier of the singer Michael Jackson. The war in far-off Afghanistan seemed more and more like a lost cause. Pundits were openly asking if it was becoming Obama's Vietnam.

If the war was out of sight and out of mind for most Americans, it was absolutely everything to the three dozen or so men in Berschinski's platoon. Their focus was as narrow as a steel blade. They were about killing the enemy and surviving to go home from a dangerous hellhole. The war's problems were especially acute in the southern part of the country where they were deployed. Maddeningly elusive Taliban insurgents were attacking towns and villages with all manner of homemade explosives, keeping the American forces off guard and tormenting the local populations. Dan's job that Tuesday was to take his platoon into a small town near the west bank of the Arghandab River, have his men dismount from their $3 million Stryker armored vehicles, and then lead a contingent on foot into orchards that were behind the town and irrigated by the river. The idea was to learn whatever they could about Taliban forces that would hide out in the orchards in the daytime, concealed by the canopy of trees from U.S. helicopters flying overhead. At night the Taliban would creep back into the town.

Berschinski's men, some of them as young as eighteen, were still getting used to this soft-spoken, unassuming lieutenant who didn't look much older than a high school kid himself. He wasn't very big, about five nine, 160 pounds. But they were learning that he was fiercely intelligent, athletic, tough, and a good guy once you got to know him. He'd only been in the war zone a month, assigned to the First Battalion of the Seventeenth Infantry Regiment, which was part of a huge Stryker brigade. The Stryker units were lightly armored and highly mobile. Berschinski was the leader of the Second Platoon in Bravo Company.

Berschinski and his men knew from intelligence reports that members of the Taliban were in the orchards, but they didn't know much else. No one had actually seen them. He had maps that showed a rough system of paths and trails inside the orchards, but basically the soldiers were walking into the unknown. Officers higher up the chain of command wanted to know more about the Taliban. How many were there? Where were they? Combat missions could be maddeningly vague. "Our mission overall," said Berschinski, "was simply to move into a new area, gather intelligence, and start making connections with the local populations. What did they need? Did they have schools? Stuff like that."

In mid-afternoon, with the sun blazing, the men started the complicated process of pulling on and hooking up their heavy combat gear. Nerves are always on edge at the start of a patrol, and there was not a lot of talking as the men worked their way into their moisture-wicking T-shirts and body armor, their camouflage shirts and trousers, their combat boots, and the helmets with the mount for night-vision goggles. The goggles themselves were carried in a pouch. Each man had an M4 carbine, and Dan carried six spare magazines loaded with twenty-nine rounds each. He also carried a smoke grenade, a first aid kit, a compass, a six-blade knife, a Global Positioning System similar to those used by civilian hikers, and a CamelBak canteen.

Berschinski had already been on several patrols through towns and farmland scattered along the river. It was hostile terrain and Second Platoon had been hit with roadside bombs nearly every time. The expectation as the men mounted the Strykers around three in the afternoon and began the drive toward town was that this patrol would not be any different. A violent encounter of some sort was anticipated. The plan was for Second Platoon to enter the orchards from the north and move south. Bravo Company's Third Platoon would head into the orchards from the south, and they would end up eventually in roughly the same area.

Things did not go well. Third Platoon was about five hundred yards down a trail into the trees when there was an explosion. Berschinski and his men heard the blast and saw smoke rising on the horizon. A feeling of dread swept over them. The young lieutenant received emergency orders by radio for his men to link up as quickly as possible with Third Platoon, which had been hit with an IED and was taking small-arms fire. One of their soldiers was missing.

Combat is almost always surreal. Despite the wonders of twenty-first-century weapons and communications, what unfolded that afternoon seemed almost primitive: young men with deadly weapons hurrying along dirt paths, through fruit trees, trying to reach comrades being attacked on a hot summer afternoon by other young men with deadly weapons. Berschinski's men came to a small wooden footbridge, about two meters long, maybe a meter wide, that crossed an irrigation canal. Berschinski sent one team across with its squad leader and watched them move on down the trail. Berschinski followed, along with his radio telephone opera-tor. He had gotten about three meters beyond the bridge when the explosion occurred. It was an enormous sound that shook the after-noon. Men went flying. Berschinski was sent sprawling and for a brief moment lay stunned on the ground. Then he began crawling in the dirt and debris, calling out the names of his men, taking inventory. One after another responded. Most seemed okay. But when he called the name of Jonathan Yanney, a twenty-year-old private first class from Litchfield, Minnesota, there was no answer. Yanney was the only one on the bridge when the bomb went off. There was no bridge left, just a huge crater. And Yanney was nowhere to be found.

Stunned and shaken, their ears still ringing from the sound of the blast, the men searched literally high and low for any sign of their comrade. Berschinski jumped into the crater. Others checked the flood walls that protected the orchards. The antenna from the radio Yanney had been carrying was spotted in a tree. Other bits and pieces of equipment were found—parts of a rifle, a battered helmet, and a boot. No Yanney. The men pushed deeper into the orchards, still looking. An order came in by radio to halt the search and link up with Third Platoon, which by then had been evacu-ated from the site of its encounter with the Taliban. Berschinski ordered his men off the trails, hoping to avoid contact with any more bombs. They trudged with their heavy packs through muddy fields, exhausted now, frightened and overheated, and filled with sorrow and anger over the loss of Yanney.

It's hard to make sense of these tragic encounters in which healthy young people, not much older than children, are lost for reasons that, at best, remain obscure. This was not the landing at Normandy. It was a reconnaissance mission that came down the chain of command without being well thought out. Just head into those orchards, guys, and see what you find. Maybe it'll be some-thing interesting. Now two lives were lost and the GIs were left to negotiate their way through Taliban-infested territory with no clear purpose, or even exact destination, in mind.

"By the time I linked up with the company commander, it was

dusk," Berschinski would say later. "I said, 'What's going on?' He said we were going to hold our position overnight and then search in the morning for the missing soldier from Third Platoon. I said we still didn't have Yanney. I assumed he was dead, but we hadn't found his body. He said we'd look for the other soldier first, his name was Troy Tom, and that we'd go get Yanney later."

Troy Tom was a twenty-one-year-old specialist from Shiprock, New Mexico, a Navajo Indian whose middle name was Orion. He'd joined the military in part to get veterans' benefits for college. The army would promote him posthumously to sergeant.

Berschinski's platoon was assigned to an area in one of three compounds that the company had set up at the edge of a small town. The houses and trails inside the compounds had been cleared and supposedly secured. Berschinski settled his men in for the night and promised they would resume the search for Yanney the next day. The men tried to relax. Some smoked. They listened to sounds coming in from the darkness outside and wondered where the Taliban was and how many insurgents there might be. Would they attack? Two or three hours passed and some of the men were dozing when Berschinski received a radio message ordering platoon leaders to assemble at the headquarters compound for a meeting with the company commander. It seemed odd, but he shrugged. Such is life in the military. Berschinski reached for his helmet, picked a soldier to accompany him, and headed outside. They walked past a guard and through a gate and about twenty yards down a trail to the other compound. The meeting was on the roof of a small building and did not last long. The platoon leaders got essentially the same message that Berschinski had received informally hours earlier: they would remain in the compounds overnight and resume searching for the missing soldiers the next day. It wasn't much of a meeting and Berschinski was ready to get some sleep. He and the other soldier, a private first class, began walking back to their quarters, Berschinski in front, the other soldier a few steps behind.

As they approached the gate, they were walking on a path that had been traversed by soldiers countless times over the previous few hours. Berschinski was about three steps from the gate when he gave out the challenge to alert the guard that he and the PFC were coming in. And then, suddenly, the explosion. The noise was deafening. There was a tremendous sense of pressure closing in on Berschinski, and then he was lying on the ground, seemingly on a slant with his head lower than the rest of his body. He knew what had happened and assumed he was in the crater that tends to be left when an IED goes off. His helmet was askew and partially covered his eyes. He had trouble hearing. He knew something really terrible had happened, but he tried to keep his wits about him. He unbuckled the chin straps of the helmet and tossed it away. He tilted his eyes backward, not wanting to look down and see something shocking.

Later, the men who ran to assist him would tell him that he had screamed, "I need help! I need a medic! I have no legs!"

On a bitterly cold day in December 2010, I drove from New York City to Cambridge, Massachusetts, to see Linda Bilmes, a senior lecturer in public policy at the Harvard Kennedy School. Over coffee, in a small conference room, we talked about the tragic hole that the United States had dug for itself with the wars in Iraq and Afghanistan. The government's lack of preparedness for these two great undertakings still struck me as astonishing. The Bush administration, hot for war in the aftermath of the September 11th attacks, had no idea of the magnitude of the task, the number of troops that would be needed, or the enormity of the casualties to come. An orchestrated crescendo for the invasion of Iraq was played for a worldwide audience, climaxed by the "shock and awe" bombing campaign, but no coherent strategy was developed. No real thought was ever given to how the wars would be paid for. The secretary of defense, Donald Rumsfeld, told the nation he didn't know if the war in Iraq would last five days, five weeks, or five months, but he was certain it wasn't "going to last any longer than that."

Bilmes was the co-author, with the Nobel Prize–winning economist Joseph Stiglitz, of *The Three Trillion Dollar War*, a book first published in 2008 that examined the staggering long-term costs of the conflicts in Iraq and Afghanistan. The authors soon found that even the $3 trillion figure was an underestimate. The levels of human suffering from the two wars and the financial toll they have exacted have been breathtaking, far higher than most Americans realized. With the meter still running, the best estimates by the time I spoke with Bilmes were that the wars would cost more than $4 trillion, and within a few years it was evident that it would be a lot more. "The costs have been much higher across the board than we had predicted," Bilmes said. "We had estimated, for example, that long-term veterans' disability and medical care would be between $400 billion and $700 billion. Now, after seeing the actual medical records of several hundred thousand returning vets, we expect it will be between $600 billion and $900 billion. That's a huge increase, and there is no provision anywhere for meeting this obligation to the veterans."

The costs could not be separated from the enormous human suffering. Three years after our conversation, Bilmes reported that "more than half of the 1.56 million troops who have been discharged to date have received medical treatment at VA facilities and have been granted benefits for the rest of their lives." I remember standing, notebook in hand, in a small hospital room in Washington, where I interviewed Luis Rosa-Valentin, a young sergeant who had been blown apart by a roadside bomb while leading a patrol in Baghdad. He'd lost both legs, his left arm, and his hearing. A friend of Valentin's with a special computer hookup would type my questions, and Valentin would read them on a small screen. Then he would answer the question out loud. "I have no memory of the attack, which causes problems for me," he said. "As you can imagine, it's a little tough to be walking down the street in Baghdad one moment, and the next you're waking up in Walter Reed with no legs, one arm, and you can't hear anything. It makes coping difficult."

The hearing loss was especially hard, he said. "I can't call anybody to say hello or tell them what's happening with me. And when people are having a conversation around me, I'm completely left out of it, unless somebody decides to write down real quick what's being said."

By 2014 nearly sixty-eight hundred American service men and women had been killed in the two wars, and tens of thousands more had been wounded. The military was trying to cope with an epidemic of mental problems—depression, severe anxiety, post-traumatic stress disorder, and other ailments. Suicides were off the charts. With enlistees for the marathon wars in short supply, troops had been ordered to serve tour after tour in combat zones with precious little time to recuperate between deployments.

There was no way to minimize or finesse the financial cost of America's obligation to care for those troops. The U.S. will be paying for them for decades.

The recklessness of the nation's approach to the wars in Iraq and Afghanistan was underscored by the federal government's willingness, even as the troops were pouring into harm's way, to dramatically *cut* taxes and sharply *increase* nonessential domestic spending. It was a policy stance that was historically unprecedented and wildly irresponsible. As Robert D. Hormats wrote in his book *The Price of Liberty:* "By supporting and signing expensive spending and tax legislation, President George W. Bush broke with a tradition that had extended from Madison through Lincoln, Wilson, Franklin Roosevelt, Truman, and, eventually, Johnson and Reagan. All of them insisted on, or at least acquiesced in, wartime tax increases, cuts in civilian programs, and sometimes both, as they devoted more resources to the nation's military requirements."

Lyndon Johnson lost his war on poverty to the war in Vietnam. It didn't matter that the economy was booming at the time. The idea that the country would go to war without giving any thought as to how the war would be paid for, and without engaging in some form of national sacrifice, would have been considered absurd. Johnson knew well what was at risk. He would later tell Doris Kearns Goodwin, "If I left the woman I really loved—the Great Society—in order to get involved with that bitch of a war on the other side of the world, then I would lose everything at home. All my programs . . . All my dreams."

By 2003, Tom DeLay, one of the most powerful Republicans in the House of Representatives, was insisting, "Nothing is more important in the face of a war than cutting taxes."

Bob and Susan Berschinski live in Peachtree City, Georgia, an idyllic suburban community thirty miles south of Atlanta, where they run a small family business. When Susan came home from work on the afternoon of August 19, 2009, she listened to a message from an unfamiliar military office that said she or her husband should call an 800 number right away. "I wasn't even sure it was a legitimate message," she told me, "but I called." She was told that her son Dan had been wounded in Afghanistan, that both of his legs had been severed. There was no other information immediately available.

The Berschinskis live in a lovely, spotless, comfortably furnished home in a rustic subdivision that can seem at times more rural than suburban. Susan stood alone in the house that August afternoon trying to absorb the shock of what she had just heard. Her hands shook and her stomach was queasy as she reached again for the phone. "I called the office and told Bob, and of course he came home right away," she said. "It was probably 3:30 in the afternoon. I had been given a phone number to call for continuous updates. It's hard to remember all the details, the state we were in. We called Dan's brother and told him. We didn't call anybody else right away. We were, you know, in shock."

Lying in the silence of the crater immediately after the explosion, before help came, Dan tried to take stock, tried as best he could to stay calm. He reached down with his right hand and tried to touch whatever he could of his body. "I don't know what I felt," he would tell me much later. "I don't know if it was dirt or a mangled portion of a leg. I don't know. I just knew it was bad. So I just kind of laid there and figured the medics would get to me, and pretty soon I could feel myself getting dragged out of the hole by my shoulder straps. Someone was pulling me out, and then I started hearing voices. I don't have any visual memory after the explosion, but I remember hearing specific people's voices. So pretty immediately my first sergeant was there talking to me, one of my squad leaders, and my company commander."

Their immediate goal was to keep Dan alive. "They kept telling me to open my eyes," he said. "I could hear commotion. I knew guys were working on me, and it's strange that I have no visual memory. But I guess I began to open my eyes because at first they were all yelling at me and calling me by my call sign—they're saying, 'Two-Six! Two-Six! Open your eyes!' And I guess I would because they quit yelling at me. But after a while I guess I closed my eyes again because they would start yelling again, and I remember that being repeated over and over. And I remember thinking, 'Well, in the movies if you close your eyes you die, and if you keep your eyes open you stay alive.' And they kept yelling at me to open my eyes, and I was like, 'I guess I'll open my eyes and give the medics a chance. I'll see what they can do.' "

The explosion had blown Dan's right leg off just below the hip, severed his left leg above the knee, shattered his left arm, broken his jaw, and inflicted terrible pelvic damage. The bleeding. The shock. The trauma. It all seemed more than this young—and until just moments earlier exquisitely healthy—body could bear. Death was just a whisper away.

While the medics and others worked desperately to stop the bleeding and stabilize the badly wounded officer, they kept glancing up, looking for a glimpse of a medevac helicopter. The call for one had been placed immediately, and obviously speed was essential. Dan was placed on a litter and carried into a field where a chopper could easily touch down. Though semiconscious, Dan understood the importance of being quickly evacuated. So it was with a sense of relief that he heard the rotor wash, the thumping swoosh, of an approaching helicopter. "I got pretty excited as I listened to it land," he said. Perhaps the medics had worked a miracle after all.

But then he heard, or sensed, the helicopter taking off without him. Something odd was occurring. There were two or three other soldiers at nearby units who also needed to be evacuated, so there were a number of choppers in the vicinity, and some were being targeted by the Taliban. The one that landed near Dan was not a medical evacuation craft. It was a small two-man Kiowa reconnaissance helicopter. The pilot volunteered to take Dan aboard and fly him to Kandahar airfield, which was only twenty kilometers away. The men attending to Dan tried to get him into the cramped helicopter, where he'd have to be strapped into a seat sitting upright. They struggled for several minutes before the medics decided that Dan would surely die in that position. He'd never make it to the airfield. The attempt was called off and the chopper took off.

"I was on the ground for at least an hour," Dan said. "From what I understand, the Kiowa was finally able to get in radio contact with an air force rescue team and they came and got me. And it was either on that bird or at the medical facility at the airfield that I was induced into a coma. The last memory I have is of my disappointment at hearing that first helicopter taking off. Then everything sort of faded out. My next memory was opening my eyes and seeing my dad standing over me."

It would be an understatement to say that the wait for news about Dan was excruciating for his parents. Both felt the army made every effort to keep them updated, but news about their badly wounded son had to make its way from such disparate faraway places as Afghanistan's Kandahar and Bagram airfields and, later, briefly, the vast Landstuhl military medical center in Germany. "They were very good about giving us as much information as they had," said Bob Berschinski. "They have a very difficult job."

At one point, remarkably, the Berschinskis were able to speak by phone with a surgeon and a head nurse at Kandahar. The conversation did not generate much in the way of hope. "Honestly," said Susan, "my sense is that they were preparing us for him to die. As the days passed, I kept expecting a car with a death team to pull up in front of the house. I froze every time I heard a car outside or someone knocked at the door. All I could think that whole week was, 'Please, don't let him die.' "

"The sense at the beginning," said Bob, "was that this kid was so messed up, the odds were against him. The army kept telling us, 'He's still alive and we're doing our best to keep him alive, but that's all we can say right now.' A day would go by and then another, and they would say, 'We can't get him stable enough to transfer. As soon as we can, we'll let you know.' But each day that he didn't die the outlook got a little brighter. Each of those days was like a gift to us."

Still, even with the knowledge that their son was hovering on the brink of death, the Berschinskis did not realize how extensive his wounds were.

A week elapsed between the time Dan was wounded and the moment when his parents finally saw him in a small, eerily quiet room at the Walter Reed Army Medical Center, which was then in Washington. As Dan emerged from the coma, he could see his dad standing over him, talking. As Dan recalled, "He said, 'You're at Walter Reed in D.C.' I said, 'Okay.' I remember my neck was in a brace, a little foam brace, and I had tubes going in my nose, which I absolutely hated. I was very confused and a little bit paranoid. I remember doctors coming in, and there was this doctor standing there teaching some interns about how to properly apply a neck brace. He put a finger between my neck and the brace, and he was like, 'See how much room there is. It's not even effective.' And my jaw was wired shut, and I remember saying through clenched teeth, 'Get the fucking brace off my neck!' I hated it, hated having it around me. And the doctor wouldn't take it off. I just remember being very angry that he was standing there talking to the kids and telling them that my brace wasn't even effective, yet he wouldn't take it off.

"I remember having a lot of crazy thoughts, like, 'Where am I? What kind of hospital is this? Why are they talking about me and not helping me?' But apparently they were helping me a lot. Really a lot. I had gotten hit on the eighteenth of August, and they flew me to Kandahar. They held me there for about six days before I was stable enough to fly. From there they flew me to Bagram, up north, and put me on a bigger plane that was bound for Landstuhl. I got to Landstuhl, and they simply transferred me from one plane immediately to another, and I came right here."

During an interview at Walter Reed, Dan went over the events of those first very strange days.

"Apparently, I was at Walter Reed for two or three days, I'm not sure, before I came out of the coma. And then it was just a blur, a quick succession of surgeries and all kinds of things that I didn't understand. I'd never been inside a hospital before this. I'd never so much as broken an arm. I really didn't understand how nurses worked or how surgeries worked, nothing about anesthesia. I was just really paranoid. I was hearing a lot of voices, odd voices, not what you'd think of as normal hospital voices. At the time, I totally thought the voices were real. Like I thought my dad was getting in fights with doctors and stuff. My family swears that didn't happen. And I remember, like, the wallpaper in the ICU. It was just weird. Changing shapes. And there were voices all around me. I had no sense of where I actually was. Since I've kind of become normal, I've been throughout the whole hospital. I've seen the ICU and everything. I know what it's like now, and it does not at all match my memory, my perceptions, when I was really hurting.

"Anyway, they immediately started doing all these surgeries. And one of the first things I remember my dad telling me, after he said hi and I was going to be okay and that I was at Walter Reed, he almost immediately said, 'Hey, they need to do surgery on your hand, on your left hand. Your pinkie is pretty torn up, and they want permission to cut it off.' And I remember thinking, 'Well, crap, I've already lost my legs, what does a pinkie matter?' And I was like, 'Yeah, of course, they can cut the pinkie off.'"

When Dan's parents got to the hospital, they were under the impression that he had lost one leg at a point below the knee and the other not too far above the knee. "That's what we had been told," said Bob. "But the way these things go, he had to have multiple surgeries. These blasts shred the flesh. They don't make a clean amputation, like getting run over by a train. A lot of times it starts off below the knee and ends up somewhere above the knee because they have to keep cutting away material until they get all the dirt and grime and everything else that gets blasted in. It has to be clean. And they have to keep slicing back until they get to clean material before they can begin to think about closing it up.

So probably that original report was correct. But by the time he got to us, it was the left side just above the knee, and the right side almost all the way to the hip. And it ended up being all the way to the hip."

Dan suffered what was called a hip disarticulation on the right side, a devastating injury that doctors feared would prevent him from walking with artificial legs. He was looking at a lifetime in a wheelchair.

The hope at first was that the remainder of the leg would not have to be removed so high up, but as Bob Berschinski explained, "The hip is a ball-and-socket joint, with the top of the femur being the ball. When Dan got to Walter Reed, he had the ball and a very short stub of femur left. But they ended up taking it out, asking our permission, which we gave, and taking it out."

The loss of Dan's legs was obviously the worst of his very serious wounds, but there were many others. During an interview in which they became quite emotional at times, Bob and Susan took turns describing them. "We already knew about his legs, of course," said Susan, "but we didn't know the extent of his other injuries. I think we knew he had a broken arm. We didn't know about the broken jaw, the broken pelvis."

"His left arm and hand were just a mess," said Bob. "They were in what's called an external fixator, which is one of those Erector set deals with the pins running every which way to hold things in place. You see them at Walter Reed all the time. There are guys who have these things on six or eight months as they try to rebuild limbs. If you can picture something like a heavy-duty cage with pins running from the cage in through the flesh to the bone. If the bone's broken in four or five places, what they'll do is line it up the way they want it to grow back, and then by running multiple pins in from this external cage, they'll fix everything in place."

"His whole left arm and hand were encased in one of those," said Susan. "And they still didn't know about possible back and neck damage, so he was in a brace, a collar."

"There was so much equipment," said Bob. "They had a device called a wound VAC, which is essentially a vacuum that fits over a wound. It produces negative pressure at the exterior of the wound, and what it does is cause the wound to seep and clean itself out. It's a counter-infection and gangrene thing."

"He had five of those," Susan said.

"He had a tube coming out of his chest," Bob said, "because one of his lungs had filled with fluid. He had a drainage tube. I counted sixteen tubes coming out of our kid."

"The only place we could really touch him was on his head," said Susan. "The only place on his body you could access was the hair on the top of his head. And he was on this drug, propofol, the one that killed Michael Jackson. They used that to produce the medically induced coma, so when he got to Walter Reed, he was still out on that."

Neither could remember exactly how long Dan remained unconscious at Walter Reed. They guessed three or four days.

"It seemed like a week," said Bob. "That whole time he had two full-time nurses assigned only to him, and they never stopped moving, keeping everything going. And they gradually reduced the propofol and brought him out of the coma. It's a medical miracle that this kid survived."

"A miracle," said Susan. "We could see little bits of him, his personality, emerging. The thing that probably upset him the most was being wired, having his jaw wired shut, because in his mind he thought that all of his being was behind the wire. He tried to explain it to me. It was terrifying to him. And he wasn't just wired the way we've seen after a broken jaw from, say, a ball field injury."

She paused for a moment, then said, "We had to suction him constantly. I mean like every fifteen seconds. Over and over. Of course, the nurses would have done that if we hadn't, but it was a way that we could help."

5 *Understating the Costs of War*

I used to run marathons.

—DAN BERSCHINSKI

I stood shivering in the February cold at the top of a ramp outside the Walter Reed Army Medical Center in Washington. It was a weekday morning and Dan Berschinski was struggling in his very early attempts to walk with artificial legs. Walk? He could barely stand up on them. There was a wide leather belt around his waist hooked to a harness-like contraption that kept him from falling in a heap. A rehabilitation therapist held fast to the belt. Dan's hands were gripped tight to the handles of a pair of metal crutches. Ever so slowly he tried to move one leg ahead of the other. The goal was to move just a few feet down the ramp.

Dan's parents had been right. It was a miracle that he was alive. Now, six months after the explosion in Afghanistan (where members of his unit were still fighting), Dan was trying with what was left of his body to fashion a new life. He shifted in the harness and grimaced as a sharp pain shot through him. All of his attention was focused on moving his right leg forward. I stared, forgetting for a moment that I was supposed to be taking notes. There was a high-stakes quality to this young man's effort to move one prosthetic limb, and then the other, just a foot or two forward. What he was trying to accomplish seemed impossible. He had only one thigh—the left one, and just part of that. His right thigh was completely gone. In all honesty, I thought he was facing too much pain and had too little strength to succeed.

Dan was disappointed when the session ended. The pain had been intense, and no real progress had been made. Back inside, with the prosthetics removed, he talked about the long and difficult road back from his close encounter with death. "I remember at first I couldn't take care of myself at all," he said. "It was like being a little kid again. I was in and out of surgery and pretty doped up, and the nurses had to do everything for me. It took a while just to get my bearings. And then I started coming to grips with what had really happened to me. Here I was twenty-four years old and a lieutenant in the army, and I'd been in charge of a combat infantry platoon and millions of dollars' worth of equipment, and all of a sudden I'm just lying there helpless. Not able to do anything."

I asked if he was in pain all the time. He shrugged and gave a weak smile. "The pain sucks, there's no doubt about that," he said. "I think people can pretty much understand how much it must suck to lose your legs. So, yes, the physical stuff is difficult. But I'll say this, the emotional or mental factor is much bigger. It's not that easy to get used to. I mean, I was a pretty capable guy. I played sports my whole life. I jumped out of airplanes. I went to Ranger school. To realize now that I can't even go to the bathroom in the middle of the night without a wheelchair is quite humbling. I guess what I mean is, sure, dealing with the pain is difficult. But what's really hard is realizing that, holy crap, I used to run marathons and now I'm struggling just to walk down that little ramp."

We were sitting in a large room, not unlike a gym, filled with amputees in various stages of rehabilitation. Some were on the handful of exercise machines scattered about. Some were flexing what was left of their legs or arms, or lifting weights, or practicing with crutches. Some, like Dan, were in wheelchairs. "There's a ton of guys here who have lost limbs," he said. "The IEDs that they're using now are so much more powerful than your traditional military-grade antipersonnel mines. Sergeant Tom, who was killed in the other platoon on the day I was wounded—his body was found about two hundred meters away from where the bomb went off. And my soldier Yanney? We never completely found his body, which still bothers me. These bombs are like twenty pounds of just blunt-force explosives buried underground. They go off, and they can literally hurl a soldier in full combat gear two hundred meters."

The scale of the problem that Dan was describing was new. The military was dealing with an unanticipated epidemic of amputations. Dan himself was part of a wave of cases in which soldiers and marines who were blasted by IEDs routinely lost more than one limb. The more powerful bombs were changing the nature of the wounds inflicted on GIs in fundamental ways. Alarming headlines began to appear about this devastating new trend, which was being hurriedly studied by a team of physicians led by a retired army surgeon, John B. Holcomb. Working with doctors and nurses at the Landstuhl Regional Medical Center in Germany, where wounded soldiers were sent before being evacuated back to the United States, Holcomb and his colleagues were seeing more and more injuries like Dan's—both legs blown off (sometimes so close to the hip that the individual would likely be confined to a wheelchair for life), along with severe damage to the genitals, urinary tract, and pelvic area. In some cases, one or both arms were lost as well. Holcomb told the *Los Angeles Times* that he and the other members of his study team had been shocked by what they were seeing. "Everybody was taken aback by the frequency of these injuries," he said, "the double amputations, the injuries to the penis and testicles. Nothing like this has been seen before."

There was talk in the military of a new "signature wound" from the wars in Afghanistan and Iraq, especially Afghanistan. A special report prepared for the army surgeon general in June 2011 used the formal description of the wound as its title: *Dismounted Complex Blast Injury.*

At the time Dan was hurt, two-thirds of war-related amputations involved just one limb, in most instances a leg. By late 2010, with the power of the IEDs increasing (and more troops engaged in foot patrols in Afghanistan), 50 percent of the amputee cases involved two or more limbs. Within months, multiple amputations were occurring in three-quarters of the cases. It was difficult for anyone, even hard-core combat veterans and military surgeons, to imagine what it was like to live with no legs and just one arm, or no limbs at all.

Whatever the multiple, the cost of treating, rehabilitating, and otherwise caring for double amputees was tremendous. For triple and quadruple amputees, the lifetime costs were astronomical.

The terrible damage that the powerful bombs were doing to the pelvic and genital areas only heightened the awful distress of the victims. To have one's "manhood blown away" was considered by many of the troops to be the worst possible injury, worse than the loss of one or more limbs. It was not at all unusual for gravely wounded troops, in the midst of combat, to ask soldiers administering potentially lifesaving treatment to "check down there and see if I'm all right." The report on blast injuries for the army surgeon general said, "The increased rate of double and triple amputees, coupled with pelvic and genital injuries, represented a new level of injury to overcome. Devastating injuries of the kind just described took their toll on unit morale. To some, the resultant burden on their family and loved ones seemed too much to accept and, anecdotally, some actually developed 'do not resuscitate' pacts with their battle buddies in the event of this type of injury."

Jeremy Schwartz, a reporter for the *American-Statesman* in Austin, Texas, captured the profound impact of such injuries in a 2012 article about a private first class undergoing rehabilitation at an army program known as the Center for the Intrepid. Schwartz wrote,

Six months after the blast in the mountains of southern Afghanistan, Matthew Leyva rolls into the rehabilitation center at the Center for the Intrepid in a mechanized wheelchair. His left arm is encased in a cylindrical cage, metal rods plunging into a forearm that is withered and discolored. He has just three fingers on each hand, empty spaces where the pinkies and ring fingers used to be. His shorts spill over his lap, his legs gone except for a few inches of femur that jut out below his midsection. A colostomy bag is tucked under his shirt.

He is 21 and had been married less than a year when he stepped on the pressure plate. The blast took more than his legs: it left him unable to have children and dependent on testosterone treatments. With his good arm, Leyva pulls his torso onto the mat from his wheelchair and practices rolling on his back and pushing himself up. If he falls and nobody is around, he will need this skill.

As with Dan Berschinski, Leyva would most likely have died if he'd suffered similar wounds in a previous war. But near-miraculous advances in battlefield medicine were managing to keep such soldiers alive. The next step—the very difficult but crucial task of seeing that their lives would again become productive and satisfying—was still being worked out. Berschinski, in an unpublished op-ed article, wrote,

Only a handful of prosthetists have the experience and skill required to design and build the high-level sockets many severely wounded, like me, need to connect our bodies to our mechanical legs. In short, the military's top-notch medical system must continue to improve or risk leaving behind those that have sacrificed so much in wars we have elected to fight . . . Generals and politicians line up to shake the hands of wounded soldiers like me. My greatest hope is that while they're shaking hands and thanking me for my service, they pause to reflect on the commitment owed to America's wounded. Otherwise the handshakes and thanks ring hollow.

Even with the remarkable advances in medicine, a substantial number of the troops who sustained devastating blast wounds were unable to survive. The horrible ways in which they died were seldom reported in the mainstream press. More than a hundred GIs who succumbed to blast wounds were the victims of what the army described as "total body fragmentation."

The problems associated with caring for America's wounded service men and women—and paying for that care—are mind-bogglingly immense, and the nation has been almost terminally reluctant to face that daunting challenge head-on. Many thousands of GIs were sent home from Iraq and Afghanistan with bullet wounds, broken bones, varying degrees of paralysis, terrible burns, or disabling (and often disfiguring) blast and shrapnel wounds. Some have come home blind or deaf, or both. Thousands have been left with impaired vision, and nearly 200,000 have suffered some degree of hearing loss short of outright deafness. The number who returned with post-traumatic stress disorder, major depression, traumatic brain injury, or some combination of the three could not be precisely determined but was estimated to have reached several hundred thousand by 2013.

Sending troops into war is like feeding human flesh into a meat grinder. Most Americans, whatever they might tell pollsters or say publicly, think it's crazy to risk life and limb in wars like those in Iraq and Afghanistan, which is why so few members of the wealthy and middle classes gave even a passing thought to having their children fight. Less than 1 percent of the population served in those wars. From the perspective of the privileged, they were wars to be fought by other people's children.

The Harvard researcher Linda Bilmes told a congressional committee in mid-2011 that the number of veterans who will be entitled to lifetime medical care and disability compensation resulting from their service in Afghanistan or Iraq (or both) was approaching 50 percent of all service members returning from those countries. It's an obligation for which the United States has not prepared. Very few public officials have even bothered to consider the enormity of the obligation. The costs of caring for the wounded and the disabled do not decrease when wars end; they *increase* in the years that follow the cessation of fighting, rising dramatically over time before peaking decades after the conflicts are over. What that means in human terms is that the agony of war can last for the rest of a veteran's life. In terms of financial costs, it represents an enormous and increasing budgetary responsibility. In Washington's perennial budget wars, that responsibility is all but overlooked.

Bilmes told the committee, "The magnitude of Iraq and Afghanistan veterans' costs is grossly understated in government projections . . . The peak funding years for conflicts are typically so far into the future that they are not included in official estimates. It is a sobering fact that the peak year for paying veterans' disability compensation to World War I veterans was 1969—more than 50 years after the armistice. The largest expenditures for World War II veterans came in 1982. Payments to Vietnam and the first Gulf War veterans are still climbing."

The VA actually lacked the capacity to properly estimate its obligations. Bilmes noted that it had run short of funds in 2005 and 2006 because of budget planning that, incredibly, had been based on data from 2001—data compiled *before the wars in Afghanistan and Iraq began.*

The grim truth was that no one accurately forecast the toll that the wars would take. The costs of caring for the wounded exploded to a degree that shocked even those who tried most diligently to make honest, rigorous estimates. Bilmes and her colleague Joseph Stiglitz underestimated the long-term costs of the wars in their book, *The Three Trillion Dollar War,* in part because they underestimated the astonishing number of veterans who would end up qualifying for medical care and disability benefits.

In a particularly poignant passage of her congressional testimony, Bilmes said,

The Iraq and Afghanistan conflicts have presented the military with its biggest challenge since conscription ended in 1973. In many respects, the all-volunteer force has come under enormous strain. Suicide among veterans is at record levels. Women troops (who make up 11 percent of the force) have been especially hard-hit: divorce rates are three times higher for female than for male troops, and more than 30,000 single mothers have deployed to the war zone. These social costs are far-reaching. They include the loss of productive capacity of young Americans who have been killed or seriously wounded in Iraq and Afghanistan, lost productivity due to mental illness, the burden on caregivers who frequently have to sacrifice paid employment in order to take care of a veteran with a disability, as well as increases in divorce, domestic violence, substance abuse, and other social problems . . . For many veterans there is simply a diminished quality of life, the costs of which are borne by the individuals and families.

James Hackemer would become a quintessential example of the sheer madness of it all. He was a twenty-five-year-old army sergeant who lost both legs and part of a hip when a roadside bomb struck his armored vehicle in Iraq in 2008. Two other soldiers also lost both of their legs in the attack. Hackemer, the father of two young girls, suffered two strokes and was in a coma for a month and a half before beginning an agonizing rehabilitation. Medical miracles kept him alive, and he seemed, against the odds, to be on the road to something approaching an acceptable recovery. His young daughters, other relatives, and friends all rallied to the young man with the neat military-style haircut who had lost nearly half his body. Hackemer did what he could, improvising daily, to get used to his new circumstances. He was quick to smile. Eventually, he was able to ride a bicycle with hand pedals. He would go out for pizza with friends and watch sports on TV. One of the things he most enjoyed was riding roller coasters. In July 2011, during a festive outing with his daughters and other relatives at an amusement park in Syracuse, New York, Hackemer was placed in a front seat of a roller coaster known as the Ride of Steel. It reached a height of two hundred feet and a speed of seventy miles per hour. A nephew in his late teens or early twenties sat beside him. It was assumed that Hackemer was securely fastened into his seat. But in fact, because of the absence of his legs, he was not. As the cars roared over a rise and hurtled into a descent, with the passengers screaming with excitement, James Hackemer was flung from his seat. He plunged the equivalent of fifteen or twenty stories to the ground and was killed.

Americans have been remarkably indifferent to the great suffering that has resulted from the wars of recent years. Politicians go

out of their way not to talk about it, and mainstream media outlets aggressively censor stories and images that might unduly upset
readers or viewers. A focus on the suffering was considered bad
taste, not to mention bad business. Some harrowing documenta-
ries have been made, but they have not had widespread circulation.
So the pain is endured for the most part behind closed doors. With
so much of the suffering concealed, and with so few families having a personal stake in the wars, the collective response has generally been one of denial and indifference.

Americans don't see videos of soldiers and marines dying or
writhing in pain, their arms or legs gone, their faces horribly
burned. We don't see their bodies trembling or torn flesh gushing
blood. We don't see soldiers lying dead in mud or sand or crumpled
lifeless in their Humvees or in the flaming wreckage of a downed
helicopter. The public is seldom given the opportunity to understand what warfare really is, what it truly entails, and without that
information it is extremely difficult to make sound judgments on
whether the wars being fought are worth the sacrifices that are
being made.

In the early moments of the 2006 HBO documentary, *Baghdad
ER,* a man dressed in hospital scrubs is carrying a bloodied arm
that has been amputated above the elbow. It's the kind of gruesome scene that one expects from a low-rent slasher movie, but in
war such scenes are an all-too-common reality. The man in the
documentary deposits the arm in a large red plastic bag. Later in
the film, which chronicled two months at the army's central medical facility in Iraq, a wounded specialist who survived a roadside
bomb attack murmurs from his stretcher, "It was the worst thing I
ever saw in my life, sir." When he was asked what he had seen, the
soldier recalled his last view of a buddy who had been killed in the
attack. "My friend didn't have a face," he said.

A nurse in the film, Captain Glenna Greene, discussed what it
was like to care for the wounded: "It just kills me, because these
are just kids, you know. I'm old enough to be their mom. And just
to see them hurt, it's very difficult."

She noted that some of the wounded were too young to legally
purchase an alcoholic beverage.

While the public was largely indifferent to the nation's warriors (beyond bumper stickers here and there and a brief "thank you for your service" at airports), it gave almost no thought at all to the staggering number of civilians—Americans and foreigners— who have been killed or badly wounded in Iraq and Afghanistan. I remember writing about Marla Ruzicka, a twenty-eight-year-old American who went to Iraq soon after the U.S. invasion in 2003. She was an outgoing woman, loaded with personality, who liked to have a good time. But as her father would tell me, she also had a passion for helping people in serious trouble. So she went to Iraq hoping to secure compensation for the relatives of innocent victims killed in the war. She also hoped to persuade the U.S. government to establish an agency that would document and report on civilian casualties. It was a forlorn hope. In April 2005, Marla and an Iraqi colleague, Faiz Ali Salim, were trapped in their car on the airport road in Baghdad when a suicide bomber attacked a nearby convoy. In the turmoil that erupted, Marla's vehicle was engulfed in flames. She and Salim burned to death.

Civilian contractors hired by U.S. companies to take over jobs once done by the military—driving, mess hall duty, routine security, and so forth—have also been killed and wounded in numbers that most Americans are not aware of. In 2012 more contractors than U.S. soldiers were killed in Afghanistan, a fact that prompted one *New York Times* reporter to write, "Even the dying is being outsourced here."

And then there were the foreigners. "One of the most remarkable aspects of American wars is how little we discuss the victims who are not Americans," wrote John Tirman in his book *The Deaths of Others*, a chilling study of the fate of civilians sucked into the savagery of war. Tirman made no effort to conceal his dismay at "the absence of concern, the want of sympathy, which is so evident in Americans' response to the human costs of war."

That indifference to the consequences of warfare is what makes it so easy to go to war again and again and again. The human carnage, the physical destruction, and the financial toll of any given war are never appalling enough to prompt the public to take a serious stand against the next war. Credible estimates put the death toll of Iraqi civilians at several hundred thousand, perhaps a million, but that was not something on the minds of most Americans.

I've interviewed countless wounded service members over the years. It's impossible not to be deeply moved by the agony and often superhuman struggles they're forced to endure. Each of their stories stays with you. The sadness. The bravery. The triumphs. The battles lost. And then there are the families of the wounded and the grieving relatives of the dead. You search in vain for some way to justify such immense suffering. But there are no adequate explanations at hand.

In October 2004, I spent some time with Eugene Simpson Jr., a twenty-seven-year-old army staff sergeant who had once been a star athlete but was left paralyzed from the waist down when his spinal cord was severed in a roadside bomb explosion in Iraq. "It hurt so bad I couldn't cry," he told me. He shook his head at the wonder of all that had happened to him. He recalled the weeping and the shrieks of pain of the badly wounded soldiers at the evacuation hospital in Landstuhl. "I'll hear them forever," he told me. "As badly as I was hurt, I really felt for them."

Simpson was in a wheelchair in the basement of his parents' home in Dale City, Virginia. When I asked him if he knew for sure who the enemy was that he and his men had been fighting in Iraq, he stared at me for a long moment. And then he shook his head. In a tone that seemed a mixture of sorrow, regret, and frustration, he said very softly, "I don't know. That would be my answer. I don't know."

A well-wisher wandered over to Dan in the large room at Walter Reed and thanked him for his service. Dan smiled, chatted, and shook the man's hand. Taking notes as they talked, I tried to read Dan's expression. He had plenty of reasons to be unhappy, but the only thing that seemed to be bothering him that day was that he hadn't done well trying to walk down the ramp. I was amazed by his apparent equanimity. When the well-wisher left, Dan said,

"You have to be patient." I thought he meant with strangers coming up to him. But he was talking about his difficult recovery. "You have to let your scars heal and recover from your surgeries. But this nerve pain on the left side is really bothering me. That's the reason I'm having so much trouble walking. We're going to have to find a solution to that. It's preventing me from progressing to my fullest ability."

He was on a mission, this young lieutenant in a wheelchair who seemed as focused as a professor who'd just erased one difficult problem from the blackboard, the problem of survival, and was already hard at work on another, rehabilitation. "It's not even that the pain is so bad," he said. "I can take the pain. It's just that, you know, my goal is to walk, and I can't let that pain stop me. The doctors will find a solution. I'm confident of that. It's just that I have to wait, which is frustrating. I have to schedule an appointment, and the doctor will say we have to do an MRI, we have to do ultrasounds. They'll say, 'Well, we think it's this problem—we'll inject a steroid. If that doesn't work, this is Plan B. If that doesn't work, we'll come up with something.' So I have to wait.

"It's a mental challenge as much as anything else. If the therapist told me, 'Okay, you just have to suck up this pain, endure it for however long, and someday you'll be good to go,' I could do that. No problem. The way I feel about things right now, I could do pretty much anything, you know, to fix myself. To walk again. But there's more to it than just putting up with the pain. Physically, it takes a long time. And there are limitations on the science, on the technology. It all takes time. And the waiting—that's really the hardest thing."

He fended off the idea that he might not be able to walk with prostheses. The doctors, trying to prepare him and his family for that possibility, told them about a marine lieutenant with similar injuries who was studying at Harvard Law School. "He just kind of gave up on the idea of walking after a while," Dan said. "He decided he wanted to move on with his life, and rehabbing and everything was going to take up too much time and distract him too much. So he's in a wheelchair."

Dan stressed that he meant no disrespect for the marine lieutenant, but the prospect of life in a wheelchair had never been acceptable to Dan or his family and thus had been rejected out of hand.
"I don't really know how long it's going to take," Dan said. "I mean,
the doctors are telling me they've never seen anyone in my situation, with the injuries I've sustained—they've never seen them
walk successfully. But I want to walk. I guess I *could* say I'm done
with rehab and I'll just get around with a wheelchair for the rest of
my life, but I don't want to. I want to walk."

One of the most noticeable things about someone who has lost
both legs is that he or she tends to look small. So much of the body
is gone. Beyond that, Dan was extremely thin. I asked him about
that.

He laughed. "Well, I was never that big to begin with," he said,
"maybe a good 150 or 160 pounds. But what happened, the main
reason I'm alive today, is that when I was walking down that trail,
we were passing by these six-to-eight-foot-high flood walls. And
what we think happened is that I stepped on the bomb at such an
angle that it blew off my legs, but instead of it shooting me way
up in the air, it threw me into a wall, just slammed me into the
wall. That broke my left arm and smashed the left side of my face,
popping my jaw out on my right side. So my jaw had to be wired
shut for three weeks, and that meant I didn't eat basically anything
that entire time. And then, you know, losing your legs and all the
traumatic injuries, the surgeries, that all contributed to me losing
a tremendous amount of weight. But I'm finally starting to get a
normal appetite, so I'm trying to gain as much weight as possible."

He grinned, then shrugged.

In all the times I'd talked to Dan, I hadn't noticed any sign that
his terrible ordeal had gotten him down. So I asked if he ever got
depressed. He seemed surprised by the question and took his time
before answering. "I'm going to say very slightly. I'm going to say
that because I think it would be impossible to not get depressed
in this situation. But I have a good attitude and a good sense of
purpose. After all I've been through, I know now that I'm going to
live. I know I'm going to have a productive, awesome life, no matter what. It will just be different from what I had expected. I've just

got to spend the next two years, or few years—whatever it takes—training and doing prosthetic work."

He was smiling and seemed oddly relaxed considering the circumstances. We'd talked a long time that day, and I figured he must be tired. We shook hands. I wished him luck and told him I'd be back to talk again soon.

6 Poverty and Inequality

This is an impressive crowd—the haves and the have-mores.

—GEORGE W. BUSH

People feel like the system is rigged against them. And here is the painful part, they're right. The system is rigged.

—ELIZABETH WARREN

Jessica Gallardo's immediate goal was to graduate from high school, a modest objective for most youngsters but a very heavy lift in her case. She was nineteen and a senior at Bushwick Community High School, a school for struggling teens in Brooklyn. The Bushwick neighborhood had been battered for years—decades, really—by the familiar panoply of urban ills: joblessness, gang violence, distressed families, and the terrible erosion of hope and possibility that so often accompanies concentrated poverty. Gentrification and an influx of artists in search of cheaper housing had changed some parts of the neighborhood, but Jessica and her family were very much a part of the older, poorer dynamic. And it was poverty that was making it so difficult for her to get through school.

When I first met Jessica in the late winter of 2013, she was scheduled to graduate the following June, but she told me, "I don't think I'm going to make it." She was working full-time to help her mother pay rent, and when she explained what her job was like, I understood why she seemed overwhelmed. She worked in what she referred to benignly as a bakery. It was actually a firm that sold some baked goods retail but was primarily a wholesale supplier for restaurants, retail grocery outlets, and other businesses. Jessica's job was to lift loaves of freshly baked bread from a conveyor machine and box them for delivery. She and several other workers would do that for eight or more hours each night. "I work from four in the afternoon to midnight," she said. "But Sundays and Mondays I work from four until one or two in the morning. And we have no breaks."

"What if you have to go to the bathroom?" I asked.

"You can only do that if another machine is not busy. Because somebody else has to come and take your place so you can go to the bathroom real fast and come right back."

I asked how much she was paid.

"Seven twenty-five an hour. Minimum wage."

As we continued to talk, it became clear that Jessica was maintaining a daily pace that was unsustainable. When I asked about her lunch break, she said, "We don't get no breaks at all. If you want to eat, you have to work and eat at the same time. So me, personally, I don't eat. I just stay with the work. But my body is in so much pain 'cause I have to stand in one spot for so many hours picking up bread and packing it into the boxes."

For that work she took home about $250 a week, which disappeared almost immediately. Jessica's father was a construction worker who'd lost his job in the recession and had been unable to find steady work since. Her mother had a minimum-wage job as a seamstress. An older sister, twenty-five, had two children and no job. There was also a younger sister. All lived in an extremely cramped four-room Bushwick apartment.

"I give my mother $100 every week," Jessica said. "I have to pay $48 each week for my taxi and $14 for my bus. I take the bus to school in the morning, but I have to take the taxi home from work because it's late at night and my neighborhood is dangerous. It's an awful grind. Terrible. And all of this is affecting school because I'm just so tired that sometimes I get to school late and I miss one class, and because of that one class I don't think I'm going to graduate."

Her voice had dropped to a murmur. She sounded very much like a kid, but her eyes, often sad, looked much older than nineteen. "I really want to graduate," she said, "but if I don't work, we won't have no place to live."

Jessica's routine was not just wearying; it was cruel. Much of her time at work was spent willing herself not to eat and not to have to go to the bathroom. "I just keep boxing the bread, boxing the bread," she said. "If you stop lifting the bread out, the machine will get full and then it will get backed up and the bread will get all crushed like garbage and the managers will get mad. Then they have to throw that batch out and start all over again, so we have to stay there longer. It's so exhausting. By the time I get home from work, it's after one o'clock and then I have to do my homework. That can take, like, till three in the morning. By then it's very hard to think. Sometimes I fall asleep while I'm doing my homework. I'm hungry but most of the time I don't eat. I'll just eat in the morning. And that's all I'll eat all day."

She began to cry.

Jessica's situation was by no means unusual. For the many millions of working poor in America, life is a nonstop excursion on the knife edge of disaster. It's an excursion accompanied by poisonous amounts of stress, which has become an integral part of the American family's cash-strapped new normal. Poverty, in all of its many forms, made a ferocious comeback in the United States in the economically turbulent first decade of the twenty-first century. In the years since Bill Clinton left office, the ranks of the poor expanded by fifteen million. By 2013 nearly fifty million Americans were poor. Another fifty million, the so-called near poor, were living just a notch or two above the official poverty line. They could feel the advancing flames of economic deprivation licking at their heels. Those two groups, the poor and the near poor, constituted nearly a third of the entire U.S. population. Child poverty was an outright scandal. One in every five American children was poor, and one in every three black children. For a while the United States had the highest child poverty rate in the entire industrialized world. In recent years it has slipped to number two, surpassed only by Romania.

Michael Harrington had supposedly opened America's eyes to the misery and degradation of poverty in the midst of widespread plenty with his seminal book *The Other America*. That was way back in 1962. John F. Kennedy was in the White House, and the establishment view was that the U.S. was a righteous, prosperous, solidly middle-class society. The image conjured by that comforting self-assessment was what Harrington called the "familiar America." As he pointed out, "It is celebrated in speeches and advertised on television and in the magazines. It has the highest standard of living the world has ever known."

The other America, said Harrington, was pretty much invisible— the forty million to fifty million people who were poor. The suffering of those tens of millions of fellow citizens was not a matter of concern to the mainstream. "Here is a great mass of people," he wrote, "yet it takes an effort of the intellect and will even to see them."

In an introduction to the thirtieth-anniversary edition of *The Other America*, Irving Howe said, "Mike's book was a *cri de coeur*, an appeal to the conscience of the country: How can you allow such a scandal to fester in this country?" That question was no less relevant—and the scandalous extent of poverty in America was no less shameful—a half century after Harrington sounded his alarm.

Substantial strides against poverty, especially among the elderly, were made in the years following publication of *The Other America*. Medicare, Medicaid, and many other initiatives shepherded by Lyndon Johnson helped reduce the ranks of the poor. But by the time Howe was writing in the early 1990s, poverty was already making its comeback. "Indeed," he wrote, "one of the most terrible developments has been the large increase of poverty among children."

By 2013 poverty had a viselike grip on much of the population, diminishing the lives of people old and young and spreading ominously to groups and communities that had long seemed immune. One in six Americans was officially poor with many others doing only marginally better. On a damp, drizzly morning in December, I visited the soup kitchen at the Church of the Holy Apostles on Manhattan's West Side. The line at eleven o'clock for the once-daily feeding stretched a half block up Ninth Avenue and then around the corner of Twenty-Eighth Street. The people on line were mostly men and mostly very quiet. I struck up a conversation with Anthony Fernandez, who was fifty and said he ate at the soup kitchen two or three times a week. "I have a job," he said. "I'm a security guard. But I don't have enough money. The job's only part-time and doesn't pay very much. And, you know, I'm separated from my wife. I have to pay child support. If I didn't come here, there would be those days where I'd just hang on for a day or two without eating, and then you get that feeling in your stomach, and you feel desperate."

Fernandez was clean shaven and neatly dressed in a white shirt, gray Windbreaker, dark slacks, and sneakers. "They're strict about your appearance on the job," he said. "You have to be clean shaven; they don't want your shirt collar to be raggedy. It's not always easy to stay clean and presentable." We were in walking distance of Penn Station, Madison Square Garden, and Macy's. "Sometimes," said Fernandez, "you have to go up to Thirty-Fourth Street and find a bathroom to shave or to wash. It's not that pleasant."

I asked if he thought things might get better soon. He was skeptical. "It's very hard to find work," he said. "The jobs are scarce, and there is so much competition. The bosses want you to have experience, they want you to do a good job, but they don't want to pay anything. They can get away with it 'cause there's always somebody waiting to take that job if you don't want it. I'm not discouraged. I'm a survivor. But there are a lot of families breaking up now because the rents are so high, and what happens is the wife and kids, they have to move in with a relative, the grandparents or something. And the man, he ends up out here in the street, sleeping on a friend's couch or whatever. I have friends who have two jobs and can't afford anything but a room to live in. I stay in a basement, and there are those days when I end up without even any food to eat."

Father Glenn Chalmers, an Episcopal priest, runs the soup

kitchen, which serves from one thousand to twelve hundred people each day. Sitting in his small comfortable office, he spoke—often in a tone of disappointment, and even dismay—of the scale and persistence of the poverty, hunger, and homelessness plaguing the U.S. "Often we have families with children showing up," he said, "especially in the summer when school is out."

He said the relentless demand at the soup kitchen was driven by joblessness, the high cost of housing, and mental health and addiction issues. "When we started in the '80s, which were the Reagan years and a time of deinstitutionalization, we thought of our mission in terms of a temporary solution to temporary problems. But that was not the case. What we're seeing now is a more or less permanent underclass, with more and more people landing in very deep trouble. We're seeing folks who are just stunned to find themselves in a soup line. People are coming to understand that they are only a job loss or an illness away from catastrophe."

As he talked about how vast the need had become, Chalmers noted that he had three children in college and that some of their friends were essentially homeless—forced to sleep on the couches of classmates or other friends because they were in such dire financial circumstances.

"I'm starting to think that Reagan won," he said, "because they always wanted the private sector to provide these social services, not the government. And that's what we're doing, but in such a limited way. We're not coming close to meeting the need."

He paused, then added, "What troubles me most is that some of us are so busy trying to keep up with the demand—raising money, providing the services—that we don't ever have the time to sit back and assess what's really going on. That's very disturbing, very troubling. We have to ask ourselves: 'Is this the kind of society we want? Is this the sort of thing we ought to tolerate?' It has become overwhelming, and yet there doesn't seem to be any national outcry. People have pretty much accepted what is truly a terrible situation. We should not allow ourselves to remain comfortable knowing that so many people are in such deep trouble. Above all, I'd like to see people get angry, really angry—angry to the point where we say, 'We can't have this. It isn't right.' "

They are only a job loss or an illness away from catastrophe. Reverend Chalmers's comment resonated with special force during an interview I did with Susan St. Amour, a fifty-four-year-old woman living in a homeless shelter in Portland, Maine. She'd been introduced to me by a friend who saw her standing on the median of a busy street on a bitterly cold morning in January 2014. The temperature was just fourteen degrees, and a stiff wind was blowing. St. Amour, who'd lost her job and been unable to find another, was shivering as she held up a sign that said, "We can't help everyone, but everyone can help someone." It was a quote from Ronald Reagan. When I spoke with her, she said, "I used to be that person who'd be driving along in a car, and if I saw someone with a sign asking for money, I'd give them a dollar or two. I never thought I'd be the one with the sign."

She'd been a supervisor in the medical billing department of a company that, as she put it, "ramped up its outsourcing and laid a lot of us off." That had been more than two years earlier. "I searched for a job," she said. "I really searched. I just couldn't get hired. You get to a certain age and you really wonder what is going to happen to you. I've been homeless for sixteen months and, I'll tell you, I can't see any light at the end of the tunnel."

As 2013 was coming to a close, the federal government was cutting back on its food stamp program, lowering the monthly allocation of benefits to recipients. It didn't matter that the need remained sky-high or that the Christmas holidays were approaching. In New York, where nearly two million of the city's eight million residents were on food stamps, the cuts represented a loss of seventy-six million meals a year. The operators of private food banks and soup kitchens described the cuts as devastating and said there was no way for charitable efforts to offset the impact to any significant degree.

The *New York Times* reported on a soup kitchen in Charleston, South Carolina, where worried discussions were taking place in November 2013 about how to cope with declining food stamp availability. According to the article, "People said they felt desperate. Many stuffed extra bread or cake into their pockets for later in the day, and traded advice on which agencies might be handing out free groceries later in the month. 'People at this level of need are already going hungry,' said Sister Noreen Buttimer, a nun who works at the soup kitchen, a Catholic charity. 'It's frightening how we think about the poor.' "

For all the talk about a troubled economy, the problem of hunger in America has not been well understood. Millions of Americans, trapped in hard times, are skipping meals and rationing their families' food. Jilly Stephens, director of the City Harvest food charity in New York, told the *Daily News*, "When I came to New York City nine years ago from working at an international aid foundation serving developing countries, I was astonished that there were people who were actually going to bed hungry in the richest city on Earth. Then I was staggered by how many were hungry."

According to the Department of Agriculture, which administers the food stamp program, nearly fifty million Americans lived in households designated as "food insecure," which meant the families did not always have access to enough to eat. Parents, teachers, and emergency food providers have told endless stories about children going to bed hungry at night or showing up at school hungry in the morning. A study conducted by the New York City Coalition Against Hunger found that nearly half of the children in the Bronx, the city's poorest borough, were in families that lacked sufficient access to food. Poor parents routinely skip their own meals to ensure that their children eat. In the documentary film *American Winter*, which followed several families that spiraled out of the middle class during the Great Recession and its aftermath, an eight-year-old boy named Ocean spoke directly to the pain caused by family hunger. Referring to his parents, who were reeling from the impact of long-term unemployment, Ocean says, "I hear them in bed sometimes saying we skipped dinner because we need to feed our kids. It makes you feel that it's your fault that they have to pay [for] food for us and that it's wasting their money for us. Sometimes when I hear that I cry."

A twelve-year-old named Tara, whose mother acknowledged eating sparingly and almost never during the daytime, says, "I worry about my mom the most. She doesn't really get to eat. I'd rather have my mom eat than me." The cameras show Tara holding up paper signs on which she has written, "Don't 4-get ur lunch mama! Don't 4-get." She pastes the signs all over the house and then tells her mother, "If you forget, I'll be texting you and you'll get in trouble."

Sasha Abramsky, a senior fellow at Demos, captured the soul-crushing impact of economic deprivation in his book *The American Way of Poverty:*

> Too poor to participate in the consumption rituals that define most Americans' lives, too cash-strapped to go to the malls, to visit cafés or movie theaters, to buy food anywhere other than dollar stores, these men and women live on America's edge. The poorest of the poor live under freeway ramps and bridges in out-of-the-way neighborhoods such as the Alphabet district of northern Las Vegas or Los Angeles's Skid Row. Others live in trailer parks far from central cities. Then there are those living in apartment buildings and even suburban houses, who for a variety of reasons have lost their financial security; for them, their deprivation remains hidden behind closed doors.

I was struck again and again by the frustration and dejection I saw in people caught up in the chronic stress and anxiety of their struggle to stay afloat. Jessica Gallardo spent most of her waking hours just going through the motions of living. "When I get home at that early hour of the morning, I want to take a shower because I smell just like the bread and I have crumbs all over me," she said. "But I have the homework to do, and I'm already so exhausted. So I take my shower in the morning. When I get up, there are crumbs all in the bed. It's so disgusting. Then I go to school, I go to work, and then at night it's the same thing all over again."

Gallardo at least had the prospect of graduating from high school and moving on. Over the past several years I've met with an extraordinary number of young men and women, from their mid-teens to age twenty-four or twenty-five, who seemed already defeated. They were teenagers and young adults who were not in school, had been unable to find work, and had all but given up hope. Long before the recession hit, there were legions of those jobless, undereducated young people all across the country. Their days and nights were long and mostly empty. I'd try to talk with them whenever I hit their cities or towns. Writing from Chicago, I noted, "You see them in many parts of the city, hanging out on frigid street corners, skylarking at the malls or bowling alleys, hustling for money wherever they can, drifting in some cases into the devastating clutches of drug selling, gang membership, prostitution, and worse."

Andrew Sum, director of the Center for Labor Market Studies at Northeastern University, has produced a long series of reports on the devastation caused by the extreme levels of joblessness among the young. For years he has urged the government and private industry to respond. The reverse has happened. Programs designed to increase employment among teenagers and young adults have been gutted or eliminated, one after another, year after year. "We've abandoned these kids," Sum told me. "We're destroying our future by not looking out for them. It's such a tragedy. What does anyone think is going to happen to these kids?"

I often noticed a disconcerting loss of affect in the expressions of young people who'd gone more than two or three years without any meaningful work and without returning to school. Interviewing them, I wouldn't hear much in the way of aspirations. Many had given up on finding a great job or in some cases any job. They didn't talk about being in love or someday marrying and raising a family. They didn't express a desire to someday own their own home.

Poverty and joblessness can drain the life out of people. In an interview that took place long before the recession hit, Angjell Brackins, a nineteen-year-old resident of Chicago's South Side, said to me, "I can't take it anymore. I get up in the morning. I take a bath. I put on my clothes. I go outside. That's it. That's my day."

She shook her head in frustration. She'd tried for many months to find a job, filling out application after application, to no avail. She said she'd be willing to do any kind of work if only someone would hire her. But one jobless month followed another, and her sense of resignation only grew.

The recession made matters infinitely more dire. Poverty among teenagers and young adults without strong education credentials spread like a wildfire through dry timber.

A 2012 report from the Annie E. Casey Foundation addressed the scale of the crisis and the precipitous extent to which the prospects for younger, less well-educated Americans had deteriorated: "Forty years ago a teenager leaving high school—with or without a diploma—could find a job in a local factory. Twenty years ago, even as manufacturing jobs moved offshore, young people could still gain a foothold in the workforce through neighborhood stores and restaurants. Amid the housing boom of the past decade, youth with some training could find a career track in the construction field. But today—with millions of jobs lost and experienced workers scrambling for every available position—America's young people stand last in line for jobs."

Conditions were desperate for the poorest youngsters. Without work, they often had nowhere to turn for support. "Youth employment," the Casey report said, "is at its lowest level since World War II; only about half of young people ages 16 to 24 held jobs in 2011. Among teens in that group, only one in four is now employed, compared to 46 percent in 2000. Overall, 6.5 million people ages 16 to 24 are both out of school and out of work, statistics that suggest dire consequences for financial stability and employment prospects in that population."

Increasing numbers of young people, with no jobs and no money, landed in the netherworld of homelessness: couch surfing or sleeping in shelters or cars or on the street. Susan Saulny of the *New York Times* wrote, "These young adults are the new face of a national homeless population, one that poverty experts and case workers say is growing. Yet the problem is mostly invisible." Her article quoted Andrae Bailey, who ran the Community Food and Outreach Center in Orlando, Florida: "Years ago, you didn't see what looked like people of college age sitting and waiting to talk to a crisis worker because they are homeless on the street. Now that's a normal thing." Kristine Cunningham, director of a shelter for young adults in Seattle, told Saulny, "I see them coming back day after day, more defeated, more tired out . . . And it's heartbreaking. This is the age when you want to show the world you have value."

The brutal economic conditions of the past several years have deprived young people of many of the opportunities that greeted postwar children coming of age in the 1960s and early '70s. Five years after the end of the Great Recession nearly half of all the unemployed in America were younger than thirty-four. In addition to the more than 5.5 million young people officially listed as unemployed in mid-2013, there were nearly 5 million who were underemployed, working sporadically, or part-time, or in very low-wage jobs for which, educationally, they were overqualified.

More than half a decade after the recession ended, the job market for young men and women remained the worst it had been in the six decades that the government had been tracking such data. Not even those who had completed college were spared. The Economic Policy Institute noted that while young college graduates fared better than high school graduates or dropouts, they still lagged far behind older graduates who had benefited from the much more robust employment opportunities of previous years. The truth is that the doors of opportunity for young Americans embarking on the adventure of adulthood have been slammed shut to an astonishing degree. When Andrew Sum and his colleagues surveyed the type of work that young college graduates were doing, they found that the most frequent category was waiting tables and tending bar, followed closely by salesclerk at a mall. "These aren't college labor market jobs," Sum said. "Do you need a bachelor's degree to pour a drink? What's costly to the society is that these college graduates are bumping down the next group, people without degrees, and so on. High school graduates and dropouts don't have much of a chance in that environment. It's really sad."

While the official jobless rates for young workers in all education categories were very high, they greatly understated the precarious circumstances of that group. Many who were out of work were not counted as unemployed, either because they'd never been able to enter the job market or because, discouraged, they had stopped looking for a job. Of those working, overwhelming numbers were in part-time or otherwise contingent work. The situation that Dean LeNoir found himself in was common. LeNoir, a twenty-six-year-old resident of Queens, New York, had earned bachelor's and master's degrees in political science. But he could not find what he felt was suitable work. When I met him, he had a temporary job at a foundation in lower Manhattan, doing data entry for $12 an hour. "I've applied so often for jobs it's not funny," he said. "I've done all I could, filled out so many applications, written so many cover letters. It's frustrating. You put all this effort into the cover letter. You want it to be perfect. And then you don't even hear back. You get to the point where you don't even want to fill out an application if you don't already know someone at a place because it seems like a waste of your time."

I mentioned that in past decades people in their mid- to late twenties had begun settling down—establishing careers, starting families, making down payments on a first home. "That's interesting," LeNoir said, "but that's not our experience. You look around and you see that all those sorts of things are being pushed back big-time with our generation. The money is just not there. My mother sometimes makes jokes, like, 'When are you going to give me grandchildren?' I do want children eventually. But I can't even think about when I might be able to support children. I can barely support myself right now."

Wave after wave of students like Dean LeNoir are coming out of America's high schools and colleges each spring. Proudly clutching their diplomas and degrees, they swarm a labor market that cannot accommodate them. No preparation has been made for this generational backlog. I interviewed a young woman named Bailey Jensen who graduated from Allegheny College in Pennsylvania in 2010. She had hoped to find work that would contribute to improving nutrition among the poor. Making a lot of money was not one of her goals. She came out of college with very high hopes, assuming that with her degree and the experience of having studied abroad for a year, she would have little trouble finding a job that paid enough to cover her modest expenses. "I was pretty idealistic," she said. "I wanted to help people, and I hoped to find work that was meaningful. The money was not a big deal to me."

She barely found any work at all and nothing that came close to supporting a decent standard of living, much less challenging her levels of competence and intelligence. "The only thing I managed to find paid minimum wage and promised a mere sixteen-hour workweek," she said, unable to hide her disappointment.

Bailey moved from Pittsburgh, where she had lived during her college years, to Portland, Oregon. The employment scene was no better. "I thought I could at least get a job in a nursery or in Home Depot's lawn and garden department. Was I ever mistaken. I couldn't even land babysitting or cleaning gigs posted on craigslist."

Two years after graduating, Bailey was bouncing from one temporary part-time job to another—as a seasonal employee at the Portland YWCA, as a waitress in a coffee shop, as a clerk in a bakery. The last time we spoke, she was living in the basement of an aunt and uncle's home. "But I'll have to leave in a few weeks," she told me. "My cousin just graduated from college and he can't find a job. So he's coming back home to live. There's not enough room in the basement for both of us."

Millions of young men and women were being forced to put their lives on hold, and for some it seemed like a permanent hold. Birthrates in the United States fell in tandem with the plunge in economic well-being, and marriage has increasingly become a preserve of the well-to-do.

Liz Charpentier, a young woman I met in Waltham, Massachusetts, where I had gone to give a speech on poverty, embodied this new reality. She was twenty-five, had graduated in 2010 from Bridgewater State College in Massachusetts, and wanted to be a teacher. "It's been difficult," she told me. "We had been led to believe that the grown-up world of work would be waiting for us with open arms. But, of course, that's not what happened. I couldn't get a job right out of college, so I worked at Starbucks and volunteered in a classroom just to keep up with what was going on and to make connections."

She readjusted her expectations and moved into an apartment with five roommates. "I managed to get a job as a teacher's assistant, which is very low pay, but I took it. I did that for a year in a sixth-grade classroom, and then the next year I got another teaching assistant position in a second-grade classroom. The plan was to work with a teacher who was planning to retire. I was supposed to be a teaching assistant for half of the year and then a long-term sub for the second half when she left. But then the district I was working for had budget cuts, and I wasn't even rehired as an assistant. I was just let go."

She spent a summer teaching in a program for third and fourth graders, but after that there was nothing, so it was back to Starbucks. "That was discouraging," she said, "but I kept my eyes open for any kind of long-term sub or even daily substitute positions, and one opened up in a town called Lawrence. So I took that. But it was only temporary, to replace a teacher who would be coming back from maternity leave. So now I'm out of work again. No job."

I asked if she could go back to Starbucks. "Maybe if I groveled," she said. "I'm going to have to find something like that just to see me through. It's exhausting. It takes a toll on your self-esteem. It's definitely not what I expected."

When I asked if she ever felt sad or depressed, she said, "Oh yeah. My poor boyfriend—the other night I just had like a total meltdown, and I was like, 'I don't want to do this anymore. I just want to know where I'm going to be in six weeks.' And he kept saying, 'Just put in your time. You're paying your dues. Something will work out.' "

Charpentier's former classmates were also struggling. "A lot of people are subbing," she said. "A lot of people are just temping in other fields. Most are still living with their parents. So I'm not the only one going through a tough time, but that's little consolation. I had a friend who graduated with a degree in psychology, and he's working at a payroll agency now. He said he couldn't find anything else. This is a widespread problem.

"Off the top of my head I would say that between 30 and 50 percent of my peers, the ones who graduated around the time that I did, have gone back home to live with their parents. It doesn't even faze me anymore if somebody my age says, 'Oh yeah, I live with my folks.' It's not ideal, by any means, but it seems to be the way that people my age are getting by."

She sighed when I asked if she had college loans to pay off. "I don't know of anyone who doesn't," she said. "That's my biggest monthly obligation, bigger even than my rent."

When the normal rites of passage into adulthood—marriage, starting a family, homeownership—are being postponed and in some cases dispensed with, there will inevitably be some long-term societal impacts. But no one can know for sure what they will be. In the meantime, millions of young people are learning to live with the anxiety of long-term uncertainty. "For me, personally," said Charpentier, "It's definitely delayed things from what I'd expected. I didn't think at twenty-five I'd have five roommates and not be married and still be paying off loans. There are three couples in our apartment. One couple is engaged but they have no plans for getting married, just indefinitely engaged. The other couple has been together since high school but they're not engaged. They seem to be waiting for things to settle down. Everything's too crazy right now, too insecure. My boyfriend and I are not engaged and we have no plans to become engaged very soon.

"People think about getting married but they just don't have the money or the stability to go through with it. It's kind of hard to get engaged if you're living with your folks. I do have a college friend who bought her first house this year, and I have to tell you that just blew me away. Buying your own home. That seems like Oz to me, a fantastical place that I will never get to."

At the bottom of the heap in this new world of ever-expanding economic distress, far below the struggling middle class and worse off than the people hovering just above or below the poverty line, were the extreme poor, the people in the category that the government calls "deep poverty." These were the folks trying to make it on incomes that were less than half of the official poverty rate. For a family of four, that was an annual income of $11,700 or less. Incredibly, there were more than twenty million people in that category in 2013. They were the people who routinely tried to get by on one meal a day, who for the most part could not even think about getting dental work done, who would seek shelter in doorways or alleys or subways when all other alternatives had run out, who could not even afford to bury their dead.

"These are folks who never get a break," said Mariana Chilton, a

Drexel University professor who has specialized in issues of hunger and poverty. "They don't just skip meals; they often go entire days without eating because they don't have enough money. They have to do trade-offs between medicine and food, heat and food, rent and food. It's absolutely unconscionable that this should be happening."

Although it seems unbelievable, nearly one in ten American children was growing up in the horror of deep poverty in 2013. Many were as handicapped by their economic deprivation as someone with a physical disability. As Sasha Abramsky put it, they were condemned "to run uphill throughout their often truncated lives."

While poverty was exacting its terrible toll on so many millions of Americans, the nation's upper strata were luxuriating in levels of wealth that might have embarrassed King Midas. Michael Bloomberg, the mayor of New York for twelve years, was worth an astonishing $31 billion when he left office on New Year's Eve 2013. His wealth had increased by more than $4 billion in just the prior twelve months. The gap between Bloomberg's wealth and the economic circumstances of most of his constituents was bizarre. Fully a third of the city's children were poor. A third of *everybody* in the Bronx, children and adults, were poor. While there were plenty of fabulously wealthy people in New York, most of the city's residents were struggling economically, even those who considered themselves middle-class. A walk through the city's many poorer precincts was often a close encounter with resignation and despair. I remember interviewing a middle-aged woman in Brooklyn whose eyes were bloodred from several days of crying. Her mother had died, and she'd been unable to raise enough money to travel to St. Louis for the funeral. "I wanted to see her that one last time," the woman said, and she started crying again.

The contrasts between rich and poor in New York could be shocking. On a bitingly cold morning a week before Christmas in 2013, I went by One57, an astonishingly tall residential building, even by New York standards. Construction on the ninety-story superluxurious tower at 157 West Fifty-Seventh Street was nearly complete. I stood across the street on the snow-encrusted sidewalk, a few steps from Carnegie Hall, and stared toward the top. The sleek, silvery exterior sparkled in the sunlight. A couple of apartments on the highest floors had reportedly sold for more than $90 million. While I was taking notes on this highest of high-end buildings, I noticed a woman with two young daughters who was asking passersby for money to buy the children breakfast. I walked over to her, and we talked for a few minutes. The woman said that her husband had died, that she was out of work, and that the family's limited savings were gone. I asked if she was homeless. "Not really," she said. The three of them were staying in the tiny living room of a friend, who had two children of her own. Nodding toward her daughters, who were jumping up and down to ward off the cold, she said, "I couldn't bear to take them into the shelters. I'm trying to find work. Then I can look for an apartment."

One57 might as well have been on a different planet from the one inhabited by the woman and her daughters. The hotel-and-condominium tower was designed by Christian de Portzamparc, winner of the coveted Pritzker Architecture Prize. Billionaires were the target buyers. Instead of kitchens, apartments came with "gourmet cooking zones." Ceilings in the penthouses were more than two stories high.

While the high rollers were bidding up the prices in luxury co-ops and condos (routinely paying $10 million to $20 million for apartments), homelessness was spreading uncontrollably. And no wonder. The *average* purchase price for an apartment in Manhattan was a mind-boggling $1.4 million. The average rent for an apartment, citywide, was more than $3,000 a month. With nearly half the city's population poor or near poor, and with low-wage work becoming ever more the norm, widespread homelessness was inevitable. The city's shelters housed more than fifty thousand New Yorkers a night, including more than twenty-one thousand children. For a variety of reasons, large numbers of homeless New Yorkers were turned away when seeking shelter or—like the woman asking for help to buy breakfast for her daughters—never applied for shelter. People doubled or tripled up if they could or—if they couldn't—

tried to find an out-of-the-way public space in which to lie down. It was "commonplace," as the *New York Times* public editor, Margaret Sullivan, noted, "to see men and women sleeping on the street."

Ian Frazier of *The New Yorker* noted in the fall of 2013 that some homeless individuals had "taken to living underground, in subway tunnels and other places out of sight."

The fabulously wealthy Bloomberg dismissed the homeless crisis with unnerving callousness. The city was having trouble finding room for its enormous homeless population, he said, because the law required New Yorkers to be too generous, too compassionate. In a remark that left even his own supporters shaking their heads, Bloomberg told his weekly radio audience, "You can arrive in your private jet at Kennedy Airport, take a private limousine and go straight to the shelter system and walk in the door, and we've got to give you shelter."

The mayor could afford to be cavalier. He was so rich he disdained the mansion provided by the city for its chief executive. Bloomberg had about a dozen homes of his own, including a lavish five-story beaux arts town house on Manhattan's Upper East Side, a thirty-three-acre estate in the Westchester County town of North Salem, and a thirty-five-acre estate in the Hamptons. He owned homes in Armonk, New York; Vail, Colorado; and Wellington, Florida. He had an estate in London and a mansion in Bermuda. Getting from one of his many residences to another was never a problem. He owned a private jet and a helicopter. It's reasonable to conclude that from the dizzying heights at which Bloomberg was used to traveling, it was difficult for him to see the men and women sleeping on the city's streets, their limos tucked somewhere out of sight.

When Bloomberg closed out his mayoralty, four and a half years after the recession had supposedly ended, poverty had reached its highest point in New York City in ten years and was still rising. But for the rich, life had never been better. As Sam Roberts had written more than a year earlier in the *Times,* "The income gap in Manhattan, already wider than almost anywhere else in the country, rivaled disparities in sub-Saharan Africa."

Manhattan, home to Wall Street, might have set the standard for inequality, but the rest of the nation was not far behind. While the middle class was merging with lower income groups, the wealthy were continuing to benefit spectacularly from public policies that had been boosting their living standards for decades. The result was a vast and growing disparity of income and wealth that had become one of the most ruinous aspects of American life and culture.

Virtually all of the economic gains in the United States of America—nearly all of the benefits of economic growth—go to a very tiny percentage of extraordinarily wealthy individuals. Bill Moyers, interviewing the former labor secretary Robert Reich, said, "The figures are so startling, I had to shake my head in disbelief when I first saw them—showing that in the first three years of the recovery from the recession brought on by the financial collapse in 2008, the top one percent of Americans took home 95 percent of the income gains. Ninety-five percent!"

Reich, who was about to release his powerful documentary, *Inequality for All*, nodded and then explained the sharp distinction between the current grotesquely lopsided distribution of income and the way things were from roughly the mid-1940s to the late 1970s, when nearly everyone benefited from economic growth: "We called it shared prosperity . . . We considered it normal. As the economy grows, we should all get something. And during those years, the economy doubled in size and everybody's income doubled. Even if you were in the bottom fifth of the income earners you did better."

"Help us understand," said Moyers, "in practical terms, what it means when the layman or woman reads that the top one percent of Americans took home 95 percent of the income gains."

"I think that most people," said Reich, "if they really understand it, will say: 'This is not the America that I should be part of. This is not an economy that is working as it should be working. Something is fundamentally wrong. And the game feels rigged somehow.' "

More than half of all the income in America goes to the top 10 percent. That doesn't leave much for everyone else to divvy up.

The top *1* percent, that tiny group securely situated at the pinnacle of the economic pyramid, hauls in nearly a fifth of the nation's income each year. Andrew Hacker, writing in the *New York Review of Books,* said, "Imagine a giant vacuum cleaner looming over America's economy, drawing dollars from its bottom to its upper tiers. Using U.S. Census reports, I estimate that since 1985, the lower 60 percent of households have lost $4 trillion, most of which has ascended to the top 5 percent, including a growing tier now taking in $1 million or more each year."

Whatever semblance of fairness or equity that might once have existed in the system has been wiped out. The typical president or CEO of a large American corporation used to earn twenty to thirty times as much as a typical worker. Now he or she earns nearly three hundred times as much. It is common for workers, with little hope of rising above their low-wage circumstances, to rely on food stamps, Medicaid, and other public assistance for some of their essential needs.

The richest Americans were not only consuming nearly all of the nation's income gains year after year; they were also stockpiling ever greater portions of the nation's wealth. The 400 richest people in the country in 2013 had more wealth—more money and more assets—than the bottom 150 *million* Americans combined. That should have been beyond disturbing in a society that claims to cherish such values as fairness, equality, and upward mobility. It should have been utterly shocking. *A mere 400 people had more than the total holdings—the homes, the cars, the savings, the stocks, the bonds—of 150 million people.* According to *Forbes* magazine (with its ads for private jets with queen-sized beds and walk-in showers), those 400 individuals were worth a breathtaking $2 trillion. That was more than the annual gross domestic product of Canada. With its Walmart fortune, the Walton clan alone was worth more than the collective wealth of the bottom 125 million Americans. These are the kinds of distortions that used to alarm people when they were associated with thuggish third-world dictatorships. Now they've become the norm in a country that for many long decades had pointed proudly to its vast and prosperous middle class as its defining characteristic.

When the professors Michael Norton of the Harvard Business School and Dan Ariely of Duke University conducted surveys about the distribution of wealth in the United States, they found that most Americans had not grasped how far the elites had distanced themselves from everybody else. The prevailing belief, for example, was that the richest 20 percent controlled about 59 percent of the nation's wealth. In reality, they controlled an extraordinary 84 percent. That left a mere 16 percent for the vast bulk of Americans—80 percent of the population—which meant that there were millions of people with absolutely no wealth at all. Much of the American population had either zero net worth or negative net worth. The respondents to the professors' survey had a sense that things were out of whack, that their society was very unequal, but they did not realize just how unequal it had, in fact, become. As Norton and Ariely noted, wealth inequality had reached historic highs, "topping even the levels seen just before the Great Depression."

Jacob Hacker and Paul Pierson, in *Winner-Take-All Politics*, reported on a survey in 2007 in which respondents were asked what they thought the CEO of a major American corporation earned. Thinking of a big number, those who were interviewed came up with an average estimate of $500,000 a year. "Not quite," the authors wrote. "In 2007, the average CEO of an S&P 500 corporation earned over $14 million."

To get a sense of the kind of money held by individuals and families at the upper extremes of America's wealth strata, consider Michael Bloomberg's $31 billion. If someone were to try to spend all of that money at the rate of $10,000 a day, it would take nearly 8,500 years to deplete Bloomberg's fortune. The money would finally be gone somewhere around the year 10,500. (If compound interest were accumulating the entire time, the fortune would never be depleted. U.S. Treasury notes alone would generate a return of more than $100,000 *an hour*.)

Bloomberg, according to *Forbes* magazine, was only the tenth-wealthiest person in America as 2014 approached. Warren Buffett, the second richest, made an astonishing $37 million a *day* in 2013. His net worth increased by $12.7 billion over the course of the year, rising to $59.1 billion. As CNBC's Robert Frank noted, "That works out to a paper gain of $1.5 million an hour."

The richest American, Bill Gates, was worth an estimated $72 billion, according to *Forbes,* more than twice as much as Bloomberg.

The very wealthiest have amassed so much money that many are clueless about how to handle it or what to do with it. According to an article by Missy Sullivan in the *Wall Street Journal*'s *WSJ.Money* magazine, anxiety-ridden rich people are seeking help from practitioners in the new field of "wealth psychology." These counselors, she said, "help the high-net-worth set sort through the complex emotions surrounding affluence." One "wealth-psychology expert," Kathleen Burns Kingsbury, told Sullivan, "In a world often biased against the wealthy, where not having to work can gnaw at an inheritor's self-worth, it's easy to get tripped up by substance abuse, eating disorders and shopping addictions."

The goal of the "money shrinks," according to Sullivan, is to try to root out self-defeating attitudes and behavior by men and women in danger of being emotionally overwhelmed by all their money. In essence, these were people worried about drowning in the vast sea of their own wealth. I imagined the anxiety that some of them must have felt while flipping through the Neiman Marcus Christmas catalog, trying to decide whether to purchase Indian Larry's hand-built Wild Child motorcycle at $750,000; or, at $1.5 million, the Ultimate Outdoor Entertainment System (including a 201-inch television screen that rises miraculously from beneath one's lawn); or the Forevermark Ultimate Diamond Experience, which, for $1.85 million, included not just a 25-carat diamond ring but dinner with top executives at the De Beers headquarters in London and a trip "deep into the heart of Africa to discover where your stone began its journey more than one billion years ago."

This vast inequality, so much greater than most Americans realized, had long since burst the bounds of fairness and rationality. America's vaunted ideals are drained of all their meaning when so few can have so much while so many have so little. That was not what America was ever supposed to be about. What's more, we've been paying a fearful price for this extreme economic imbalance. In the post-recession era it became impossible to hide the tragic

fact that the disparities in wealth and income were seriously harm-
ing enormous numbers of people. Among other things, they were
undermining the health of large segments of the population and
shortening many lives. A week before Thanksgiving 2013, Dr. Steven Woolf, director of the Center on Society and Health at Virginia
Commonwealth University, testified before a U.S. Senate subcommittee on the profound impact that economic conditions were having on the physical well-being and life expectancy of Americans.
"The lower people's income," he said, "the earlier they die and the
sicker they live . . . American children are less likely to reach age
five than children in other rich nations. Our babies are less likely
to reach their first birthday. Our rate for premature babies is similar to sub-Saharan Africa and our teenagers are sicker than teens
elsewhere."

The relationship between socioeconomic status and health is
complex but undeniable. Research over the past several years has
shown that the types of jobs people have, their incomes, the neighborhoods in which they live, and the levels of their education all
have an effect on the quality of their health and their life expectancy. As the epidemiologist Michael Marmot wrote in his book
The Status Syndrome, "Where you stand in the social hierarchy is
intimately related to your chances of getting ill, and your length
of life."

This is not simply a case of wealthy people being better able to
take care of themselves. In highly unequal societies, *all* people will
pay a price—the rich, the middle class, and the poor—though it is
true that the poor will suffer most. Extreme economic inequality
undermines trust and social solidarity. It increases stress and fos-
ters an obsession with material gain. The British researchers Richard Wilkinson and Kate Pickett, in their book *The Spirit Level: Why
Greater Equality Makes Societies Stronger,* explored the ways in which
large differences in wealth and income heightened social anxieties.
They wrote: "Instead of accepting each other as equals on the basis
of our common humanity as we might in more equal settings, getting the measure of each other becomes more important as status
differences widen. We come to see social position as a more important feature of a person's identity . . . Indeed, psychological experi-

ments suggest that we make judgments of each other's social status within the first few seconds of meeting. No wonder first impressions count, and no wonder we feel social evaluation anxieties!"

Under such circumstances, people are more likely to experience feelings of shame and inadequacy, to inflate their own importance and become excessively self-absorbed, egotistical, narcissistic, to equate their self-worth with their material goods, and to look down on others with less, and up to others with more.

What researchers are finding is that economic policies and other socioeconomic factors can have as great an impact on the physical well-being of citizens as public health policies. The Web site of the Center on Society and Health offered examples that were both dramatic and heartbreaking, including the following: "In New Orleans, a person born in the city's Lakeview neighborhood has a life expectancy that is a stunning 25 years longer than one born near Iberville, just a few miles down Interstate 10. In Washington, D.C., residents of one neighborhood near Metro's Red Line can expect to live 9 years fewer than those who live only a few stops further away." The quality of the health of everyone in between can be plotted on a continuum that charts their economic circumstances. Money has become destiny in a way that was never intended by most Americans.

Woolf and Paula Braveman, director of the Center on Social Disparities in Health at the University of California, San Francisco, conducted a joint study in 2011 on the relationship of social and economic factors to health disparities. They noted that since 1980 the United States had fallen from fourteenth in life expectancy among industrialized countries to twenty-fifth in 2008, "behind such countries as Portugal and Slovenia." By 2013 it had slipped to twenty-sixth, according to the Organization for Economic Cooperation and Development. Even the wealthy in America were living shorter lives than in many other countries.

On a beautiful autumn afternoon in 2013, I sat down in Central Park with the Nobel Prize–winning economist Joseph Stiglitz to talk about his book *The Price of Inequality.* Stiglitz had argued for many years that America's extreme imbalances of wealth and income distorted and hampered the economy in a variety of ways. Most obviously, they kept money out of the hands of potential consumers, including home buyers and young people just starting their adult lives. The economy also performed less efficiently, less creatively, and far less productively as decisions in both the private and the public spheres increasingly favored the very well-off as opposed to the majority of the population. Investments in public goods like infrastructure, affordable housing, education, clean energy alternatives, and research and development—investments that would have strengthened the nation's long-term health and economic competitiveness—were consistently rejected in favor of policies and initiatives that funneled more and more wealth into the few private hands at the top. Most of the rest of the population fell further and further behind.

"No one would argue that that's a sign of an economy that's doing well," said Stiglitz. He noted that the median income of a full-time male worker was lower in 2013, when adjusted for inflation, than it had been in 1968. Median family income, which had been bolstered by the entry of women into the workforce, was lower than it had been in the mid-1990s.

"We'd always been the country where more people were making it into the middle class than anywhere else," said Stiglitz. "In large part that was because our kids were able to get a college education, and that was seen as an important part of our competitive advantage. Now you look at the statistics, and we're not number one in any way, and certainly not in the percentage of kids graduating from college. Who is it that gets into what is now the elite, the group that can compete with the rest of the world? Well, more and more that's out of the reach of the kids from the middle class, let alone those on the lower rungs of the economic ladder."

He leaned forward with a look that seemed to express amazement at the folly of it all. "We've put our young people in a terrible position," he said. "They're saddled with these college loans that can't be discharged, even in bankruptcy. And when the macroeconomy is not working well, like now, even if they do well in school, they might not get a good job. So if the economy is not run well and you don't get a job and then you can't pay the loans, well, then your life is messed up. And that's what we're doing to people."

By 2013 student loan indebtedness in the United States had surpassed $1.2 trillion. That was more than the nation's total amount of credit card debt. Student debt amounted to 6 percent of the entire national debt. More than two-thirds of America's graduates were carrying trunk loads of debt along with their caps and gowns as they left school. In many cases, those debts would last a lifetime.

Stiglitz warned that the disparities of wealth and income had reached such extremes that they were standing in the way of a full economic recovery and, more important, were changing something fundamental about the country itself. As he put it, "The American dream—a good life in exchange for hard work—is slowly dying."

On one of my follow-up calls to Jessica Gallardo she told me that she had not graduated from high school. "The workload was too heavy, and I didn't get enough credits," she said. "But I'm not giving up. I'm still going to class, a little older than the other students. But I'm not giving up."

She'd tried to find a job that paid more, and with less onerous working conditions, but with no luck. "It's sort of a race against time," she said. "If I can't get another job, and my family falls behind in the rent, I don't know what I'll have to do. Leave school maybe."

There was nothing unusual about Jessica's difficult situation. With so few decent jobs available for their parents and other older relatives, teenagers were routinely being pressed to help out with family finances. Andy Martier, a teacher at Jessica's school, told me about an eighteen-year-old boy whose family was living in a homeless shelter. The teen had been working part-time as the family tried desperately to scrape together enough money to move into an apartment. Then the boy lost his job.

"I met with him and we talked for a while and he was really down," said Martier. "I was able to give him $40 from a fund I'd put aside for just such emergencies. When I gave him the money, he burst into tears, just out of control crying. He was grateful, but he also felt humiliated because he'd had to take money from someone who was not his family. People don't know how bad it is out here. This is not what you see on television. It's like a depression."

7 The Public Schools

If you think education is expensive, try
ignorance.

—DEREK BOK, *Harvard president, 1971–1991*

Jessie Ramey and Kathy Newman did not seem like rabble-rousers,
and neither was spoiling for a fight in 2011. Ramey taught history and women's studies at the University of Pittsburgh. Newman
was an associate professor of English at Carnegie Mellon University. Both were married and had young children in the Pittsburgh
public schools. They were pretty content with their lives. But then,
like a plague set loose from the state capital in Harrisburg, came
the devastating cuts to public education ordered by Pennsylvania's
newly elected governor, Tom Corbett.

I had run into Newman at a conference in New York, and she
urged me to take a look at what was happening in her state. "You
won't believe it," she told me.

Corbett, a Republican, took office in January 2011. Republicans
had also captured both houses of the state legislature. Riding the
wave of Tea Party momentum from the summer and fall of 2010,
the GOP in Pennsylvania felt that the way had been cleared for
an attack on public spending. Corbett had been eager, for a variety of reasons, to target education, so he pounced. His first budget
proposal stunned public school families. A mother with two small
children in the Pittsburgh school system told me, "It was like a
blow to the solar plexus." She recalled a late-night talk with her

husband when they'd actually considered leaving the state. "We couldn't believe it," she said. "We couldn't believe they'd treat the schools that way. Education had always meant so much to us."

Corbett's budget called for reductions totaling nearly $1 billion in state aid to public schools—cuts so large that jobs, classes, and activities that had long been taken for granted would have to be dismantled. Teachers by the thousands would be forced into unemployment. Support personnel would be fired. Enrichment programs and access to school libraries would be restricted or eliminated. And this would occur in a state that, compared with others, already languished in the bottom ranks of aid to public education. It was a breathtaking proposal. And most of it, despite bitter protests, would stand.

The cuts caused tremendous anguish. Just when parents and teachers had begun to think that the worst of the Great Recession was over, the budget cuts drove the public schools into a state of extreme and prolonged distress. According to the Pennsylvania Association of School Business Officials, an astonishing twenty thousand teachers and other staffers were pushed out of their jobs in 2011 and 2012. "Furloughed" was the euphemism of choice.

Some districts were hit harder than others, with schools in poorer areas hit the hardest because they relied the most on state aid. By 2012, when the full impact of the cuts was felt, the reports coming in from districts around the state sounded like a bloodletting. Art and music classes were the quickest to be eliminated by hard-pressed schools. Also cut were science and foreign-language classes and precollege business courses. Tutoring programs for students in need of special help were closed. It became common for youngsters to show up at school and find that sports programs and other extracurricular activities had been eliminated. In many cases, fees for participating in such activities were imposed or increased. You could no longer just "try out" for a sports team. Your family had to come up with cash in order for you to play. The job cuts were brutal. In addition to teachers, schools fired nurses, psychologists, guidance counselors, librarians, teacher aides and janitors.

Principals and teachers began to feel they were under siege. In Reading, one of the poorest cities in America, teachers at an elementary school were pulled one by one from a student assembly and given the word that they were being laid off. Bridget Manbeck told the *Reading Eagle,* "The worst part was the kids. We were laid off and the kids knew right away." Manbeck was a twenty-five-year-old third-grade English teacher. She was upset but tried to remain stoic for the sake of the children. "I didn't want to break down in front of them," she said. "These kids are losing people who believed in them when they may not have had that at home."

Parents and students held candlelight vigils in a number of districts to "mourn" the loss of teachers and other school personnel who had been fired. One furloughed teacher, tears pouring from her face, told me it felt like the barbarians had breached the gates.

With the school system buckling, a lot of parents in Pennsylvania became radicalized. "The cuts were a flash point for us," said Ramey. "They were truly draconian, and they lit a fire under a lot of parents. They forced us to think seriously about the value of public schools, about public schools as a public good, and about the consequences if we were to somehow lose them. They were cutting the legs out from under our system and we knew we had to fight back."

The parents would soon learn that what was happening in Pennsylvania was a particularly stark example of an insidious long-term trend in public education in America. Pennsylvania's schools had been underfunded for years, especially those serving poorer children. The new cuts accelerated the drainage of resources and began saddling middle-class districts with many of the woes that had previously been most common in poorer ones. More broadly, the state's schools had also been swept up in the so-called reform movement that had spread across the country, accelerated by the passage of George W. Bush's No Child Left Behind law in 2001 and then again by the Obama administration's Race to the Top competition. A seemingly endless brigade of wealthy individuals, foundations, corporations, and politicians (including Governor Corbett in Pennsylvania and many of his most generous financial supporters) had clambered aboard the "reform" bandwagon, championing charter schools, high-stakes testing, online and for-profit education, and a sustained and often bitter assault on traditional public schools and their teachers.

The combination of deep budget cuts to traditional schools and the diversion of attention and resources to testing and a wide range of privatization initiatives took a toll that very few of the nation's mainstream leaders were willing to acknowledge. Among the casualties was the teaching profession itself, which was being deeply and painfully demoralized.

As teachers themselves—college instructors—Jessie Ramey and Kathy Newman were especially sensitive to what was happening. "The school my son goes to, Linden, is an old historic landmark, over a hundred years old," said Newman. "He's in third grade. We found out we were going to lose four homeroom teachers, our dedicated science teacher for kindergarten to fifth grade, an art teacher, our band program, which starts in third grade, and half of our music program. And our librarian would only be there one day a week instead of five."

She made the point that every time a course or an activity is eliminated, and each time a teacher disappears from the front of a classroom, children are cut off from a stream of vital and often delightful experiences. Diminish a child's schoolroom activities and you diminish her life experience. Newman noted that her daughter, a five-year-old, loved art, but because of the budget cuts "art is only taught once every six days at Linden."

Newman met Ramey at a gathering of Pittsburgh parents from the city's East End, an area with a high concentration of colleges and universities, hospitals and cultural institutions. They established an instant bond. Both felt, as they asked questions, listened to other parents, and offered their own opinions, that it was important to strike back aggressively against the governor and other state officials who were setting in motion a range of policies that were badly damaging the schools. Not only was the state cutting school funding, but Corbett had come into office very closely aligned with a range of individuals and organizations intent on draining public dollars from traditional public schools in other ways. They were committed to the creation of more charter schools and for-profit online schools. They supported school voucher programs and tax schemes that would funnel public education dollars to private interests.

"There were so many issues," Ramey said. "But in the beginning we were focused almost entirely on the budget cuts. That was the immediate crisis. The effects of those cuts were historic, truly unprecedented. They were cruel. But we weren't sure what to do. How do you fight the state? How do you fight your own government?"

The increasingly energized parents from the East End looked for other groups that were fighting the cuts and found that there were a lot of them, all over Pennsylvania. Ramey and Newman did what they could to help pull the many disaffected strands together. They arranged strategy sessions, many of them held in the living room of Newman's home in Pittsburgh's Squirrel Hill neighborhood. They began organizing joint projects and protests. Ramey started a blog that, to her surprise, became both an indispensable source of information and a rallying tool for concerned parents statewide. The tone of the blog was often indignant: "Just look at the increased class sizes; the cuts to arts, languages, and even core subjects; the loss of tutoring; and the number of school districts that have resorted to eliminating early childhood education and kindergarten. And you tell us the schools are not hurting because of funding cuts?"

The parents in Pittsburgh soon learned that theirs was by no means a small, geographically isolated issue. They were in touch, through social media and in many other ways, with activist parents across the country. What was happening in Pennsylvania was an especially toxic dose of what was happening to public education in much of the United States. Traditional public schools were under fierce attack, and the teachers in them were being vilified. The activists weren't getting much press anywhere, but I found their commitment heartening. In an era of widespread political cynicism, they were engaged in the purest form of democratic protest. They were fighting back, forcefully and intelligently, against an assault on what they perceived as an essential public good.

The truth was that the parents in Pittsburgh had come to the game late. Corbett's budget cuts were already being enacted before the first of their protests was under way. But Ramey, Newman, and their growing network of allies were determined to fight anyway. Perhaps some cuts could still be fended off. More important, the parents wanted to establish some real measure of control over a system that was crucial to their children's lives. As one mother put it, they were not willing to remain passive as elected officials applied a wrecking ball to their children's schools.

Pennsylvania's movers and shakers were about to meet the people you seldom hear from in the endless debates over major public issues: the ordinary, everyday people who make up the bulk of America's population. They would hear from the parents, the students, the workers—the people most directly affected by the decisions handed down by the elite.

Schenley Plaza in Pittsburgh's Oakland neighborhood is surrounded by classic symbols of intellectual life. If you're standing in the grass-covered plaza, you can look one way and see, right across the street, the main branch of the Carnegie Library of Pittsburgh. Look the other way and there is the University of Pittsburgh's Hillman Library, an extraordinary resource focused primarily on the humanities and social sciences. And there, soaring majestically in front of you, is the Cathedral of Learning, a forty-two-story late–Gothic Revival structure that anchors the campus and houses, among other things, the university's renowned department of philosophy. It was the perfect place to protest cuts to education. But the parents were nervous. This was the first public demonstration that they'd attempted, and the weather was not cooperating. It was a Saturday in early February 2012, and a fierce snowstorm with biting winds had hit southwestern Pennsylvania earlier in the day. The assumption was that the protest would be a bust. But the parents had underestimated the anger generated by Corbett's budget cuts. More than 250 parents and children showed up in the cold and the snow, and so did the local media. The storm had let up, but the wind was still blowing, stinging already flushed faces, as students spoke movingly about what was happening in their schools and about the latest news out of Harrisburg. Corbett, incredibly, was proposing another $100 million in education cuts, on top of the nearly $1 billion that was already in place. One student wept as she spoke about the program cuts at her school. Arthur Mueller, a sophomore whose favorite activity was performing in the high school band, told the crowd, "We couldn't go to the state marching band finals because we couldn't afford a bus." As one student after another took the microphone, onlookers waved signs that proclaimed, "Some Cuts Don't Heal." One woman asked if she was still in America.

The governor's proposed new round of cuts seemed wildly destructive. Nearly all of the $100 million in reductions would come out of kindergarten and early-childhood programs. There was little disagreement among educators, on the right or the left, about the importance of such programs. "It just made no sense," said Ramey. "If there is one thing that we know, it's that early-childhood education is absolutely where we should be investing *more* resources. That's truly the way to turn around the lives of students who would otherwise end up struggling."

That first protest was considered a big success and would lead to many more. Corbett had emerged, in the eyes of parents, as more villainous than ever. "For an awful lot of parents, that plan to cut $100 million from early-childhood education was the point of no return," said Ramey. "It was pretty galvanizing."

What the parents saw was not a simple budgetary calculus, a retrenchment in spending resulting from a downturn in revenues because of economic hard times. What they saw was the highest officer of the commonwealth brutally squeezing the life out of their children's future. As I followed their efforts, I came to think that the fact that they were protesting was as important as the issues they were protesting about.

Corbett's harsh approach to public education was part of a disastrous national trend that had been accelerated by the economic downturn. America's commitment to traditional public education was declining in state after state. Nationwide, public schools lost more than a quarter of a million staffers and administrators from

2010 to 2012. More than 150,000 of them were teachers. A study of education spending in forty-six states by the Center on Budget and Policy Priorities found that cuts in aid to public schools had been "widespread and very deep." Nearly two-thirds of the nation's school districts were providing fewer dollars per student in 2012 than they had in 2008. In many districts, parents who could afford it were digging into their pockets for cash to pay for services and even staff positions that would otherwise have been lost. The Center on Budget and Policy Priorities noted, "At least 23 states have deeply cut pre-kindergarten and/or K–12 spending. Mississippi will fail for the fourth year in a row to meet statutory spending requirements enacted to ensure adequate funding in all school districts. The three previous years of underfunding have cost over 2,000 school employees their jobs."

More than a hundred districts, many of them in rural areas, reduced the school week to four days. Nearly half of all districts in California cut back on art, drama, and music programs.

My former colleague at the *New York Times* Nick Kristof went back to visit his old high school in rural Yamhill, Oregon, in 2011. He found that the number of school days had been reduced to 167 from the typical 180. The school newspaper was gone. Students were being saddled with a fee of $125 to participate in a team sport. The school district's business manager told Kristof, "It's like a long, slow bleed, watching things disappear." The superintendent of schools, Steve Chiovaro, ruefully noted, "Every year we say: What can we cut? What can we reduce? We've gotten to the point where we can no longer 'do no harm.' We're starting to eviscerate education."

As the economy slowly improved, many school districts began restoring some of the cuts. But there was no effort to restore either the financial or the political commitment to a robust public school system that had once been a hallmark of American education. That was not just shortsighted; it was aggressively self-destructive. Backtracking on education is the societal equivalent of mainlining heroin. Laura D'Andrea Tyson, a professor at Berkeley who served as chairwoman of the Council of Economic Advisers during the Clinton administration, expressed her alarm when she wrote, "A core American value is that each individual should have the opportunity to realize his or her potential. Birth needn't dictate destiny. Education has been the traditional American pathway to opportunity and upward mobility, but this pathway is closing for a growing number of Americans in low- and middle-income families."

Jessie Ramey stressed another crucial value. Without adequate funding, the United States loses public education as a cornerstone of its democracy, the foundation of an informed citizenry. The resistance to the cuts in Pennsylvania intensified. Although scrupulously well mannered, Ramey, Newman, and the other parents in Pittsburgh's East End were growing increasingly angry as the teacher firings and loss of services continued rolling through their schools. One woman took me aside at a rally and whispered that she was *pissed off about all this.*" Parents swapped endless stories about children who were upset over the loss of classes they'd once had, or about teachers they missed, or about showing up at the locked door of a school library and peering through a window at books they were unable to access. Ramey wrote on her blog about the governor's "vampiric budget." At house parties at which nothing stronger than coffee and herbal tea was served, the parents rolled up their sleeves and defiantly flexed their civic muscles. Sara Goodkind, a parent I met at Newman's house, said, "We realized we weren't going to get anywhere just fighting at the local level. We all agreed that we had to take it further."

Frederick Douglass had counseled that "power concedes nothing without a demand." The parents would make sure that their demands were heard.

With Ramey and Newman and a handful of others taking the lead, the Pittsburgh parents worked closely with an established statewide organization called Education Voters Pennsylvania. "They had sponsored a series of call-your-legislator days, which had been quite effective," Ramey said. "So we started arranging our own call-your-legislator and then write-your-legislator days for our parents and students."

Soon the members of the state senate and the general assembly found themselves inundated with calls, letters, texts, tweets, e-mail, and Facebook postings decrying the budget cuts. "We were not going to be ignored," said Newman. "We might not win, but it wouldn't be for lack of trying."

Some of Governor Corbett's public pronouncements fed the parents' fury. Using various forms of budgetary doublespeak, he would at times suggest that state funding for the public schools was actually increasing. Such assertions drove the parents wild. Ramey would pump entries into her blog explaining how a particular program could receive a modest increase in funding while overall state support for education was being dramatically reduced. Corbett had actually dismissed some of the complaints about budget cuts as an "urban legend." Ramey wrote, "Sadly, this is no urban legend. In fact, some of the school districts that are being hit hardest by these state cuts are outside the urban core." She then rattled off a long list of suburban and rural school districts that had sustained cuts of $1 million or more, districts with names like Baldwin-Whitehall, East Allegheny, McKeesport, Penn Hills, Plum Borough, Armstrong, Apollo-Ridge, Big Beaver Falls, Belle Vernon. She noted that there were many other districts that had lost nearly a million. And the governor, she noted, wanted still more cuts.

Ramey's blog (yinzercation.wordpress.com) became a cornerstone of the statewide movement, serving a function similar to that of the pamphlets and essays that rallied the citizenry in the early days of the Republic. "PUBLIC EDUCATION IS A PUBLIC GOOD!" the blog blared. "HELP SAVE OUR SCHOOLS!" Many of the postings went viral. Articles and essays from the blog, all written by Ramey, were frequently picked up by the *Huffington Post* and *AlterNet*.

"You could tell we were having an impact," Ramey said. "We were getting feedback from the top officials in state government, and after a while it became obvious we were getting under the governor's skin."

More and more protests were organized. Students held mock bake sales to highlight the enormity of the cuts. They gave away cupcakes and cookies while handing out flyers that said it was impossible to sell enough pastry to offset the cuts in any meaningful way. Newman pulled together a group of students and parents for a trip to Harrisburg, where they spent the day calling on legislators, distributing cookies and talking points, and giving interviews to the press. Student posters were ubiquitous at all the demonstrations: "We want our library back." "We miss our science teacher." "Art was my favorite subject." "I'm a drummer without a band."

And then, suddenly, unexpectedly, came a gift from the public relations gods. Sara Segel, one of the protesting parents, recalled being in a Target store one afternoon in the spring of 2012 when she got an e-mail from Ramey and Newman. It said Corbett and his wife were going to receive a lifetime achievement award from the Pittsburgh Opera for, of all things, their extraordinary contributions to the arts and education. The man whose budget cuts were visiting wholesale destruction on student art and music programs, and that were driving teachers out of their jobs and closing school libraries all over the state, was to be held up as a sterling example of all that was positive and good about the arts, culture, and education. "Oh, the irony!" said Segel. "I said to myself on the spot, 'Oh my God, this is a gift.' "

The Corbetts were to be honored at a lavish $750-a-plate black-tie dinner. Ramey raced to her computer. She wrote in her blog,

> Believe it or not, the Pittsburgh Opera is planning to honor Gov. Corbett with a lifetime achievement award for his contributions to . . . wait for it . . . EDUCATION! I kid you not. The Opera announced that Corbett "will be honored for his early work as a teacher as well as his long-standing protection of the public interest" and that, "as Governor, he has recognized the economic, educational, and social value of the arts."
>
> Is the Opera so out of touch that it doesn't realize Gov. Corbett has actually *devastated* public education, cutting $1 BILLION from Pennsylvania's schools these past two years? These cuts have crippled local school districts, which have been forced to slash arts education.

She noted that 44 percent of the state's school districts had already eliminated courses and others were already planning eliminations:

The first to go? Arts, music and foreign languages—the very things students need to become educated citizens who will appreciate the arts, be patrons of the arts, and become future artists themselves. Last week, 1,000 people gathered in Upper Darby, outside of Philadelphia, to protest the state cuts that have forced that district to eliminate all elementary arts and music programming, as well as foreign languages in the middle schools. *This* is Gov. Corbett's true legacy to the arts. And look at what is happening right here in Pittsburgh: our flagship arts school, CAPA [the Creative and Performing Arts school], is cutting private music lessons. Taylor Allderdice is laying off its marching band director. Elementary schools across the district are losing music, art, library, and language instruction. How in the world are our kids going to become opera lovers?

She went on:

It's also farcical to hear the Opera and Gov. Corbett himself touting his credentials as a former teacher. He taught high school for *one year* in the Pine Grove Area School district out in Schuylkill County. That school district, by the way, has lost $1.1 MILLION in education cuts these past two years. The de-funding of public education in Pennsylvania is a tragedy of operatic proportions. Instead of celebrating Gov. Corbett, the Pittsburgh Opera ought to stage *The Beggar's Opera* to recognize how public schools have become beggars, hoping to salvage their arts curriculum with donations. That opera is an 18th century classic still popular today for its themes of political corruption and poverty. Sounds just right.

The outrage spread quickly. The opera's Facebook page was bombarded with angry posts. A *Huffington Post* article said, "The lifetime achievement award creates an unfortunate atmospheric of 'Let Them Eat Cake' obliviousness." Parents, students, and a host of civic organizations began mobilizing. And their big project was a planned demonstration—an "Operatic Extravaganza," as Ramey put it—outside the Pittsburgh Opera's headquarters on the night of the awards gala. "This will be a super fun event," Ramey promised, "with people dressed in opera costumes, activities for kids, and lots of student performing groups."

Sara Segel had been correct. The opera's award to the governor was a gift that kept on giving.

The weather could hardly have been nicer on the evening of May 12, 2012. It was a beautiful night for a gala, and you couldn't help but notice, if you were outside the opera around 6:00 p.m., that an awful lot of the people who were showing up were members of Pittsburgh's economic and cultural elite. Many arrived in luxury vehicles—limousines, Mercedes, BMWs. "It was a warm night, and the women were wearing beautiful gowns, like they were going to the Academy Awards," said Newman.

The hundreds of protesters who were on hand to greet the guests had something less refined in mind. They ranged in age from toddlers to the elderly. Many were long-standing lovers of the arts, but they were committed, for one night at least, to raucous, if not outlandish, behavior. The spirit of the protest was captured by a political cartoonist, Rob Rogers, who, referring to Corbett's lifetime achievement award, said in a comic strip, "That's like giving Godzilla an award for urban planning."

Horned helmets and other bits and pieces of opera garb were ubiquitous among the protesters, who sang, staged mock sword fights, and applauded loudly at every derisive reference to Corbett. Student musicians brought their instruments and played as loud as they could while onlookers waved signs decrying the loss of school music programs. The crowd was serious one moment—listening to speakers lamenting the cuts and explaining (often with great emotion) the importance of a solid, well-rounded education—and then, in the next moment, matters would give way to a general hilarity, including abominable renditions of famous arias.

The rally drew extensive television and newspaper coverage and was considered a "smash hit" by participants. As the protesters were leaving, a four-year-old, with the remnants of a cotton candy in one hand and his other holding on to his mother's jacket, asked, "When are we gonna do it again?"

Corbett's first round of cuts, which ended up totaling about

$900 million, remained in place. But the protesting parents real-
ized a major victory when the governor and his allies felt they had
to back down on the additional cuts, the $100 million that would
have come out of kindergarten and early-childhood education programs. A powerful new force in Pennsylvania politics had emerged,
and the state's leaders recognized that it would have to be dealt
with. The parents had become well organized statewide, not just
at the local level. They were smart and relentless and had a sharp
sense of public relations. And they were masters of social media,
able to mobilize at virtually a moment's notice. They had come out
of nowhere to make the voices of ordinary people heard, which, as
one parent put it, "is the essence of a true democracy."

On a cold, dreary morning in January 2013, I met the education
historian Diane Ravitch for breakfast at a quiet neighborhood restaurant in Brooklyn Heights, just across the East River from lower
Manhattan. A thin coating of slush was on the sidewalk and a light
rain was falling as we walked into the blessedly warm restaurant.
We found a table near the back and sat down for a long conversation. Late in her career, the highly respected Ravitch had executed
a full-blown philosophical pivot. For years she'd been a strong sup-
porter of the "reform" movement that championed charter schools,
high-stakes testing, rigid teacher accountability, and school choice.
But what she found after many years of near-obsessive attention to
public education was that those corporate-style practices—which
advocates had promised would revitalize the nation's schools, end
racial and ethnic achievement gaps, and even begin to wipe out
poverty—were not working. Children were not learning more.
Achievement gaps were not closing. And the charter and online
schools were taking money and other critical resources away from
traditional public schools.

   "Yes, there is a crisis in American education today," Ravitch told
me, "but it's not what a lot of people think. The crisis has been
caused by this so-called reform movement that is pushing so many
bad ideas that don't work and will actually harm children."

Among the worst of the ideas was the reliance on standardized tests as the key to educational excellence. This was not just a basic tenet of the movement; it had become a doctrine of absolute faith that permeated the public education establishment.

The testing craze had gotten its unfortunate foothold in the public schools toward the end of the twentieth century. It was seen as a way of imposing accountability on a public school system that policy makers and a new generation of reformers insisted was failing. The relentless testing that they saw as an answer—in many cases, as *the* answer—was toxic from the beginning. But it took a truly harrowing turn when President George W. Bush signed his far-reaching No Child Left Behind program into law.

Despite wide support from the right and the left, the testing components of No Child Left Behind defied common sense. They required states to test students in reading and math every year in grades three through eight and at least once in high school. The most glaring flaw in the law was its imposition of a mandate that could never be met. By law, test scores at every school had to improve every year. This steady improvement, according to the law's architects, would culminate in every student in the United States demonstrating proficiency in reading and math by 2014. That was not just unreasonable; it was delusionary. No such achievement was humanly possible. No country has ever, could ever, achieve 100 percent student proficiency—by 2014 or any other time. But No Child Left Behind demanded it and imposed severe punishment on schools that did not demonstrate the required annual gains, what the law benignly called "adequate yearly progress." Teachers and principals were fired in schools that repeatedly missed their goals. A huge number of struggling schools were given the educational equivalent of the death penalty. They were shut down. Many had been important civic cornerstones of their neighborhoods and communities. When 2014 arrived and nothing even approaching the mandated progress had occurred, it was impossible to contend that 100 percent proficiency had been anything but a fantasy.

No Child Left Behind was the most extensive federal involvement in public education in the nation's history, and no aspect of the law was more disruptive than its testing requirements. The tests were supposed to measure student accomplishment and the effectiveness of teachers and principals. The sanctions against those who did poorly would, in theory, prompt them to do better. The threat of being held back, of being forced to go to summer school, of not graduating from high school, was supposed to make students work harder, study more. At the same time, the fear of being fired would—in the view of the proponents of testing—create such pressure on teachers and principals that they would up their game. Those who couldn't cut it would be driven from the profession.

The testing craze spread like a fire out of control. It didn't matter that there was no evidence, empirical or otherwise, that the tests with their dire consequences would improve the quality of education in America. Some states went beyond the federal requirements and began establishing additional tests of their own. Teachers whose students did poorly on the tests were denounced, ridiculed by newspaper and magazine writers, television commentators, elected officials, and other instant education experts. Teachers' unions were excoriated for allegedly protecting the malefactors. Some districts established so-called teacher-proof curricula, which obliged teachers to rigidly follow carefully scripted teaching guides. The idea was to have each subject taught in exactly the same way, at exactly the same pace. Everyone would be on the same page, literally. The mandate: raise the test scores, or else.

"You don't think that has been demoralizing to teachers?" Ravitch said to me. "They're under constant attack and they feel a real sense of powerlessness."

The testing, she noted, had expanded far beyond any sense of reasonable proportion. It had become "the primary measure of school quality."

Principals and teachers became obsessed with their students' scores. Inevitably, they began teaching to the mandated tests while radically narrowing the rest of the curriculum. The only thing that mattered was to get those scores higher and higher.

The results were hardly edifying. In 2011, after a decade of No Child Left Behind, even Joel Klein, who presided as chancellor over the "radical reform" of New York City's public schools, had to acknowledge that very little real progress had been made. In an article for the *Atlantic* magazine, he wrote that nationally, despite years of effort, "the gains we have made in improving our schools are negligible." Klein was a former federal prosecutor who was appointed chancellor by Michael Bloomberg, a powerful mayor who had acquired unprecedented control of the city's school system. With Bloomberg's blessing, Klein had opened charter schools, closed schools that he determined were doing poorly, gone to war against the city's teachers, and genuflected before the mighty god of testing. (In some cases Klein had to actually close the new schools he had created, because they were doing poorly.) Klein and Bloomberg had thought—had even bragged—that their reforms were bringing about near-miraculous improvements in student achievement. Speaking of the relative performance of minority and white children, Bloomberg said in 2008, "We've done everything possible to narrow the achievement gap—and we have. In some cases, we've reduced it by half." A year later he was saying, "We are closing the shameful achievement gap faster than ever." But reality soon set in. As the *New York Times* reported in August 2010, "When results from the 2010 tests—which state officials said presented a more accurate portrayal of students' abilities—were released last month, they came as a blow to the legacy of the mayor and the chancellor, as passing rates dropped by more than 25 percentage points on most tests. But the most painful part might well have been the evaporation of one of their signature accomplishments: the closing of the racial achievement gap." When it became clear that all his radical reforms had failed to produce radical improvements, Klein blamed the teachers, politicians, bureaucrats—everyone except the reformers whose cherished reforms had achieved so little.

Ravitch seemed to seethe as she talked about all this. Her voice was low and even, and her comments measured. But she readily acknowledged that much of what was going on in public education made her angry. "Tests measure the achievement gap," she said. "They do nothing to close it. It's absurd to think they would."

The obsession with tests, she said, was a way of ignoring the real problems in the schools: the massive budget cuts, for example, and the way the schools have changed over several decades. "When people talk about the good old days of America's public schools," she said, "they're talking about days when, first of all, the schools they attended were not desegregated. They didn't have kids with disabilities, and very few kids who didn't speak English. So things have changed, and tests are not the answer to those changes."

Ravitch shook her head. So much of what was occurring in schools was unnecessary, counterproductive, destructive, she said. The teaching to the test. The refusal to acknowledge the powerful impact of poverty. The tendency to believe that anyone can be a teacher, that training and long years of experience count for nothing, might even be a handicap.

"It's all of these things together that make me so outraged," said Ravitch. The intensity of the look in her eyes beneath her short, neatly cut white hair made me think of the abolitionists of old.

Ravitch made the point that the nation's elite private schools, which had been attended by many of the men and women in the forefront of the new era of reform, did not use standardized tests. "What do those schools know," she asked, "that the people imposing this on the public schools can't figure out?"

Ravitch was not opposed to testing students. But the fact that the tests had such enormous consequences attached to them appalled her. It was as if the people exercising the most influence over the nation's schools had allowed themselves to become infused with the peculiar idea that a first-class education meant nothing more than an arbitrarily established passing score on a multiple-choice test. "Testing doesn't improve instruction," Ravitch said. "The tests are a measure. That's all. We should not be treating testing as the goal of education. It's not. The goal of education is to help children develop to their fullest capacity. Testing doesn't do that."

Ravitch hammered that point again and again in her writing and many public appearances. In a blog post for the *New York Review of Books*, she stressed the danger of viewing standardized tests as anything more than diagnostic tools of limited and wildly varying quality. The results of the tests, she said, should never be confused with the rich and complex reality of a well-educated individual. "The scores tell us nothing about how students think, how deeply they understand history or science or literature or philosophy, or how much they love to paint or dance or sing, or how well prepared they are to cast their votes carefully or to be wise jurors."

It was a caution that went unheeded. The unshakable faith in testing became a nightmare for serious educators. Policy makers who knew little or nothing about how to teach children, especially those from impoverished backgrounds, or with disabilities, or other issues that could make learning a challenge, were calling the shots.

It was often difficult for serious educators to believe how radically things had changed. The Tuckahoe Middle School in suburban Henrico County, Virginia, was considered by parents, teachers, and administrators to be a fine school. But a year after No Child Left Behind took effect, it was branded a failure because it tested only 94 percent of its students, rather than the 95 percent mandated by the law. As the *New York Times* reported, "The school has a sizable number of immigrants—many from Bosnia—who do not know English well. Virginia law permits them to be exempted from state tests once, to give them time to learn English. Even if Tuckahoe had wanted to test them, the state had not developed a test for limited English speakers."

Tuckahoe's principal, Kurt Hulett, was understandably frustrated. "It did not make sense," he said, "to have them take a test they could not understand." Virginia asked the federal government to sign off on a onetime, one-year exemption that would allow the state to develop an alternative test for immigrants. As the *Times* put it, "Federal officials would not budge."

In district after district, schools began adapting to the imperative of the tests. Brenda Baker, a veteran English teacher at the Ernie Davis Middle School in upstate Elmira, New York, complained to the *New York Times*'s Abby Goodnough that much of her time was spent helping other teachers strengthen their students' test-taking skills. Referring to the eighth-grade reading exam, Baker said, "I eat, drink and sleep that baby."

The many problems surrounding high-stakes testing—in general, not just in education—have long been well-known. Ravitch mentioned Campbell's law, a rule formulated by the social science researcher Donald T. Campbell: "The more any quantitative social indicator is used for social decision making, the more subject it will be to corruption pressures and the more apt it will be to distort and corrupt the social processes it is intended to monitor."

When you start promoting or firing teachers and principals based on test scores, the tests themselves become the object of attention instead of the quality of the education that the tests are supposed to measure. "Performance is slanted to meet the measure," said Ravitch. "The policy makers don't seem to understand that. The more some indicator like a test is used to punish or reward people, the more the very thing that's being measured gets corrupted."

That's what has been happening in America's public schools. Creativity and innovation were often left behind as traditional lesson plans were narrowed or discarded and teaching to the test became the norm. Eventually, and probably inevitably, a series of cheating scandals erupted. In Atlanta, two years of celebrated improvements in student test scores were found to have been the result of rampant cheating by teachers and principals in scores of schools. On Good Friday, March 29, 2013, a grand jury in Fulton County, Georgia, indicted thirty-five Atlanta educators, including Beverly Hall, a nationally known administrator who had been Atlanta's superintendent of schools during the period when the alleged cheating occurred. They were charged with racketeering, false swearing, theft, and influencing witnesses as part of a wide conspiracy to boost the school system's test scores and avoid detection by authorities. The inflated scores had lifted Hall to the heights of American educators. She had been the nation's Superintendent of the Year in 2009. But an investigation by the *Atlanta Journal-Constitution* prompted a state investigation that revealed a grotesque cheating operation that, according to investigators, involved more than 150 teachers and principals. The cheating was driven, officials said, by the district's manic desire to demonstrate the "adequate yearly progress" mandated by No Child Left Behind. Teachers erased wrong answers and filled in correct ones. Struggling students were placed next to kids who were considered smarter and encouraged to copy the correct answers. In some cases, according to investigators, teachers just gave the children the answers. At least one principal was believed to have lost his job because he refused to cheat. Atlanta's scandal was the worst in an epidemic of cheating that had spread across the country. School systems with large numbers of poor children were often the places where cheating was found. Cities touched by the scandals included New York, Philadelphia, Houston, and Washington. But smaller systems in such diverse states as Nevada, Massachusetts, and Indiana also turned up evidence of cheating.

For all the test prepping and potentially brutal professional consequences, the tests themselves had virtually nothing to do with whether students were being well educated. As with the Tuckahoe Middle School in Virginia, there were many schools that performed well but were branded failures because their test scores slipped or some other mandate of No Child Left Behind had not been met. In 2011 more than 70 percent of all the public schools in New Hampshire were identified as failing.

Michael Winerip of the *New York Times* profiled one of the "failing" New Hampshire schools, the Oyster River Middle School in Durham. "This year," Winerip wrote, "Oyster River got serious about test prep. In September the school announced a new motto, 'Fill the Box.' Students have been told that their best chance for a high score on the state English test is to use all the blank space allotted for the essay. 'You have to write as much as you can,' says Jay Richard, the principal. 'People have studied these things.'"

Richard's comment was a remarkably clear example of education being upended by mindless testing. Rather than being taught how to write well, kids were told to write as much as they could as fast as they could. Serious scholars could only despair. Among those interviewed by Winerip was Linda Rief, who had taught English at Oyster River for twenty-five years. She denounced as "complete stupidity" the idea that the volume of writing could somehow be equated with the quality of the writing. Rief had devoted her entire adult life to teaching and in 2000 had been named Teacher of the Year by the New Hampshire Council of Teachers of English. But the public school landscape had changed, and policy makers were not much interested in the insights and advice of veteran educators like her.

8 *Poverty and Public Education*

Even young babies growing up in low-income neighborhoods already evidence elevated chronic stress.

—*Researchers* GARY EVANS, JEANNE BROOKS-GUNN, AND PAMELA KATO KLEBANOV

The warmth generated as Deonne Arrington walked the halls of her school was extraordinary. At age forty-seven, and with her arms outstretched for a hug or to give a reassuring squeeze on a pair of young shoulders, she seemed more like the perfect mom than a principal. Somehow she knew the names of nearly all of the four hundred students at Lincoln Elementary, a prekindergarten-to-fifth-grade school in the tough East Liberty neighborhood of Pittsburgh. I walked beside her, taking notes, on an afternoon in February 2013. Lincoln was one of several struggling schools that I was visiting to get a better sense of what was happening beneath the veneer of the testing phenomenon.

Arrington had a smile and a high five or an encouraging word for every student she encountered. Some of them were tiny. "Are you going to make the honor roll this month?" she would ask. A child would smile shyly and nod. "That would really put a smile on my face," Arrington would say.

I chuckled. When I was in school, you'd try to flee if you saw the principal coming. With Arrington, the opposite was the case.

The kids seemed irresistibly drawn to her. *"Miss Arrington! Miss Arrington!* Hi! We're making cupcakes. Do you want me to make one for you?" Smaller children would sometimes wrap their arms around her legs as if they would never let go.

"What are you reading?" Arrington would ask. "How's your mom doing?"

Watching Arrington in action, I marveled at her ability to remain upbeat. There was almost an idyllic quality to her interaction with the children, which contrasted with the troubling reality of many of their young lives. It would have been easy for a casual onlooker, walking the brightly lit halls gaily decorated with children's artworks, to get a wrong impression. The backgrounds of some of the children, many of them, were hellish.

"Ours is a high-impact school," said Arrington, "which means that more than 90 percent of our students are impoverished. There's a lot of stress and deprivation that they have to deal with, and that has an impact on their schoolwork."

Ninety-eight percent of Lincoln's students were African American. Two percent were white. The combination of concentrated poverty and racial isolation is almost always toxic when it comes to education. But the ever-expanding crowd of corporate-style reformers has shown no interest in reducing the isolation of black and Latino students. Segregation in public schools, fed by housing and income patterns, is on the rise, and that increase has been exacerbated by the expansion of charter schools, which—for all their professed concern about achievement gaps and disappointing outcomes—tend to be even more rigidly segregated than traditional public schools. Ashira Mayers, a seventh-grade student at an all-black charter school in Brooklyn, told the *New York Times,* "We will sometimes talk about why don't we have any white kids? We wonder what their schools are like. We see them on TV, with the soccer fields and the biology labs and all that cool stuff. Sometimes I feel I have to work harder because I don't have all that they have. A lot of us think that way."

Racial, cultural, and economic isolation inevitably leave a stain. Arrington told me about a time three years earlier, during her first year as principal, when she led a group of eight- and nine-year-olds into the school library. "I thought they would enjoy it," she said. "We didn't have a librarian, but there were books all around us, and I just assumed from my own experience that the children would love to come in and read. I was so wrong. They were not at all interested. In fact, they were mad, very angry and upset that they had to be there. They couldn't see the point. They weren't used to books. In most cases there were no books in their homes. And for many, there had been no history of adults reading to them when they were very little. So we've had to work hard to develop a love of reading among our children. That's been one of my biggest emphases."

Other problems were more serious. During a particularly cold stretch of weather, children were showing up at school without warm clothing. "It was like the Arctic out there," one teacher told me. "The kids were trying to tough it out. They'd come in shivering so badly—it was pitiful." Arrington and some of the teachers, using their own money, bought coats, hats, and gloves for the youngsters who needed them.

Then there was the continuing problem of children coming to school when they were sick. In most of those cases, Arrington said, the parents couldn't afford to take time off from work. Given a choice between sending their youngsters to school with the flu (or worse) and losing two or three days' pay, the parents (in most cases, single mothers) sent their kids to school.

Some kids, perfectly healthy, are chronically late for school; others seem loath to come to school at all.

"When we ask kids why they're late, they say, 'We overslept,' " said Arrington. Letters go out to parents. Phone calls are made. Conferences are called. The parents are told, "It's important that your child get to school on time." "Our reading classes are first thing in the morning," said Arrington. "The children who miss ten or fifteen minutes every day are missing an hour's worth of instruction every week. They can't afford that. So one of the things I'm planning to do now is buy alarm clocks for the children. We've also been suggesting to parents that they use their cell phones as alarms."

She thought for a moment, then added, "We have truancy elimination meetings, where we invite the parents to come in. But that doesn't always work. As a last resort we have to take the parents to the magistrate, who will compel them to send their kids to school."

Arrington sighed when I mentioned the children who are chronically absent. "The parent doesn't have to share that information with us," she said, "so we seldom really get to the bottom of it." She noted that a parent might be working an odd shift and is not at home in the morning to get the kids up and out. Some young children are cared for by older siblings. Getting the younger ones off to school may not be a priority for the older child.

Some parents are drug addicted or alcoholic. Some are seriously ill. Some homes are plagued with violence. Self-styled reformers are often willfully blind to the complex realities of poor children's lives.

"Our children have serious stresses to deal with," Arrington said. "We had four fires over the Christmas break." She paused, as if amazed herself. "*Four fires!* So what happens? With all their possessions gone, the children don't come back to school. As soon as we hear about it, we get our counselor out to the family. We have to get clothes for the children and get them all ready again for school. Remember, these are poor families. Three of my teachers took children out shopping for clothes. Staff members use their own money. They'll take up a collection. As principal, I try to match what the staff comes up with.

"I remember this one mother. I'd had some tough conversations with her because her daughter was often late. The mom had it in her mind that the school was out to get her. Then she had a fire. The little girl came in to tell me. The next day we gave the mother a gift certificate for $200 and we got some food to the family. Even the other children tried to help. They chipped in and got a coat for the little girl. She couldn't fit in it. It was the wrong size. But it was the thought that counted."

We turned a corner and came upon a boy standing alone a few feet from a classroom door. He was about nine or ten and had the saddest look on his face. "He's supposed to be inside that class," Arrington told me. She went up to the boy and said a few words in a soft voice. Then I heard her ask if he would be willing to go back into the classroom. He seemed undecided. "That would really put a smile on my face," she said. "Can you do that for me?" He seemed reluctant, but he nodded. Arrington guided him back into the classroom.

Later she would tell me that the class was for youngsters with mental or emotional difficulties. The previous Friday, the boy, who was already dealing with emotional issues, told teachers his father had been shot and was in the hospital. School officials would later learn that it was not actually the boy's father who had been shot but another male figure who was important to him. The boy was devastated.

Stress and the mental health issues it can lead to are serious problems at Lincoln Elementary. Children are grappling with anxiety, grief, depression, chronic fearfulness, and many other challenges. "In September," said Arrington, "several of our children were playing on the football field, and there was a shooting, right on the field where they were playing. So, of course, they were upset. And they bring all those kinds of concerns to school with them."

Keeping things together at the school can sometimes require a heroic effort by the children and the adults caring for them. Arrington has managed to reduce tardiness and truancy over the past couple of years. She has tried to make reading a big deal. Photographs of students and charts showing the books they've read are posted on the corridor walls. Awards are handed out. There is a Principal's Book Club. Still, the school's standardized test scores have languished. "Hopefully, this year we can get them up," Arrington told me.

Arne Duncan was not happy. New international assessments of student academic performance had been released a couple of weeks before Christmas 2012, and American youngsters had not done nearly as well as Duncan had hoped. No one could accuse the nation's six-foot seven-inch basketball-loving education secretary (he was often on the court with President Obama) of not working hard. He was a tireless promoter of the administration's education policies, including its massively promoted Race to the Top initiative, which was supposed to correct the many embarrassing failings of No Child Left Behind. But the big payoff that Obama and his education secretary had hoped to achieve had not occurred. Despite what Duncan routinely described as "real progress," he was forced to acknowledge "that learning gains in fourth grade are not being sustained through eighth grade." Referring to the international test scores, he noted that mathematics and science achievement had "failed to measurably improve between 2007 and 2011." He called the results "unacceptable."

There was a déjà vu quality to Duncan's comments. Two years earlier, after the results of another international test were made public, Duncan had ruefully complained that the disappointing scores of American students showed that they "were poorly prepared to compete in today's knowledge economy." He added, sharply, that Americans needed "to wake up to this educational reality, instead of napping at the wheel while emerging competitors prepare their students for economic leadership."

Despite all the attention focused on education over more than thirty years, American kids have baffled reformers by continuing to disappoint in the international testing arena. The lagging scores provoked endless hand-wringing, year after year, decade after decade. At the end of 2011, Michelle Rhee, the former chancellor of the Washington, D.C., school system and one of the fiercest of the test zealots and charter school champions, was writing in the *New York Times*, "The past year was a sobering one for American educators, as we learned that the United States is falling farther behind in international student rankings."

Could things really have been that bad? And if so, why, after so many years?

The idea that American public education was in a virtual state of collapse, the victim of incompetents, freeloaders, and worse, had become the conventional wisdom. *Newsweek* ran a cover in March 2010 headlined "The Key to Saving American Education." It showed a blackboard with one sentence written over and over: "We must fire bad teachers. We must fire bad teachers . . ." The accompanying article opened with a big red F and an ominous lead sentence:

"The relative decline of American education at the elementary- and high-school levels has long been a national embarrassment as well as a threat to the nation's future."

There seemed to be no end to the lamentation. From his lofty perch as the richest person in the United States, Bill Gates summarily declared that American high schools were obsolete and vowed to bring them—kicking and screaming, if necessary—into the twenty-first century. Bill Bennett, who served as secretary of education under Ronald Reagan, apocalyptically declared, "Our schools should get five years to get back to where they were in 1963. If they're still bad, maybe we should declare educational bankruptcy, give the people their money and let them educate themselves and start their own schools."

The hysteria went back at least as far as the release in 1983 of the profoundly influential report *A Nation at Risk*, a thirty-six-page document that Diane Ravitch called "the all-time blockbuster of education reports." Terrel Bell, Reagan's first secretary of education, had set up the National Commission on Excellence in Education in 1981 "to examine the widespread public perception that something is seriously remiss in our educational system." The commissioners' results were unfortunate because they got some important things very wrong, and their mistakes led to decades of further erroneous assumptions and misguided corrective efforts. The problem was in the commission's basic analysis, spelled out in *A Nation at Risk*. It mistakenly concluded that educational achievement in the United States was declining. The final report, written in language calculated to alarm, was a national sensation. It warned, "The educational foundations of our society are presently being eroded by a rising tide of mediocrity that threatens our very future as a nation and as a people. If an unfriendly foreign power had attempted to impose on America the mediocre educational performance that exists today, we might well have viewed it as an act of war."

According to the report, the men and women responsible for America's public school system were engaged "in an act of unthinking, unilateral disarmament imperiling the nation's economic health." The authors pushed the idea of impending doom as hard as they could, asserting, "Our once unchallenged preeminence in commerce, industry, science, and technological innovation is being overtaken by competitors throughout the world."

It was nonsense, but the press pounced. All sorts of disasters were imagined, including the collapse of the economy and the triumph of America's economic competitors, especially Japan, where students routinely scored much better than our own on international achievement tests.

Politicians and commentators alike insisted that something had to be done. And it was in that atmosphere of alarm and confusion that the seeds of the modern education reform movement were planted. The belief spread that American schools were lousy, and if the schools were lousy, then radical efforts would have to be made to improve them or find alternatives. From those seeds would sprout the corporate-style initiatives of high-stakes testing that would transform the very nature of classroom teaching, charter schools that would be showered with public dollars while being subject to minimal public oversight, vouchers and tax credits that would make it easier for students to exit the traditional public schools, and brutal nonstop attacks on teachers and their unions.

Bad premises lead to bad outcomes, and the premise of *A Nation at Risk* was uncommonly bad. This was made clear by, among others, Richard Rothstein, a research specialist and former education columnist for the *New York Times*. He demonstrated, in a devastating critique on the twenty-fifth anniversary of the report, that its authors had "misidentified" what was really wrong with American public education "and consequently set the nation on a school reform crusade that has done more harm than good."

The biggest mistake was the contention that educational achievement in the United States was deteriorating, that American kids were doing less well in school than they had in previous years. It was true that from 1963 to 1980 the nation's average SAT scores had dropped, but that was not because students were learning less. As Rothstein explained, "*A Nation at Risk* based its analysis of declining student achievement entirely on average SAT scores which had dropped by about half a standard deviation from 1963 to 1980. But much of the decline had been due to the changing composition of SAT test takers—in the early 1960s, the preponderance of SAT test takers were high school students planning to apply to the most selective colleges."

At the time that *A Nation at Risk* was being drafted, many more kids were going to college, which meant that a smaller percentage of applicants was being drawn from the nation's socioeconomic elite. Doors were being opened much wider to the middle and working classes and the poor. Such an expansion would inevitably depress average scores on achievement tests. There was no reason to equate such a reduction with a decline in the quality of teaching across the nation.

"By 1983," Rothstein pointed out, "the demographic composition of SAT test takers had mostly stabilized, and average SAT scores were again rising, not declining." He added, "Trend scores from the National Assessment of Educational Progress (NAEP) also show a more complex picture than *Risk* described. In elementary and middle school math, average scores rose for both black and white students, starting in the late 1970s. This trend might not yet have been fully understood by *Risk* commission members—they might have concluded that the upturn then barely detectable would be short-lived. But the rise has certainly continued subsequent to 1983."

For black students, "the improvement has been so dramatic," Rothstein wrote, "that black fourth grade math scores [in 2008] are higher than white fourth grade scores in 1978. In other words, if white math achievement had been stagnant, the black-white achievement gap would have been entirely closed. The continued gap is due to substantial improvement in white scores as well."

Rothstein is no apologist for the public school system. He has readily acknowledged that there are widespread problems that need correcting and that student performance should be better. But his work has demolished the idea that at the time of *A Nation at Risk* the quality of American schools was in some sort of precipitous decline. More important, his most recent work has shown that Arne Duncan, Michelle Rhee, and most of the others in the current school reform movement apparently misread the data from the latest rounds of international achievement tests. American kids on the whole were not doing more poorly than their peers in other countries. That mistaken belief occurred, Rothstein wrote, because the test results had too often been viewed superficially. American test scores are dragged down because the U.S. has so many poor students and such a staggering degree of economic inequality. A deeper analysis that takes into account the social and economic backgrounds of the test takers in each country leads to a more nuanced and very different view of American scholastic achievement. Rothstein and Martin Carnoy, a professor at the Stanford Graduate School of Education, made a detailed study of the backgrounds of the test takers in an extensive database compiled by the Program for International Student Assessment. Their comprehensive report was published by the Economic Policy Institute in 2013. Among its findings were the following:

- Because in every country, students at the bottom of the social class distribution perform worse than students higher in that distribution, U.S. average performance appears to be relatively low partly because we have so many more test takers from the bottom of the social class distribution.
- If U.S. adolescents had a social class distribution that was similar to the distribution in countries to which the United States is frequently compared, average reading scores in the United States would be higher than average reading scores in the similar post-industrial countries we examined (France, Germany, and the United Kingdom), and the average math scores in the United States would be about the same as average math scores in similar post-industrial countries.
- Disadvantaged and lower-middle-class U.S. students perform better (and in most cases, substantially better) than comparable students in similar post-industrial countries in reading. In math, disadvantaged and lower-middle-class U.S. students perform about the same as comparable students in similar post-industrial countries.
- The performance of the lowest social class U.S. students has been improving over time, while the perfor-

mance of such students in both top-scoring and similar
post-industrial countries has been falling.

We have most often been comparing apples with oranges when
analyzing the results of international achievement tests. There
is not much to be learned by comparing the raw scores of an
eight-year-old from an intact family in an affluent suburb of Hel-
sinki with those of a poor kid living with a single mother in a
run-down tenement in the South Bronx. Finland has a first-rate
public school system, but it also has a child poverty rate of just
4 percent. The child poverty rate in the United States is 23 percent.
One in every three black children in America is poor. Blanket com-
parisons of youngsters in such radically different societies are spe-
cious. More informative assessments can be made by comparing
students in the U.S. with students in other countries whose personal backgrounds are similar. The database analyzed by Rothstein
and Carnoy offered a trove of information that enabled them to
compare the scores of students from roughly similar backgrounds,
and their subsequent analysis cast the international test results in a
decidedly different light. American students were not, in fact, lagging far behind their peers in other countries. In many respects,
they were doing better.

Like sailors misreading their guidance systems, American observers have been drawing incorrect and often dire conclusions from
international achievement tests for decades. Those errors have had
powerful consequences. "From such tests," Rothstein and Carnoy
wrote, "many journalists and policymakers have concluded that
American student achievement lags woefully behind that in many
comparable industrialized nations, that this shortcoming threatens
the nation's economic future, and that these test results therefore
suggest an urgent need for radical school reform."

Misconceptions in recent decades about American student
achievement and the overall quality of the nation's schools mir-
ror the mistaken notions that led to the erroneous conclusions of
A Nation at Risk. In a widely covered speech to the National Gov-
ernors Association in 2005, Bill Gates said, "When I compare our
high schools to what I see when I'm traveling abroad, I am ter-

rified for our workforce of tomorrow." The former secretary of state George Shultz co-authored a 2012 *Washington Post* op-ed that mournfully declared, "Current U.S. students—the future labor force—are no longer competitive with students across the developed world." Another former secretary of state, Condoleezza Rice, headed a task force with the former New York City schools chancellor Joel Klein that declared, in language reminiscent of *A Nation at Risk*, that "educational failure puts the United States' future economic prosperity, global position, and physical safety at risk." In short, according to Rice and Klein, the breakdown of the public education system was a national security threat.

There is, in fact, a big problem with public education in the United States, but the test-obsessed, pro-privatization reformers have paid it precious little attention. The real crisis is the poverty that is holding back achievement at schools like Lincoln Elementary and thousands of others across the country. That challenge has been all but ignored while policy makers continue to insist that the public education system itself has broken down.

Without that persistently wrongheaded view, it is unlikely we would have been swept into the dangerous currents of a radical reform era that has undermined rather than strengthened America's schools. The uncomfortable truth is that children in well-resourced schools do very well academically, while the performance of low-income students in racially isolated, poorly resourced schools is often dreadful. Poverty is the number one problem with education in the United States. That was the case at the time of *A Nation at Risk*, and that remains the case today. The achievement gap between high-income and low-income American students is far greater than the gap between whites and blacks, which has narrowed in recent decades. And while the schools that teach low-income children need to be improved and need better funding, there is ultimately no way to make a sweeping transformation in the academic lives of poor children without also addressing their family lives, their home environments, and the difficult personal issues that they bring to school each day.

A child who is chronically hungry is not likely to be a first-rate student. A child with undiagnosed vision or hearing problems will have trouble keeping up with classmates. A child whose mother was just beaten up by a drug-addicted live-in boyfriend will have all kinds of trouble concentrating on math and reading. A child who is worried about dodging bullets or negotiating the terrain of rival street gangs when going to and from school will have a very hard time acing a fourth-grade reading test. Children who are homeless, neglected, anxious, depressed, tired, or dealing with any of the other endless agonies associated with poverty will typically—not always, but typically—have a much tougher time learning than their more affluent and environmentally fortunate peers.

It's important to emphasize that these are not children who can't succeed. But their path up the mountain of success is much steeper and far more exhausting. This is not something that the policy makers with the most influence on public education have been willing to address. They have looked for technocratic solutions. They have shown no desire to deal forthrightly with poverty. And they appear to be horrified at the mere thought of honestly confronting the subject of race. Bill Gates told the National Urban League, "Let's end the myth that we have to solve poverty before we can improve education. I say it's more the other way around: improving education is the best way to solve poverty."

The consequences of such attitudes can be devastating. The Michelle Rhee experience in Washington, D.C., was a case in point. Rhee dismissed as "complete crap" the idea that poor children are often prevented from reaching their potential because of their family and environmental circumstances. "It's easy to blame external factors as the reason why poor minority kids aren't achieving at the same level," she said. "It's a false premise. You have to put supports and mechanisms in place around those kids, but I refuse to allow adults in the system to use that as an excuse."

As chancellor of the public schools in Washington, D.C., from 2007 to 2010, Rhee tried to show that the schools alone could overcome academic underachievement, regardless of the poverty-stricken backgrounds of so many of the district's children. Her goal was to eliminate the achievement gap between Washington's public school students, who were overwhelmingly poor and African American, and their wealthier counterparts in other school systems, including the affluent suburban districts surrounding D.C. Success would be demonstrated by getting the test scores in Washington way up, and Rhee's preferred method for doing that was to go after teachers and principals with an extraordinary and often mean-spirited ferocity. "She was like a flamethrower," said one teacher.

In a *Frontline* documentary on PBS called "The Education of Michelle Rhee," the district's assistant superintendent, Francisco Millet, said, "Principals were scared to death that if their test scores did not go up they were going to be fired."

They had every reason to be afraid. Rhee had a veritable fetish for firing people. She fired 24 principals during her first year on the job. One of them was Marta Guzman, who was the principal of the Oyster-Adams Bilingual School, a highly regarded elementary school that Rhee sent her own two daughters to. During her three years as chancellor, Rhee fired 36 principals, 22 assistant principals, 241 teachers, and 98 men and women in the district's central office.

In a chilling scene in the documentary, Rhee actually fired a principal on camera. Apparently unaware—or unconcerned— about the inherent cruelty of her behavior, Rhee invited the PBS correspondent John Merrow and his crew to record the dismissal. In the scene, which was aired by PBS, the principal was seated across a desk from Rhee. The viewer could see his blurred outline. Rhee faced the camera as she talked to him, her hands folded calmly on the desk. "So, I'll tell you that from the very beginning," she said, "from when we first met, I had concerns about your ability to do this job."

The camera then cut to a different scene in which Rhee told Merrow, "Within the first seven minutes I knew that this guy had little chance of making it long term."

Then the camera cut back to the original scene in the office. Rhee told the principal, "The folks who have been in the school, from staff and faculty who are at the school, are saying that the school's out of control—that there is no structure, no order, not a good culture that's being created. That sits squarely on your shoulders."

Moments later she leaned forward and bluntly declared, "I'm terminating your principalship *now.*"

To call the scene disturbing would be an understatement. The

absence of any sign of human feeling for someone whose career she
was blithely flushing down the drain raised serious questions about
Rhee's fitness to be chancellor. Why publicly humiliate the man? It
was fair to wonder under what circumstances (and for whom) her
feelings of empathy emerged. Did they automatically kick in when
dealing with the children in her charge? Was she capable of really
understanding what some of those kids were going through? How
did she feel about their parents?

Merrow asked Rhee, on camera, "What do you feel at a time like
that?"

She replied, as if surprised, "At a time like that?"

"When you're firing somebody," Merrow said.

Rhee smiled. "I feel like I'm doing the right thing."

Merrow pushed the point. "Any compassion?" he asked. "For
the guy? For the person you're—"

Rhee replied, "Compassion?" She squinched up her face. "Um,
I would not say that compassion is—I have hired and fired more
people in my lifetime probably than almost anyone else." She gave
a little laugh. "I think that when you're doing the kind of work that
I'm doing, where the lives and futures of children hang in the balance, you can't play with that. This is not about giving people jobs
or ensuring that people maintain their jobs. This is about educating
children."

Rhee would, in effect, be fired herself—by the voters of Washington, D.C. She resigned as the district's schools chancellor in
October 2010, after the man who had hired her, Mayor Adrian
Fenty, lost the Democratic primary in his bid for a second term. The
primary results were, in large part, a referendum on Rhee's con-
troversial tenure as chancellor. While most voters were unhappy,
it was difficult to render an objective judgment of Rhee's impact
on the city's schools. What had worked and what had not worked
was not at all clear. She had taken over one of the most troubled
systems in the nation and had only been chancellor for three years.
What was clear was that for all the conflict and turmoil that marked
her time in office, the system as a whole wasn't markedly better
when she left. The district's schools were still among the worst in

the nation. Washington's on-time graduation rate in 2011, 58 percent, was the lowest in the entire country. Not surprisingly, some of the poorest-performing schools were in the poorest neighborhoods. As the *Washington Post* noted at the time of Rhee's departure, "Twelve percent of sophomores at Spingarn High School in Northeast Washington are proficient in math, 17 percent in reading. At Johnson Middle School in Southeast, 14 percent of the students are proficient in reading and 14 percent in math."

Michelle Rhee's cold-blooded, corporate-style approach to fixing schools was a hallmark of the reform movement. The technocrats would tell from the test scores who was successful and who was not. People who didn't measure up would be punished. Schools would be closed, if necessary, the same way one would close an under-performing clothing store or fast-food franchise.

The problem is that schools are not fast-food franchises. And they're not supposed to be test-prep factories, filled with robo-teachers and mindlessly obedient, bubble-scribbling students. Walmart stores and cookie-cutter fast-food outlets may be a corporate executive's dream, but they're not good models for schools. I'd always thought of the ideal school as a warm and welcoming institution (not unlike Pittsburgh's Lincoln Elementary) committed to learning and cooperation and creativity. I'd always been taught that the whole point of a first-class education was to develop the capacity of children and teenagers to learn about the myriad wonders of the world, to think critically and independently, and ultimately to become productive citizens and lead rewarding lives.

President Obama seemed to agree back in March 2011 when he said,

One thing I never want to see happen is schools that are just teaching to the test. Because then you're not learning about the world, you're not learning about different cultures, you're not learning about science, you're not learning about math. All you're learning about is how to fill out a little bubble on an exam and the little tricks that you need to do in order to take a test. And that's not going to make education interesting to you. And young people do well in stuff that they're interested in. They're not going to do as well if it's boring.

The president's comments seemed critical of the very policies his administration had put in place with his Race to the Top initiative. Race to the Top relied even more heavily on standardized testing than No Child Left Behind. The author of an *Education Week* blog that quoted the president wrote the following:

Is President Obama aware:
- that Race to the Top requires states to tie teacher pay and evaluations to student test scores? If ever there was a recipe for teaching to the test, this is it!
- that his Secretary of Education is proposing to evaluate teacher preparation programs by tracking the test scores of the teachers they produce?
- that his administration's plan for the new version of No Child Left Behind continues to place tremendous pressure on schools attended by the poorest students, ensuring that there will still be extremely high stakes attached to these tests?
- that his Department of Education is proposing greatly expanding both the number of subjects tested, and the frequency of tests, to enable us to measure the "value" each teacher adds to their students?

I could find no way to reconcile the disconnect between President Obama's astute assessment of the critical problems with high-stakes testing and his own education policies, which were based overwhelmingly on such testing. His posture seemed inexplicable. He was too smart and too engaged to not understand that children trapped in the destructive maelstrom of poverty was *the* fundamental issue, that family income and home environment were by far the strongest factors determining how well a child would do in school. The president's policies seemed to ignore that reality, which had been demonstrated repeatedly in studies over several decades. Back in the 1980s a pair of psychologists at the University of Kansas, Betty Hart and Todd R. Risley, made the astonishing discovery that children whose parents were professionals had, by the age of four, been exposed to approximately thirty-two million more words than children growing up poor. *Thirty-two million.* Children in professional homes were talked to three times as much as the average poor child. That so-called word gap profoundly influenced the vocabulary of the children and their prospects for academic success. In a 2011 interview with National Public Radio, Dr. Hart (who died in 2012) was asked if she had been demoralized by the findings of her study. "Horrified might be a better word," she said. "Horrified when you see that the differences are so great, and you think of trying to make up those differences."

There were myriad factors, in addition to shortfalls in vocabulary, that were holding poor children back. A 2011 article by researchers from Columbia and Cornell noted that "low-income children face a bewildering array of psychosocial and physical demands that place much pressure on their adaptive capacities and appear to be toxic to the developing brain." Burdened with these challenges, poor kids tend to endure far more stress than their better-off counterparts, and they bring that stress with them to school. The authors of the article—Gary Evans, Jeanne Brooks-Gunn, and Pamela Kato Klebanov—noted, "Even young babies growing up in low-income neighborhoods already evidence elevated chronic stress."

There is no question that many poor children do well academically and go on to lead terrific lives. But that is not the rule. In general, poverty has a devastating effect on academic achievement. As Richard Rothstein has pointed out, if you send two groups of youngsters to equally high-quality schools, "the group with the greater socioeconomic disadvantage" is likely to do less well academically than the more fortunate group. Rothstein noted,

Children in low-income families are more prone to asthma, resulting in more sleeplessness, irritability, and lack of exercise. They experience lower birth weight as well as more lead poisoning and iron-deficiency anemia, each of which leads to diminished cognitive ability and more behavior problems. Their families frequently fall behind in rent and move, so children switch schools more often, losing continuity of instruction.

Poor children are, in general, not read to aloud as often or exposed to complex language and large vocabularies. Their parents have low-wage jobs and are more frequently laid off, causing family stress and more arbitrary discipline. The neighborhoods through which these children walk to school and in which they play have more crime and drugs and fewer adult role models with professional careers. Such children are more often in single-parent families and so get less adult attention. They have fewer cross-country trips, visits to museums and zoos, music or dance lessons, and organized sports leagues to develop their ambition, cultural awareness, and self-confidence.

None of these are challenges that cannot be overcome. But they won't be overcome by ignoring them. And they can't be overcome by focusing obsessively on a technocratic corporate agenda for improving schools.

While talking with Deonne Arrington about the students at Lincoln Elementary, I thought of a meeting I'd had with a group of youngsters from New York City several months earlier. The kids were from the Bronx, about twenty of them, thirteen and fourteen years old. They'd agreed to talk to me about their lives, and we got together over pizza at the Community Service Society in Manhattan. At one point I asked if the youngsters were generally happy with their lives. Only five raised their hands. When I asked why the others were unhappy, the answers came hesitantly and in subdued tones of voice. They would say because their neighborhoods were not safe, or because one or both of their parents had died, or because there was no father in their lives, or because their families were poor. Several of the children began to cry. One girl said she'd been raped years before. She looked down at the conference table we'd gathered around and murmured, "I never feel safe." Another girl said, "I saw someone on my block get shot. After that I didn't want to go outside. When I go to school, I always look at that spot where he was lying on the ground. It hurts to think about it."

The kids spoke of drug dealers and gang members and people

they had known who'd been shot and killed. Several of the young-sters, boys and girls, said they never wanted to get married because they saw domestic life as never-ending strife and grief.

The adults who had come to the office with the children seemed stunned. They began passing out tissues. One said, "Even I didn't realize it was this bad."

9 *War's Madness Runs Deep*

The price of empire is America's soul and that
price is too high.

—J. WILLIAM FULBRIGHT

Bob Berschinski, Dan's father, was on the phone, and he was
excited. "You have got to see this video!" he said. After months
of struggle, Dan had walked. Just a few steps, but he had walked.
"He's made real progress," Bob said. "I'm telling you, you have to
see it." He sent the video as an e-mail attachment.

The clip showed part of a municipal celebration for Dan. The
people of his hometown, Peachtree City, Georgia, had arranged a
welcome-home weekend for the young officer to coincide with its
annual Memorial Day observance. There was a motorcycle escort,
speeches by dignitaries, including the mayor, Don Haddix, and flags
everywhere. The video opened with Dan and a few others seated
on a platform in front of an audience at city hall. He was in a black
wheelchair, just a few steps from a simple podium and microphone.
He wore camouflage fatigues and a black beret, and he'd been fitted
with prosthetic legs that ended in a pair of tan Timberland-style
combat boots. I had a weird feeling as I sat in my apartment in
Manhattan and watched the clip. There was something disturbing
about the video, but I couldn't put my finger on it. I knew Dan's
family was happy with it, over-the-moon happy, so I felt uncomfortable feeling uncomfortable. When Dan was introduced, he put
his hands on the arms of the wheelchair to shift himself forward

in the seat. He reached for a black cane, and then a second cane, which he handed to a white-haired gentleman seated to his left. "Can you hold this for a second?" Dan asked. Then with his left hand on the arm of the wheelchair and his right hand on the cane, and with the audience beginning to applaud, he lifted himself from the wheelchair. Then he took the other cane back. First with his left foot and then his right, he began to walk toward the podium. The applause grew to a standing ovation. It was only a few steps to the podium, but when Dan reached it, everyone watching knew that it had been a triumph.

The crowd continued to applaud as Dan stood at the microphone. "Thank you," he said. "The therapists at Walter Reed would not be happy with those steps." He smiled. He reached back with his left hand to squeeze some of the stiffness from his hip. "Hoo!" he said in a spontaneous high-pitched tone. "Up until this moment I thought getting shot at was the most nerve-racking thing. But, uh, this is kind of intimidating."

Bob Berschinski would later try to explain to me how emotional he and his wife, Susan, had felt as Dan looked out at the audience and began to speak. "We thought we had lost him," Bob said. "And now here he was. And walking those few steps when, you know, he wasn't supposed to be able to."

Dan began his remarks with a story about his early days in the hospital. "I've spoken with a lot of people since my injury, and one thing I hear a lot is that people think I have a great attitude and outlook towards life. I want to share a funny little story with you, and it might explain where my good attitude comes from." He described what it was like to come out of the induced coma at Walter Reed a week after being wounded. "I was surprised to find out not that I had lost my legs," he said, "because I already knew that, but that my jaw was broken and had been wired shut. After several days and several major surgeries, I was finally lucid enough to realize that having my jaw wired shut meant that I couldn't eat any kind of normal food—no solid food, no mashed potatoes, no soups, just Gatorade and broth." He looked at the crowd with a nervous grin. "One day I'm in my hospital room, in between surgeries, and my brother's there with me. He's talking—more accurately, Rob is talking to me and I'm just kind of mumbling back as best I can—when my dad walks into the room with a McDonald's cheeseburger in his hand. My brother turns to my dad and he says, 'Dad! Are you seriously going to eat that right here in front of Dan?' To which my dad quickly replied, 'You don't seem to mind *walking* around in front of him.' "

There was a burst of laughter, and then the audience applauded. "So that's a little snapshot," said Dan, "of what it's like in the Berschinski family. I also think it's a telling example of why I've been able to endure this new change in my life. We don't take things too seriously."

With that, he proceeded to get very serious. "My family and friends who know me best will tell you that I never really enjoy being the center of attention, and it's true. I really don't. So this moment, this whole weekend, is a bit much for me to handle. But this weekend isn't just about me. It's actually about the men and women I have reluctantly come to symbolize." He said the tributes and the ceremonies should be about all the soldiers and marines and other service members called to serve and perhaps to die in war zones overseas. "It's about those who have gone before, those who are there right now, at this very moment, and those who will go when, despite our best intentions and utmost desire, our country calls on them for more service and sacrifice."

I had never seen Dan get emotional. He'd always had a more or less matter-of-fact attitude when describing what had happened to him. So it came as a surprise when his voice began to tremble and he appeared to be tearing up. That happened when he began talking about the men who had been under his command. As he put it, "The dozen or so soldiers who in the late fall of 2008 decided to reenlist despite the fact that our battalion was headed for an imminent deployment. Despite the fact that several had already been wounded in previous tours in Iraq and Afghanistan. Despite the fact that many of those men had beautiful young wives and children that they were going to leave behind. And despite the fact that I, a brand-new platoon leader with absolutely no combat experience, would be leading them in Afghanistan."

And then he told the story of Jonathan Yanney, the twenty-year-old private first class who was killed while crossing the footbridge in the orchard just seven or eight hours before Dan himself was wounded. He spoke about the trust he had in Yanney, whose job as the platoon's forward observer included such critical tasks as establishing radio contact with the helicopter units that would often come flying in very low when the platoon was in contact with the enemy. Yanney would also stay in touch with the artillery forces firing their deadly rounds over the platoon and into enemy positions. The emotion I had never seen in Dan in all the hours I had interviewed him about himself emerged as he talked to the audience about Yanney and how that young man had been forever lost in the split second it took for the bomb to explode.

Dan asked that the homecoming weekend, "from this moment on," be dedicated to Yanney and all of the young men and women who had made such tremendous sacrifices in the service of the U.S. And then he reached for his canes and walked painfully slowly back to his seat.

I sat back in my chair and took a sip of coffee, which had been sitting on my desk for the longest time and was now cold. What did I think of the video? Of course, I was happy that Dan had taken those important early steps in his personal campaign to walk again. And I was happy for his family. But there were other feelings. I was frustrated by the easy acceptance of the welcome-home event for this wounded soldier as something normal in American life. I was dismayed by the widespread attitude that, yes, it was tragic and a shame that Dan Berschinski should have suffered such terrible wounds, but, hey, however unfortunate, that sort of thing has to be expected. That's what happens in war. No way to avoid it. And the right and proper thing to do is to have a public event honoring Dan's service and expressing gratitude for his sacrifice. It bothered me that there seemed to be no collective sense that it was insane to allow the maiming of men like Dan and the killing of men like Yanney to continue so many long years after the attacks of September 11, 2001. What the hell were we still doing in Afghanistan? What was the point?

And it wasn't just Afghanistan. I took another sip of coffee. Why, as a nation, did we keep fighting these endlessly self-destructive

wars? From Vietnam to our current era. It was truly a form of
madness—year after year, decade after decade. Madness.

That afternoon I pulled the background material I'd collected
on Norman Morrison, who had tried, in a bizarrely tragic way, to
sound an alarm half a century ago. On the afternoon of November 2, 1965, Morrison drove with his year-old daughter, Emily,
from their home in Baltimore to the Pentagon in northern Virginia. To describe Morrison as intense would be an understatement. When he got wound up about something, he could become
frenzied, difficult to be around, even desperate. Later he would be
dismissed by many as mentally ill. Morrison was a Quaker official,
executive secretary of the Stony Run Friends Meeting in Baltimore,
who had been profoundly distressed by the war in Vietnam. He
was thirty-one years old, married, and deeply religious. His two
abiding issues of conscience were racial justice and world peace.
The unfolding tragedy in Southeast Asia, which he felt powerless
to stop, had driven him to the breaking point. Morrison and his
wife, Anne, had two other children, Ben, six, and Tina, five. Earlier that day, over lunch, the couple had discussed a news article
by a French priest who had described how his church in North
Vietnam and parts of the surrounding village had been bombed
by American planes. According to the priest, at least seven of his
parishioners had been killed. The Morrisons were also upset by a
Pentagon report acknowledging that forty-eight South Vietnamese
civilians had been killed by American pilots in a bombing that officials said was a mistake.

I remembered that period of our history only too well. As
Morrison was driving south from Baltimore, I was busy jumping
nervously and awkwardly to the tune of drill sergeants in basic
training at Fort Dix, New Jersey. My fellow recruits and I were
being hurriedly trained for Vietnam, being taught the rudiments
of every feasible way to "maim, kill, and destroy" the enemy, thus
saving the free world. As the days grew shorter and the temperatures colder, we spent seemingly endless hours drilling with rifles,
bayonets, machine guns, hand grenades—all the while listening
to instructors bellowing about what the "gooks" were planning to

do to us when we finally made it into the jungles. I remember one friend saying to me, "At least the jungle will be warm."

I was a skinny kid with thick glasses being toughened up with buddies like Paul Conover, a moonfaced, fun-loving character from my hometown, Montclair, New Jersey, and Michael Farmer, a love-sick seventeen-year-old from Atlantic City. It was all for naught. We wouldn't save the world, and my two friends wouldn't even save themselves. I never went to Vietnam. Through the luck of the draw I was sent to Korea, where I served fourteen months, mostly out of harm's way. Farmer would serve two tours in Vietnam, lasting just a few months into his second tour before being killed. Conover would also go to Vietnam. He came back a basket case. He wasn't just depressed. Whatever had happened to him over there seemed to have damaged his very soul. Eventually, he would shoot his wife to death and then kill himself. Madness born of war. It was ever thus.

Norman Morrison found a space in a Pentagon parking lot and climbed from the car. Carrying a gallon jug of kerosene and Emily, who was dressed in blue coveralls, he walked toward a Pentagon entrance that opened onto a mall that led down to the Potomac River. By then it was late afternoon. With the jug in one hand and Emily in his other arm, Morrison walked back and forth outside the entrance. Back and forth, this way and that. He was not far from the third-floor office of Secretary of Defense Robert McNamara. A chilly breeze was blowing in off the river. Ten minutes went by. Fifteen. Morrison kept pacing. A little before five, with the sky darkening, civilian workers and military figures began leaving the building, pouring out of the exits in waves. No one paid much attention to the man with the baby and the jug of kerosene. About a quarter after five, Morrison, standing in a small garden, placed Emily on the ground and doused himself with the contents of the jug. Then he set himself on fire.

He went up like a torch, the flames yellow and blue, leaping nearly a dozen feet into the soft darkness of the November evening. Onlookers at first had trouble realizing what was happening. Then there were shrieks to protect the baby, and Emily was quickly scooped up. A couple of soldiers rushed toward the spectral blaze and began beating at the flames. By the time the fire was out and an ambulance summoned, Morrison was dead.

McNamara did not see the awful scene that erupted less than a hundred feet from his window. But he would later describe Morrison's act as "an outcry against the killing that was destroying the lives of so many Vietnamese and American youth." If that's what it was, few paid any attention. The war would go on for years until fifty-eight thousand Americans and two to three million Vietnamese were dead. Half a century later we're still paying the tab for the Vietnam War and people are still suffering because of it. Philip Caputo, the author of *A Rumor of War*, a best seller about his experiences as a marine lieutenant in Vietnam, would write, "When we marched into the rice paddies on that damp March afternoon, we carried, along with our packs and rifles, the implicit convictions that the Vietcong would be quickly beaten. We kept the packs and rifles; the convictions, we lost."

The madness ran far deeper than most Americans realized. No degree of horror, no amount of death and suffering or financial cost or societal damage, has been enough to counter our compulsion to wage war. Hardly anyone in the U.S. could have imagined that America's response to the terror attacks of September 11, 2001, would mean nearly a decade and a half of war in Afghanistan, with U.S. troops still fighting and dying there in 2014. Or that nearly forty-five hundred American GIs would die in a war in Iraq launched just a year and a half after the invasion of Afghanistan. Those wars, which led to the loss of many hundreds of thousands of lives, including countless innocent civilians, were among the most catastrophic failures of foreign and domestic policy in the nation's history. How could such critically important matters have gone so wrong?

In the introduction to *The Long War*, a collection of essays about America's national security policies since World War II, Andrew Bacevich wrote, "Time and again, members of the foreign policy elite have misperceived the world and misconstrued American interests, thereby exacerbating rather than alleviating threats. Time and again, they have misunderstood war and the consequences likely to flow from the use of force." We have watched these tragic fiascoes unfold with stunning frequency since the middle of the last century. The hard truth is that the politicians and generals who lead us into these wars know precious little about what they are doing. They go to war the way novices enter the stock market, maximizing the benefits and minimizing the risks. William Goldman's famous line about the entertainment industry comes to mind: Nobody knows anything.

In his 1995 memoir, McNamara wrote of his own scandalous level of ignorance at the time of the Bay of Pigs invasion in Cuba in 1961, less than two months after he became defense secretary. "The truth," he said, "is that I did not understand the plan very well and did not know the facts." America's young president, John F. Kennedy, was no better informed than his defense secretary. (When McNamara was first offered the defense job, he protested that he was not qualified. "Who is?" Kennedy replied, adding that there were no schools for defense secretaries, just as there were none for presidents.) The Bay of Pigs operation was a CIA absurdity cooked up while Dwight Eisenhower was president. The invasion—by Cuban exiles with (if you can believe it) the *disguised* support of U.S. air and naval power—was supposed to be a secret. It wasn't. The CIA might as well have flown planes over Cuba trailing banners announcing to Fidel Castro that the exiles were coming. Leaks sprang up with ridiculous frequency and were widely circulated in news accounts. James T. Patterson, in his award-winning history of America's post–World War II era, *Grand Expectations*, wrote, "News stories were full of predictions that invasion lay ahead. Pierre Salinger, Kennedy's press secretary, later observed that the invasion was the 'least covert military operation in history.' He added, 'The only information Castro didn't have . . . was the exact time and place of the invasion.' Kennedy, Salinger noted, 'was upset by the lack of secrecy. "I can't believe what I'm reading," he complained. "All he [Castro] has to do is read our papers. It's all laid out for him." ' "

That was not considered sufficient reason for calling the invasion off. Kennedy, to his everlasting regret, gave the Cuban adventure the go-ahead. It was a debacle. The fifteen hundred CIA-trained exiles who landed on the island's southern coast were quickly overwhelmed by Castro's forces. More than a hundred were killed and twelve hundred were taken captive in a madcap operation that was farcical but not a bit funny. Kennedy was humiliated, and the fiasco heightened Cold War tensions immeasurably. When Patterson described the invasion attempt as "one of the most disastrous military ventures in modern American history," it was not an overstatement. The ramifications would be both tragic and profound. David Halberstam, in *The Best and the Brightest*, recounted a conversation between Kennedy and *New York Times* columnist James Reston after the president had suffered through a disastrous series of meetings with Soviet Premier Nikita Khrushchev, in Vienna two months after the Bay of Pigs. Khrushchev had used the summit to rage against the United States over its arrogance, its imperialism, and the presence of U.S. forces in Berlin. Kennedy, unprepared for such an unrestrained outburst, left the summit shaken. According to Halberstam, he told Reston,

I've got two problems. First, to figure out why he did it, and in such a hostile way. And second, to figure out what we can do about it. I think the first part is pretty easy to explain. I think he did it because of the Bay of Pigs. I think he thought that anyone who was so young and inexperienced as to get into that mess could be taken, and anyone who got into it, and didn't see it through, had no guts. So he just beat hell out of me. So I've got a terrible problem. If he thinks I'm inexperienced and have no guts, until we remove those ideas we won't get anywhere with him. So we have to act.

Kennedy told Reston that he would show Khrushchev and the world that the United States was not weak and that its president was in no way faint of heart. He said he would increase America's military budget and send even more troops into Germany. (He did both.) But that would not be all. According to Halberstam, Kennedy "turned to Reston and said that the only place in the world where there was a real challenge was in Vietnam, and 'now we have a problem in trying to make our power credible, and Vietnam looks like the place.'"

Nothing has changed in all the long years since then. Kennedy's view became the prevailing view—that the only way to make American power credible was to use it. Again and again presidents have felt the need to demonstrate to the electorate and the world that they were not fainthearted when it came to warfare. No one was more explicit on this point than Lyndon Johnson. If the United States pulled its forces out of Vietnam, he said, "then I would be seen as a coward and my nation would be seen as an appeaser, and we would both find it impossible to accomplish anything for anybody anywhere on the entire globe." Richard Nixon stressed his commitment to victory in Vietnam by declaring in 1969, "I will not be the first president of the United States to lose a war." George W. Bush had absolutely no idea what he was getting into when he launched his wholly unnecessary war in Iraq, but that didn't matter. "Fuck Saddam," he said. "We're taking him out." The inevitable casualties, the oceans of blood, the mindless slaughter of innocent civilians by the hundreds of thousands were no deterrents. The utter senselessness of it all has been breathtaking. The Cold War has disappeared, along with the Soviet Union. America has the greatest militarized empire the world has ever known, a colossus if ever history has seen one. But we're no better now at avoiding absurd, costly wars, and no better at fighting them, than we were in the years when Kennedy, Johnson, and Nixon were president.

Matthew Hoh, who was born in 1973 (at the height of the Watergate scandal), was destined to receive a full helping of wartime insanity, twenty-first-century-style. In the summer of 2009, the same summer in which Dan Berschinski was so gravely wounded, Hoh was a highly regarded State Department official posted in Afghanistan. His job was to vigorously represent America's wartime interests, and he'd always been a quintessential team player.

But the American effort in Afghanistan, fatally disrupted by the 2003 invasion of Iraq, had been botched to a fare-thee-well. There didn't seem any way to put the pieces back together. The Afghan government was dysfunctional. And chaos bordering on incoherence was the defining characteristic of the policies coming out of Washington. By 2009, Hoh was locked in a deep crisis of doubt about the war. "That," he would tell me much later, in a tone of deep chagrin, "was absolutely the last thing I needed."

Hoh was the very model of the young, experienced, gung-ho advocate for American military policy. He was thirty-six years old in 2009, a former Marine Corps captain who had served in combat in Iraq and then, as a civilian, had returned to Iraq to supervise reconstruction efforts even as the war continued to rage. In Afghanistan, he was the senior American civilian in Zabul Province, a Taliban stronghold.

Hoh was a golden boy, a favorite of some of the most important people in the Foreign Service. In their eyes, he was immensely appealing, a well-educated combat veteran who understood the nuanced imperatives of diplomacy and policy making. It didn't hurt that he was tall, athletically built, and engaging—the all-American boy. Old-timers, burdened since Vietnam with the troubled legacy of the best and the brightest, thought Hoh was the kind of young man who would benefit from the lessons of history and get matters right this time around. The Obama administration saw him as a comer. Matt Hoh was someone to watch.

So Hoh had a lot to lose. If he went public with his doubts about the Afghanistan war (and, in truth, they were more than just doubts; his support for the war had collapsed), he'd be destroying a career of tremendous promise. His real problem was that he was as tough and smart as his superiors believed—too smart and too sane to deny the reality all around him, and too principled a public servant to keep his dire assessment to himself. Hoh's assignment had brought him into almost daily contact with ordinary Afghans and their village elders, with Afghan government officials, and with American military and civilian personnel. There was no way to conceal the fact that after nearly a decade of fighting, the war was going very badly. Al-Qaeda had long since been routed, but the

Taliban was resurgent. The government in Kabul, our ally of sorts, was hopeless—a raging kleptocracy that was corrupt through and through, not to mention gratuitously brutal, incompetent, and lacking in popular support. The Afghan military, which we were supposed to be building up to the point where it could stand on its own (thus allowing U.S. forces and their NATO allies to depart), was a joke. Hoh was a patriot and not given to defeatism. He'd loved being a marine officer, commanding men in combat. There was no way that he wanted to believe that the war in Afghanistan had veered so far off course that it was no longer worth fighting. But by the summer of 2009, he found it impossible to fend off that depressing conclusion.

I hadn't yet met Hoh, but all the evidence I was seeing pointed to the same conclusion. Every time I looked closely at what we were doing in Afghanistan, I could hear the demoralizing echoes of Vietnam. In the 1960s and 1970s, despite the astonishing power of its military, the United States had come up empty against an army of lightly armed, pajama-clad peasants. Now, immensely more powerful, with weapons that in the Vietnam era would have been viewed as the wizardry of science fiction, America was finding itself baffled and bewildered in its blood-soaked, trillion-dollar fight against the elusive Taliban. In 2009 we were also still fighting in Iraq, which was an even bloodier fiasco, costing the lives of thousands of Americans and scores of thousands of Iraqis. To what end?

Hoh's experience as a marine, a diplomat, and ultimately a dissenter was a case study of the madness of it all. He had witnessed close-up, and from a variety of perspectives, the nonstop violence and death and the gruesome dehumanization that are the inevitable handmaidens of war. He would not come through it unscathed. In one of our first conversations, I pressed him about the time he'd almost been killed himself, back in 2006, when he was a company commander in Iraq. He spoke of it matter-of-factly, but his eyes telegraphed more of an emotional impact than the rest of his demeanor suggested. On December 3, 2006, Hoh hitched a ride on a navy helicopter in Haditha, a city in Al Anbar Province, one of the most dangerous regions in the country at the time. The twin-rotor

CH-46 Sea Knight helicopter, with sixteen people aboard, began its liftoff from an enormous hydroelectric dam that formed a roiling lake from the waters of the Euphrates River. Something went wrong immediately and the chopper lost power. Before it could get fully airborne, the rear landing gear clipped a four-foot wall at the edge of the helipad.

As Hoh recalled, "It didn't sound right from the moment it took off, or tried to take off. When it hit the wall, everybody on board looked at one another."

The chopper hovered momentarily, wobbled, pitched forward, and then started to descend, falling toward the water forty feet below. It hit the surface of the lake hard, belly first. The passengers, including several service members and a pair of civilian contractors, listened almost in shock as the crew began issuing emergency evacuation instructions. "Water started coming in the back," said Hoh. "I was wearing my body armor and I had my pack in front of me with eighty or ninety pounds of gear. And I had my rifle."

It was difficult in the increasing chaos to hear all of the instructions. "I'm trying to decide what to do," Hoh said. "You're a marine, so you know about water landings that have gone terribly wrong, where everyone in the helicopter dies. I saw a couple of the other guys go off the back of the helicopter, and I'm a good swimmer, so I just dropped my rifle on the deck and I went off the back, too."

The white-capped water was choppy, breathtakingly cold, and extremely deep. "It was just freezing," Hoh recalled, "and there was a strong undercurrent. I was scared to death." Still strapped in heavy body armor, he began swimming toward the dam fifty yards away. The undercurrent and the body armor made him feel as if he were pulling against a lead weight, straining against a force determined to drag him under. As he swam, he could hear voices screaming for help.

The water was filthy and was known to contain fecal matter contaminated with the bacterium that causes cholera. "I swallowed a ton of that water," Hoh said. But he made it to the dam and was hauled gasping and coughing from the lake. As he struggled to catch his breath, he looked around for a friend of his who had been on the helicopter, a major from Grosse Pointe Park, Michigan, named Joseph McCloud. Most people called McCloud by his middle name, Trane. Hoh didn't see him. He scanned the water. Rescuers had dived off the dam and were trying to help those who were still struggling. Trane was nowhere in sight. Hoh dumped his body armor and plunged back into the water. Exhausted, he joined a rope line of rescuers. It was too late. Four of the passengers had drowned, including Major McCloud, who was thirty-nine years old, married, and the father of three young children.

The crash got very little attention. For most of the press, such incidents were not worth covering. America at war had long since ceased to be big news. A helicopter crash in Iraq that was not the result of enemy fire, and in which only four people had died, was a yawner.

Hoh tried for a long time to maintain the fiction that there was something sensible about the wars and the way they were being fought. But by 2009, the weight of all that he had experienced and seen in Iraq and Afghanistan, and all that he knew of America's wartime history over the past half century, made that impossible. Over the course of several interviews, he tried to explain what it was like to be caught in the throes of a moral compulsion that flew in the face of everything he was supposed to stand for. "As a Foreign Service officer and former marine captain, I had an obligation to continue supporting the war in Afghanistan," he said. "But by the summer of 2009, I was tired of waking up feeling guilty about taking part in it. Our troops were fighting and fighting hard, but there was no available route to success. I knew it wasn't right, and yet there I was going along with it."

Hoh's reluctant take on Afghanistan was that lives were being destroyed in a seemingly endless conflict for no discernible good reason. Americans had been united in support of the initial invasion, ostensibly to hunt down and destroy the forces that had killed nearly three thousand Americans in the attacks on the World Trade Center and the Pentagon. But the mission, badly undermined by the war in Iraq, had morphed into something incomprehensible, and the American public had tuned out. Top wartime policy makers couldn't even agree on a basic strategy. Was it counterterrorism or counterinsurgency? Al-Qaeda was no longer in Afghanistan.

Did we now have the limited goal of trying to defeat the Taliban, which had proved remarkably resilient, or were we trying to build a sparkling new democracy in a country that all too often was reminiscent of the Stone Age?

"Our policy narrative just wasn't based in reality," said Hoh. "We were making the same mistakes in Afghanistan that I had seen us making in Iraq, with the same mix of hubris and arrogance and ignorance. The official narrative was that we were defending the U.S. We were losing fifty to sixty good young American men and women every month. How did those deaths make the U.S. any safer? What was the benefit of spending $150 billion a year on this war and losing all those lives? When you see the damage that this has done to so many of our kids, and how it's crippled our ability to deal with so many crucial problems at home, it just breaks your heart."

One of the places Hoh had visited as part of his duties in Afghanistan was the remote Korengal valley in Kunar Province in the eastern part of the country. The fighting there was a perfect example of tragic wartime folly. Hardly anyone in America had ever heard of the Korengal valley. It was just six miles long and home to just a handful of villagers. It was a region so remote that its inhabitants spoke their own language. And yet the Korengal had come to be known as the valley of death. American troops, for reasons no one seemed to understand, had been there for years. The valley was a place of great beauty and, once the troops arrived, great suffering. But it held no strategic value that anyone could see. Dozens of American soldiers had died in the valley, and many more had been badly wounded. The events in the valley, once it was transformed into a war zone, were surreal. There were helicopter crashes, ambushes by insurgents, and endless firefights, grenade attacks, and bombings. Sebastian Junger, the best-selling author of *The Perfect Storm*, wrote a book about the American presence in the valley. And he joined with the combat photographer Tim Hetherington (who would be killed himself in 2011 in a rocket-propelled grenade attack in Libya) to make a heartbreaking documentary about U.S. troops in the Korengal that won a grand jury prize at the Sundance Film Festival. Through it all, no one knew what the hell the Americans were trying to accomplish there.

In early 2009, the chairman of the Joint Chiefs of Staff, Admiral Michael Mullen, pointedly asked the obvious question: Why had the United States been fighting for so long in a region as isolated and thinly populated as the Korengal valley? No one had an answer. At the time, Hoh was attached as a civilian to a military brigade in Jalalabad in eastern Afghanistan. Mullen ordered the brigade to investigate, and Hoh worked on the project. The findings were disturbing.

"We'd been in there since late 2004," Hoh said, "and we were given all these stories and reasons why. Some people said suicide bombers traversed the valley to get to Kabul. Others said we were getting valuable intelligence and that there were high-value targets there. I eventually spoke to a guy who was the first officer to lead his platoon in there, and he was very clear. I said, 'Why'd you guys go into the valley?' And he said, 'Because we hadn't been in there before.'

"He went in, and in eight months they had two TICs—troops in contact. Two actions happened. So you look at that and you say, 'How the hell did we get from this period when in eight months we only had two TICs to this becoming the valley of death—the deadliest location in Afghanistan for American forces?' "

The answer could not have been simpler. "What happens," said Hoh, "is that our forces establish a presence, and anywhere we're at attracts the insurgency."

Junger's book, titled simply *War*, captured the extreme isolation of the valley and its people and why the inhabitants were so willing to welcome insurgents once the Americans showed up: "Most Korengalis have never left their village and have almost no understanding of the world beyond the mouth of the valley. That makes it a perfect place in which to base an insurgency dedicated to fighting outsiders. One old man in the valley thought the American soldiers were actually Russians who had simply stayed after the Soviet army pulled out in 1989."

These were folks who had never heard of 9/11. They could not have been less interested in what was going on in the United States. They had no comprehension of what the United States was like or even where it was. "They wouldn't have been fighting us if we weren't there," said Hoh. "They just saw us as dudes with guns coming into their valley. When you've got a population that isolated, you should be sending in anthropologists, not soldiers."

Young Americans who should have been going to college and dating, starting their first jobs, and building a future were dying in that godforsaken valley. It was wrong and not what the United States was ever supposed to have been about. A young soldier named Misha Pemble-Belkin, nicknamed Peanut Butter, was among the troops followed by Junger and Hetherington in their documentary. At one point he described, on camera, in a voice as soft as the murmur in a confessional, the awful sorrow and frustration of trying to comfort a friend who was mortally wounded, who was dying in front of his eyes. "You could see it in his face that he's slowly dying," Pemble-Belkin said. "He was turning really ghost-looking. His eyes started sinking in his head, and he started to get real brown around his eyes. And he kept saying, 'I'm getting really dizzy. I want to go to sleep.' That's some rough shit to hear, coming from one of your best friends and you're watching him die right in front of you. That's some fucking shit."

Pemble-Belkin's unit had built a shabby outpost in the Korengal that they called Restrepo, which was also the title of the documentary. It was named after Private First Class Juan Restrepo, a medic and aspiring doctor, just twenty years old, who was shot twice in the face and killed soon after his platoon arrived in the valley. PFC Restrepo had been immensely popular with the men in the platoon. In addition to being the guy who braved enemy fire to look after the wounded, he was unusually kind and almost obsessively committed to the overall welfare of his colleagues. "If you got sick he would take your guard shift," Junger wrote. "If you were depressed he'd come to your hooch and play guitar. He took care of his men in every possible way." The men looked up to this young guy who looked out for them in his short time with them, this fellow who was barely out of his teens. They loved him. And then he was gone.

Commenting on his death, a soldier who was particularly close to Restrepo said, "For a long time I hated God."

When Admiral Mullen ordered the investigation into what the army was doing in the valley, he also asked what would happen if the troops left. "Everyone knew what would happen," Hoh told me. "You could ask anyone you wanted to, from the company commander up to the assistant division commander. Everyone would say the same thing: 'Nothing happens if we leave.' There was no debate. It seemed like everyone just shrugged and said, 'Nothing happens.' "

In April 2010, after a half decade of pointless fighting, the United States pulled its forces out of the valley. That long period of indiscriminate maiming and killing and who knows how much psychological damage had made no difference in the war one way or the other. Under the headline "U.S. Retreat from Afghan Valley Marks Recognition of Blunder," the *Washington Post* wrote, "In 2010, a new set of commanders concluded that the United States had blundered into a blood feud with fierce and clannish villagers who wanted, above all, to be left alone. By this logic, subduing the Korengal wasn't worth the cost in American blood."

Matt Hoh knew that the Korengal valley fiasco was not an isolated blunder. It reflected a much wider problem. The war itself had become a marathon blunder and was no longer worth the cost in American blood. But policy makers, including America's new president, Barack Obama, wanted no part of that perspective. For any number of reasons, politics paramount among them, they had to maintain the charade that American soldiers and marines were fighting and dying in defense of freedom, democracy, and the American way. I remember Hoh raising both hands in frustration as he offered his counterargument: "Yes, of course, al-Qaeda had been based in Afghanistan in 2001. But we were still telling the same old story in 2009—that we were there to keep the United States safe and that the people we were fighting were connected to 9/11. But that was no longer the case. Our troops were not fighting al-Qaeda. Al-Qaeda was no longer there. So in 2009 that narrative bore no relevance to the reality of al-Qaeda and the security of America. The reality was that the people we were fighting in

Afghanistan had nothing to do with 9/11. They just happened to be on one side of a multisided, multilayered civil war. But that old 9/11 narrative was still there."

An awful lot of people—American service members and untold numbers of innocent civilians—were dying beneath the banner of that false narrative. As an American diplomat, Hoh was charged with helping to carry out policies that not only justified those deaths but would lead to many more. "I couldn't do that," he said. "After a while, I just couldn't do that anymore."

With a four-page letter on September 10, 2009, a document that sent a brief but noticeable tremor through the upper ranks of the Obama administration, Matthew Hoh told his superiors he was quitting the State Department. Lives were being expended, he said, in a war that no longer made sense. In a particularly poignant passage, he wrote, "Thousands of our men and women have returned home with physical and mental wounds, some that will never heal or will only worsen with time. The dead return only in bodily form to be received by families who must be reassured their dead have sacrificed for a purpose worthy of futures lost, love vanished, and promised dreams unkept. I have lost confidence such assurances can anymore be made."

Hoh's letter sent his superiors scrambling. The new president had no intention of de-escalating the war. He was intent on ratcheting it up. Hoh's resignation would be an embarrassment. If it was accepted, he'd become the first high-ranking government official to quit in protest over the war.

The American ambassador to Afghanistan, Karl Eikenberry, met with Hoh and urged him to reconsider. He offered Hoh a job in Kabul on Eikenberry's own senior staff. Hoh said no. Next came Richard C. Holbrooke, the president's special representative for Afghanistan and Pakistan. Hoh met with him in Washington. Holbrooke used a cleaned-up version of one of Lyndon Johnson's favorite arguments, that it was better to be inside the tent pissing out than vice versa. Like Eikenberry, he offered Hoh a prominent post on his own team. He said a young man with Hoh's talent and credentials could have a real impact. *Inside the tent.* Hoh wavered. The U.S. government was making him feel like a very important individual. Holbrooke would later tell the *Washington Post* that he agreed with much of Hoh's analysis of what was happening in Afghanistan, although he didn't accept his conclusion that the war was no longer worth fighting. "We took his letter very seriously," he said, "because he was a good officer. We all thought that given how serious his letter was, how much commitment there was, and his prior track record, we should pay close attention to him."

Hoh accepted Holbrooke's job offer. But almost immediately he knew he'd made a mistake. In Washington he'd be climbing inside the bubble, floating further and further away from the reality of the war, the fighting, the killing, the filth, and the futility. He wanted the killing brought to an end. He wanted the damage that the war was doing to the United States to cease. He also knew that whatever the higher-ups were promising, he'd be muzzled. He'd be trapped in the insidious contradiction that David Halberstam had described when writing about McNamara and his rationalizations about Vietnam, "the conflict between the good intentions and the desire to hold and use power."

So Hoh changed his mind again and quit.

When Hoh left the State Department, the *Washington Post* ran a long front-page article cataloging his career and the reasons for his departure. Most of the press coverage of the resignation was sympathetic, and it wasn't long before the Obama administration's attitude toward Hoh, friendly and solicitous at first, went into a deep freeze. Efforts were made behind the scenes to discredit him, but they weren't successful. Neither was Hoh's attempt to influence U.S. policy for the better. As Jonathan Alter put it, "The autumn of 2009 was when Afghanistan became Obama's war." The president, unable to embrace anything other than further escalation, plunged deeper into the quagmire.

In a major speech on August 17 to the Veterans of Foreign Wars, the president said of Afghanistan, "This is not a war of choice. This is a war of necessity."

Despite the disaster in Iraq and the passage of nearly eight years since the attacks of September 11, 2001, the momentum among policy makers for more war was overwhelming. Virtually everyone in a position of power was counseling escalation. There were fraught discussions over the merits of counterterrorism versus counterinsurgency, but no one with any real influence was suggesting that the president wind the war in Afghanistan down. Even the vice president, Joe Biden, who was seen as a cautionary voice, was telling the president to send more troops—just not as many as the generals were asking for.

In his VFW speech, Obama asserted, "Those who attacked America on 9/11 are plotting to do so again. If left unchecked, the Taliban insurgency will mean an even larger safe haven from which al-Qaeda would plot to kill more Americans. So this is not only a war worth fighting. This is fundamental to the defense of our people."

At the time that he spoke, the American economy was hemorrhaging jobs, the national budget deficit was spiraling to new heights, and American forces were still fighting and dying in the Korengal valley with no members of al-Qaeda anywhere in sight. Dan Berschinski's legs would be blown off in his catastrophic encounter with an IED on the day after the president's speech.

Matthew Hoh and other opponents of escalation had little chance of being heard above the pro-war din in Washington. The feeling had spread from the generals to the policy makers that the United States could "win" in Afghanistan, that the military would defeat the insurgency, and that somehow—through a combination of American dollars and sheer willpower—a vibrant central government would be established in Kabul. It was a typically American fantasy, based on a misconception of Afghan society and the nature of the insurgency and grounded in the idea that we had both the right and the capacity to impose our vision and values, at gunpoint, on a foreign people.

Hoh was trying to make the case for a gradual withdrawal of American forces, along with stepped-up efforts to establish a cease-fire and begin serious peace negotiations with the insurgents. That was not what the president had in mind. On December 1, before a solemn gathering of four thousand cadets in their dress gray uniforms at West Point, Obama officially announced the further expansion of the war. He said he would send an additional 30,000 troops to Afghanistan in early 2010, bringing American troop strength to 100,000, double what it had been when he took office. He then immediately and very peculiarly noted that he would begin to draw down those troops in eighteen months. The pundits got a kick out of that. NBC's David Gregory cracked, "The cavalry is coming, but not for long."

America's new president had upped the wartime ante considerably. A lot more blood would be spilled and tens of billions of dollars spent on what was already the longest war in American history—a war that was already lost. Nine days later, Obama was in Oslo, Norway, in white tie and tails, accepting the Nobel Peace Prize.

10 *Hurricane Sandy and Other Disasters*

We are facing an infrastructure crisis in this country that threatens our status as an economic superpower and threatens the health and safety of the people we serve.

—*former New York City mayor* MICHAEL BLOOMBERG

What does infrastructure do? It produces jobs.

—*former Pennsylvania governor* ED RENDELL

In the weeks and months after the bridge collapse, Mercedes Gorden's life seemed to blur into one surgery after another. She was in and out of the hospital, most of her time spent either prepping for surgery or recovering. She loathed her wheelchair, but even with crutches she could barely walk. The pain in her legs and feet and back seemed as hot and constant as electricity surging through a power line. "I don't fit into my tennis shoes anymore," she told me. "My feet are bigger now, after all the surgeries."

She shrugged. We were having dinner at a restaurant in Minneapolis. Mercedes apologized for being tired. "I'm back at work now, but I get so tired. I'm really sorry."

Among Mercedes's hopes, once it was clear that she had survived the catastrophe, was that she'd be able to walk down the aisle at her wedding. I had wondered, when I first started interviewing her, about Jake Rudh, her fiancé. I knew of many cases where a healthy young couple had been engaged, or married, and then one had suffered grievous, long-lasting injuries. Often the relationship didn't last. It was the sort of thing that happened all the time with men and women in the military who came back wounded from overseas. Mercedes had smiled when I asked her about it. Then she teared up. With Jake it had never been an issue. "From day one," she said, "he became my full-time caretaker."

They were married fifteen months after the accident in a ceremony that was joyous but also constrained by an underlying sadness for the thirteen people who had lost their lives. Jake, who joined us at the restaurant about a half hour after Mercedes and I had arrived, said to his wife, "You walked down that aisle. That was really a big deal."

"You mean I hobbled down the aisle."

Jake laughed. "You were able to be out of the wheelchair. It was great."

I was trying to read their faces across the table. Mercedes was in some respects her usual ebullient self, telling stories and laughing easily. She'd said she was tired. I wondered if she was in pain sitting in the booth for a long stretch.

"So how are you doing now?" I asked. "The wheelchair's gone. You're back at work full-time. But what about the pain?"

Mercedes fingered her cocktail. "It depends. It's different from minute to minute, hour to hour. It depends on the weather, on how active I've been, or inactive. I'm a different person every time I stand up. I might stand up and hobble, and the next time I'm practically normal. I don't always feel like my real self. Or maybe I don't remember my real self. It's bizarre. All the metal's out of my body now—the pins and screws—except for one pin in my heel. The metal would set off the machines at the airport. It happened in Costa Rica on our honeymoon. I showed them my scars, and that pretty much satisfied them. When I told them what had happened, they were like, '*Oh, man!*' "

I asked about the psychological impact of everything that had happened, and it was the first time I'd seen a look of sadness cross Mercedes's face. "At first I didn't know how profoundly it had affected me," she said. "Maybe I was dealing with so much in the beginning. I just didn't realize. But then it just sort of began to hit me. I didn't have any suicidal ideation, you know? But I can definitely see why people with mental illness or chronic pain kill themselves. I actually found an understanding of that. Not that I was at that place. But I really got it."

She'd been taking medication for psychological distress ever since the accident, she said. At one point she tried to wean herself off it. She didn't really think it would be a problem. But it was. "It was just the worst feeling," she said. "I felt helpless. I was falling into a deep black abyss that I could not pull myself out of. I became afraid of everything. I was afraid of the dark. I'd never been afraid of the dark, not even as a child. I was afraid of my husband leaving me. I had panic attacks. I had absolutely zero appetite. I couldn't eat. Not at all."

That made her laugh. "I did lose weight, so at least there was a nice upside. I had put on thirty-five or forty pounds, so I lost some weight. But I really couldn't eat anything, and that was horrible. And I couldn't sleep. And if you can't eat or sleep, and you're afraid all the time, you kind of want to die. I went back on the medication. I had to. I was afraid of having some weird freak-out. I was not in control of my emotions."

Problems remained, even with the medication. One of them was a phobia common to victims of bridge and building collapses—a fear of structures suddenly giving way beneath them. "That just will not go away," she said. "I have a fear of everything falling out from underneath me, whether it's an elevator, a bridge. If I'm on a floor above the first level, I feel like the floor could collapse. A balcony—everything. I don't trust anything to be 100 percent stable. I can be in bed and feel like my bed is going through the floor. I wouldn't be surprised if that happened. That's how silly my mind is now."

Crossing a bridge in a car is a nightmare. "It's almost unbearable," Mercedes said. "Overpasses are like the scariest things in the world for me. If I'm on an overpass and I'm not on the solid part, I'm panicky. I'm hot. I'm trying to distract myself."

Mercedes took Jake's last name when they married. The couple's goal, she said, "is to have a child and a happy life and to raise our child well."

The marriage has not been easy but Mercedes seemed awed by Jake's commitment. (He slept in her hospital room in the days immediately following the bridge collapse.) "I don't want to talk about how wonderful he's been," she told me. "I'll start crying."

Jake seemed similarly awed by Mercedes's "heroic" struggle to come back from the devastation of her injuries. "She's beyond amazing," he said. "I look back at those early days, and even though they were trying times, we tried to make the best of each day. And we laughed. Whereas it certainly wasn't fun, I want to say we had fun with what we were given."

"Don't take anything too seriously," Mercedes said. "You have to enjoy life."

"When things get trying between the two of us," said Jake, "we look back at what we've already been through. It's not going to touch what we've already been through as a couple."

I was folding my notebook when Mercedes added, "I keep telling myself I've had my quota of hardship. But you never know."

As Mercedes and the other survivors of the bridge collapse went through the various stages of their physical and psychological rehabilitation, the state of Minnesota, with funding from the federal government, was engaged in the urgent task of replacing the Interstate 35 bridge. When disaster strikes, policy makers somehow find a way to accomplish the things that they'd known all along needed to be done. Construction crews worked twenty-four hours a day seven days a week to build a spectacular ten-lane, state-of-the-art span. They did it in just eleven months. The project, paid for by the federal government, came in under budget and ahead of schedule. The new bridge was praised both for its design and its many technological features, including a sophisticated anti-icing system and a remarkable array of "smart-bridge" sensors to deliver data on the

myriad stresses imposed by traffic and weather. In a ceremony at
the new bridge a few days before it opened, the federal transportation secretary, Mary Peters, said, "It shouldn't take a tragedy to
build a bridge this fast in America."

Similar comments were made after Hurricane Katrina all but
destroyed New Orleans in 2005. The city's levees, gates, pumps,
and other flood protection components were reengineered and
replaced at a cost of $14.5 billion *after* the floodwaters had receded.
This is a perpetual pattern, and it results in the needless loss of life
every day. When he was governor of Virginia, Tim Kaine told a
national conference of political and economic leaders examining
the need to rebuild the nation's vital infrastructure systems that
Americans were "the best reactors in the world." When a crisis
occurs, "we will act," he said, "we will belly up to the bar, we'll
do what we need to do." But in the absence of a crisis, policy makers and the general public seemed chronically unwilling to act, to
invest the funds and the energy necessary to meet some of the
nation's greatest challenges—in this case, its failing infrastructure.
In the fall of 2012 it was the mid-Atlantic coast that bore the tragic
brunt of this neglect.

The wind picked up around eight o'clock that Monday evening
in October. Rico and Frankie Blancaflor could hear the windows
begin to rattle in their newly purchased, nearly century-old house.
Their baby, eighteen-month-old Eli, started to fret. Darkness had
closed in over Montclair, New Jersey, an upscale suburb a dozen
miles due west of New York City. Soon it began to rain. Hurricane
Sandy was arriving.

"It was a little bit scary," Rico told me. "You look out the window,
and you see those big trees swaying. And then, all of a sudden, the
lights went out."

The storm's progress had been closely watched by meteorolo-
gists and was obsessively covered on television. Yet it still hit the
Northeast like a sneak attack. No one was prepared for the extent
of the destruction. Entire neighborhoods were destroyed. Much

of lower Manhattan and nearly all of the city of Hoboken were flooded. Venerable beachfront communities in New York and all along the New Jersey shore were ripped apart by storm surges of astonishing power. When it was all over, more than a hundred people were dead.

Rico and Frankie lit candles, then settled down with Eli in the living room to wait out the storm. "We didn't have any television or radio," Rico recalled, "so we really didn't know what was going on, other than what was happening on our block."

The storm had traveled north over the Atlantic Ocean, just off the East Coast. On Monday evening it banked sharply to the west and slammed with tremendous fury into the mid-Atlantic region. Several factors contributed to the enormous potency of the event. A cold-weather storm was closing in on the East Coast from the west, while at the same time an Arctic system was blowing into the area from the north. There was also a full moon that Monday night, and Sandy's landfall coincided with high tide. It was a hellish convergence. The storm surge that barreled in from the dark Atlantic was epic in its intensity. "It seemed," as one stunned observer would later recount, "as if the water was determined to batter the coastline into submission."

The wind-driven waves roared into Atlantic City, which had been evacuated, and into the Jersey shore towns that stretched north all the way to New York Harbor. Floodwaters poured into Hoboken, New Jersey, and Staten Island in New York, and into lower Manhattan and Brooklyn and Queens. Sustained winds were clocked at eighty miles per hour. The Hudson and East Rivers on either side of Manhattan overflowed. Infrastructure everywhere began to give way. Salt water poured into the New York City subway system and the Brooklyn Battery Tunnel. The trains were shut down and the tunnel closed. Cars floated in the streets of Manhattan's financial district. A man who lived in a housing complex a block from the ocean in Queens told the *New York Times*, "We could be fishing out our windows tomorrow."

With the power gone, Rico and Frankie had no heat in their house. They built a fire in the living room fireplace and prepared to spend the night on the floor. They took turns sleeping as the storm raged, one lying beneath the covers beside Eli while the other stayed awake to monitor the fire. Down the block, a huge tree toppled over and crashed into the home of a neighbor. "We found out later," Rico said, "that it just missed their baby's room."

The electrical grid in New York, New Jersey, Long Island, and suburban Connecticut was quickly overwhelmed. Trees and overhead power lines went down at an astonishing rate, and underground substations in many cases were incapacitated by flooding. More than six million people lost power. When the lights went out at the NYU Langone Medical Center on Manhattan's East Side, officials turned to their backup power system, which had been installed to cope with just such emergencies. It failed. The hospital's 215 patients had to be evacuated in the middle of the storm. A distress call for ambulances went out, and soon a long convoy had materialized outside the hospital. Moving so many patients under those conditions was hair-raising, but no lives were lost.

My wife and I were at home in a high-rise building on Manhattan's Upper West Side, which did not lose power. Unable to sleep, I turned on the television around three or four in the morning and was astounded to see live footage of an entire neighborhood in the borough of Queens in flames. Breezy Point is a gated, largely working-class community on a peninsula between Jamaica Bay and the Atlantic Ocean. A fire believed to have started when floodwaters caused a short in the electrical system of an unoccupied bungalow began burning out of control and then, whipped by the winds, spread from one house to another. Firefighters could not get through the flooded roadways to properly fight the blaze. I remember thinking that some portions of the Great Chicago Fire of 1871 must have resembled the conflagration that I was watching on TV. The Breezy Point fires burned for hours, reducing entire blocks to smoking rubble. When it was all over, 126 homes had been destroyed.

Hurricane Sandy ruthlessly exposed the vulnerabilities of a woefully inadequate system of public works. As the storm raged, steadily mounting failures plagued the electrical grid, telephone service, transportation networks, roads and tunnels, hospitals, and even police and fire departments, which in some cases were unable to respond to emergencies because of flooded roadways and power outages.

The brutal winds and mammoth storm surges generated by Hurricane Sandy would cause tremendous problems under any circumstances. But the physical damage and human suffering were made much worse by a succession of breakdowns that could and should have been prevented. The urban, suburban, and oceanfront infrastructure, built for the twentieth century, was not even close to meeting the imperatives of the new century with its new needs, including the demands of a changing climate. Once the storm was over, power company executives could not quickly get the lights back on for the millions who had lost service. In some cases power was out for weeks. The Port Authority Trans-Hudson light rail system, an absolutely crucial commuter line that carried more than a quarter of a million riders between New York and New Jersey every day, would not get back to full service for months. New York's governor, Andrew Cuomo, described the storm as "frightening" and said it should result in "a fundamental rethinking of our built environment."

For millions of individuals who were not touched by tragedy, and whose property was not badly damaged, the most maddening breakdown was the marathon loss of electric power. "It makes you crazy," said Queens resident Lydia Wade. "You're like living in the dark ages. The sun goes down, it gets dark out, and you feel like you've lost touch with civilization."

In Montclair, Rico and Frankie Blancaflor were without power for eight days. "You take so many things for granted when you have electricity," Rico said. "Refrigeration, for example. You lose power and your food starts to spoil. So you need lots of canned food. Before the storm hit, Frankie and I put tons and tons of ice into the refrigerator. It was like an improvised icebox. That lasted for a while. We were finally able to get a little portable generator, but you needed gasoline to power that, and there were gas shortages. So there I was, like everybody else, waiting in line at the pumps for hours."

Rico worked for a foundation in lower Manhattan. With the PATH trains out, he commuted by bus. When he got off the bus at night near his home, the neighborhood was completely dark.

Pitch-black. No streetlights. No traffic. No lights in the surrounding homes. He started wearing a headlamp for his commute.

"It worked great," he said, "but they were laughing at me in the office. They couldn't believe I had a headlamp."

A sustained loss of electric power can be unnerving. "You can feel like you've lost all control," said Anisa Mehdi, whose home in Maplewood, New Jersey, was without power for more than a week. "As the days and nights go by, the uncertainty about when power will be restored really weighs on you. There's a sense that the natural order of things is breaking down and you are helpless to do anything about it."

For families with money the absence of electricity was a maddening inconvenience. For poor people it was a disaster that was often life-threatening. In New York City's high-rise apartment buildings, thousands of poor and low-income residents were trapped for days in utterly hellish environments—no power, heat, hot water, or elevator service. For the elderly and infirm it was a nightmare. For many who were on high floors, there was no way to leave the building.

Drinkable water would run out after two or three days. Cell phone batteries would run down, and there was no way to recharge them. Toilets that couldn't be flushed would fill with waste. In an article about residents stranded in the city's public housing projects, the *New York Times* wrote, "In apartment 8F of one tower, Daniel O'Neill, a 75-year-old retired teacher who uses a wheelchair and who still lacked reliable electricity, cut in half the dosage of his $132-a-month medicine, which he needed to stabilize his swollen limbs."

That was three weeks after the hurricane. A worker from the Federal Emergency Management Agency who eventually came upon O'Neill was horrified by his condition. "That leg looks like it could turn into gangrene," the worker said. He promised to get help.

The conditions in a privately owned high-rise complex near the beach in the Far Rockaway section of Queens became an Internet sensation when a volunteer rescue worker posted a five-minute video on YouTube. The complex, known as the Sand Castle, was without power for almost two weeks. During that time it became a place of increasing fear as tenants, many of them elderly and in some cases disabled, struggled to cope in an environment that resembled a war zone. The stench generated from rotting food, backed-up toilets, unwashed bodies, and uncollected garbage caused volunteers who entered the building to mistakenly think there were corpses in a number of apartments. In fact, only one man died, an eighty-nine-year-old World War II veteran named Thomas Anderson who had lived alone on the thirteenth floor. "Mr. Anderson," the *Times* wrote, "spent his last days largely alone in the dark, trapped high above the ground without heat, dependent on the haphazard good will of others for his survival."

One of the most disturbing truths confronting policy makers in the aftermath of the hurricane was that a similar catastrophe was almost certain to happen again, and perhaps soon. The seas along the East Coast were steadily rising, storms were becoming more intense, and the aging system of public works was weakening. State officials in New York said they believed it would cost $30 billion over ten years to replace the power grid in and around New York City with a more reliable and more resilient smart grid. Billions more were needed for the construction of new oil and gas pipelines to ensure the timely delivery of fuel during weather emergencies and for the modernization of wastewater systems that were problematic under the best of circumstances. Many of those systems were overwhelmed by Hurricane Sandy, resulting in raw or inadequately treated sewage, including human waste, flowing into the region's waterways.

But it didn't require a storm the size of Sandy to blow the lights out. Big-time power outages have become a chronic problem in the United States. I remember the sunny Thursday afternoon in August 2003 when a sudden blackout hit New York City. I was reading a report in my office on the tenth floor of the New York Times building on West Forty-Third Street. With the elevators out, I walked down the ten flights of stairs and then the half block to Times Square. Bewildered office workers had joined the disoriented throngs already in the streets. Almost everyone had a cell phone, but none of them were working because cellular towers had lost power. That freaked out a lot of people. Less than two years had elapsed since September 11, 2001, and terrorism was on nearly everyone's mind. A woman asked me if I thought the nation was under attack again. I told her no. I thought it was just a blackout, like the ones that had darkened the city in 1965 and 1977. But bigger, maybe.

It was bigger, all right. The blackout started when overloaded transmission lines in Ohio sagged into unpruned trees. Fires erupted, and a series of equipment breakdowns, including computer problems, caused what should have been a local outage to cascade. Lights went out in parts of the Midwest, much of the Northeast, and parts of Canada. Fifty million people in eight states lost power. Bill Richardson, who had served as energy secretary in the Bill Clinton administration, ruefully commented, "We are a major superpower with a third-world electrical grid. Our grid is antiquated. It needs serious modernization."

Frightened subway riders in New York City found themselves stranded on stalled and darkened trains. A woman who made a long and difficult walk down the stairs of the high-rise MetLife building on Park Avenue in Manhattan suffered an apparent heart attack. Paramedics couldn't revive her and were unable to quickly locate an ambulance. The woman died.

New York was exceedingly strange that night. No subway service. No dramas or musicals in the theater districts. None of the spectacularly animated billboard lighting that ordinarily transforms Times Square from night into day. As the sun slipped out of sight, workers at Zabar's, the legendary food emporium on the Upper West Side, were out on the sidewalk giving away huge amounts of ice cream. "We're in a lot of trouble here," one of the workers said. "All this food, and no way to keep it from spoiling."

Although tighter controls were imposed on energy systems in the wake of the 2003 outage, blackouts have become routine occurrences in the United States. Bill Richardson's comments were hardly an exaggeration. America's electrical grid is not even close to being able to shoulder the demands of the twenty-first century. In some parts of the country it seemed that anytime there was a storm, the lights went out. A severe rain and ice storm that hit the Northeast a couple of weeks before Christmas in 2008 caused blackouts that affected 1.4 million people. A series of powerful thunderstorms that swept through the mid-Atlantic region during a heat wave in June 2012 left more than 4 million people without power. Virginia, in particular, was hit hard, suffering the largest non-hurricane-related power outage in the state's history. It can be difficult to believe that the system responsible for delivering electrical power to the most advanced nation on earth could be so unreliable. But it is. The winds rise, the rain or the snow comes down, and the lights go out. The simple fact is that America's electrical grid is frail and overburdened. It was built for the needs of the twentieth century, when the United States had a much smaller population. In its present condition it is no match at all for the relentless demands of today's high-tech society.

Terrible tragedies like Hurricane Katrina, the Interstate 35W bridge collapse, and Hurricane Sandy threw a grim spotlight on the penny-wise and pound-foolish nature of policies that blocked the maintenance and rebuilding of America's essential infrastructure. There has been an almost willful refusal to acknowledge the screaming need for a massive, long-term rebuild America campaign. With the economy still weak, there was an equally desperate need for the jobs that would be created by such a program. As many economists have pointed out, the costs of borrowing for public works projects could hardly have been lower than they were in the lean years following the Great Recession. A joint study by the former Treasury secretary Lawrence Summers and J. Bradford DeLong, a professor of economics at Berkeley, showed that with interest rates near zero, government investments in such large-scale projects as infrastructure modernization would most likely be self-financing.

In light of those realities—the aging, crumbling infrastructure, the critical need to boost employment, and interest rates as low as they can go—the unwillingness of government officials to embark on an intense nationwide rebuilding program is breathtakingly shortsighted. Laura D'Andrea Tyson, who served as chairwoman of the Council of Economic Advisers in the Clinton administration, described for *New York Times* readers what she characterized as "the infrastructure twofer: jobs now and future growth." She noted that the Congressional Budget Office considered investments in public works to be "one of the most cost-effective forms of government spending in terms of the number of jobs created per dollar." At the time she was writing, Tyson was a member of President Obama's Council on Jobs and Competitiveness, a bipartisan group of business and labor leaders. According to the council, each $1 billion in government spending on infrastructure resulted in the creation of four thousand to eighteen thousand jobs.

Tyson dismissed the notion that because of government deficits the U.S. could not afford a major infrastructure rebuilding campaign. With interest rates so low, she said—in an echo of Summers, DeLong, and many other economists—efficient infrastructure investments will bring returns that "will reduce future deficits through job creation and higher growth."

The Economic Policy Institute, in a report titled *Transportation Investments and the Labor Market,* illustrated the beneficial employment effects that are typical of funds appropriated for large-scale projects: "These investment dollars are used to hire construction workers, planners, architects, engineers, project managers, and foremen, who in turn use their new income to boost their own spending. A key point is that this effect is not limited to the industry *directly* receiving investment funds. For example, every job directly supported in the construction industry supports two additional jobs in supplier industries, such as accounting, office supplies, and construction capital manufacturing . . . Additional jobs are created as these workers spend their income back into the economy."

A virtuous cycle is set in motion with such investments. Newly hired workers invest in new homes or redecorate existing homes. They purchase new vehicles, clothes, school supplies for their children. There is an upturn in business at restaurants and other service establishments in the vicinity of project sites. Many, if not most, of the new hires are drawn from workers who were previously idle or underemployed, and most of the new jobs pay wages that would support a middle-class standard of living. A significant portion of the jobs would be in sectors that do not require a four-year college education.

A study sponsored by the Rockefeller Foundation that analyzed the potential benefits of rebuilding the nation's decaying water infrastructure found that an investment of $188.4 billion over five years "would generate $265.6 billion in economic activity and create close to 1.9 million jobs."

I remember a moment when Ed Rendell, at the time the governor of Pennsylvania, became emotional as he outlined some of the benefits to be gained from meeting the nation's infrastructure challenges. I was interviewing him in the Governor's Mansion in Harrisburg. A blinding snowstorm had prevented us from making an aerial tour of roads and bridges, locks and dams, and industrial sites across the state. As he talked, Rendell started jabbing a forefinger to emphasize his points. "We don't have a lot of time to make up our minds here," he said. "We have to act if we're going to provide a decent future for our children and grandchildren. What kind of country are we going to leave them? We've got to act in terms of energy. We can't even keep the lights on."

He suddenly broke into a husky laugh and shook his head. Flames were crackling in the fireplace, and through a window we could see the relentlessly falling snow. "On a day like today," said Rendell, "the yahoos will tell you there's no such thing as global warming."

The closer one looks at America's system of public works, the worse the situation seems. Consider, for example, something as vital as the water supply. The dangerously decrepit state of the nation's vast and intricately linked water systems would shock most ordinary observers. "Every year," according to the Rockefeller Foundation study, "sewer overflows contaminate U.S. waters with 860 billion gallons of untreated sewage, an amount that could fill 1.3 million Olympic-size swimming pools or cover the entire state of Pennsylvania with one inch of sewage."

Broken-down drinking water and wastewater systems are an ongoing threat to the public's health and safety. Aging and corroded pipes, some more than a century old, are bursting somewhere—often with explosive force—every couple of minutes. On a frigid December morning in 2008, a sixty-six-inch water main burst with tremendous force beneath River Road in Bethesda, Maryland, just outside Washington. The explosion and sudden rush of water—more than 150,000 gallons per minute—destroyed a section of the road and sent boulders, tree limbs, and other dangerous debris roaring into traffic. Fire trucks and boats were summoned to rescue motorists stranded in the rising water. A helicopter had to be used to rescue a firefighter in a boat that was about to be submerged. Witnesses to the flash flooding found it hard to believe that no one was killed.

Just four months later a bustling section of downtown Baltimore had to be shut down when a giant water main break flooded parts of the area with up to two feet of water. Streets were closed, traffic was snarled, and several buildings were evacuated. Even Baltimore's city hall had to be closed.

Similar disasters are common. A water main break on a spring night in 2013 overwhelmed a neighborhood in Akron, Ohio. Several people trapped in their cars and flooded homes in the city's West Hill section had to be rescued by boat. Two weeks earlier, Hoboken, New Jersey, which hadn't fully recovered from the catastrophic floods of Hurricane Sandy, was hit with a pair of devastating water main breaks that occurred just eight hours apart. In addition to the flooding and the physical damage (including a sinkhole that swallowed a car), the city's entire population of fifty thousand was left for a time without water or with very low water pressure.

Charles Duhigg of the *New York Times* covered a disaster that hit Washington, D.C., in 2010. "A cold snap," he wrote, "had ruptured a major pipe installed the same year the light bulb was invented." Water from the broken pipe was gushing into the air at a residential street corner. As workers tried to fix the problem, other pipes in the city began to burst. Duhigg noted that in Washington a pipe breaks, on average, every day.

While water main breaks are ubiquitous and very often spectacular, leaking pipes are a constant and even bigger problem. They're costly, and they cause tremendous damage. Seven billion gallons of drinking water escape each day from old, corroded, and rusting pipes. That wasted water, already purified, represents an economic loss of more than $2.5 billion annually. Leaked water, whether purified or not, creates all sorts of problems. It undermines the ground above it, causing potholes and sinkholes. It spreads viruses, bacteria, and other pollutants. And, because of the energy used to pump it, the lost water represents a tremendous waste of electrical power.

Dilapidated sewer systems are also an enormous problem. They're failing at an alarming rate, contaminating waterways and, in many instances, drinking water systems. Contaminants cause disease, and millions of Americans are sickened each year—either from drinking contaminated water or from swimming in contaminated waterways. Most of the drinking water in the United States is safe. But the nation's high standards for drinking water are increasingly jeopardized by the deteriorating state of its water systems. Jeanne VanBriesen, a water quality expert at Carnegie Mellon University, addressed this issue in the *New York Times* when she wrote, "Public works in American cities and towns are a marvel, but they didn't just happen. They are the result of significant investments our parents and grandparents made in state-of-the-art technology—well, state-of-the-art in 1900 or 1950. We've been coasting on those investments for a long time, and there is no way to put off the need to repair, replace and upgrade much of these systems."

America's infrastructure challenge is daunting. The needs are monumental. Schools are in disrepair. Deepwater ports no longer meet the standards demanded by the container traffic of the new globalized economy. Nearly a decade after the tragedy of Hurricane Katrina, dams and levees across the nation received a near-failing grade from the American Society of Civil Engineers. Despite concerns about budget deficits and the national debt, hundreds of billions of dollars would have to be spent over the next couple of decades to bring America's vast system of public works into decent shape. The economic losses of failing to meet that imperative in a rational, systematic way would be much higher. While the infrastructure is aging and steadily deteriorating, the population and the needs of industry are steadily growing. That is an unsustainable dynamic. More important than the economic damage, the dollars lost, if the United States fails to find the will and the resources to rebuild its infrastructure, would be the lost opportunity to shore up the great promise and vitality of America. The nation is losing its edge, and the decrepit state of its infrastructure is one of the clearest outward signs.

It wasn't always like this. Almost from its very beginning the United States has been willing to invest whatever has been necessary to maintain and advance the quality of its critical infrastructure, from the earliest post roads to the Erie Canal to the interstate highway network to air travel and space exploration. Nothing was allowed to stand in the way of progress, not even wars or depressions. Abraham Lincoln, in the midst of the Civil War, threw the support of the federal government solidly behind the creation of the transcontinental railroad, a stupendous advance in an era of stagecoaches and wagon trains. The railroad, a priority of Lincoln's despite its enormous costs (driven higher by widespread corruption and mismanagement), helped fuel westward expansion and led eventually to the emergence of streetcars and mass transit. The social, cultural, and economic returns from that bold infrastructure initiative were incalculable.

Franklin Roosevelt, in the midst of the Great Depression, turned to public works on a colossal scale as a way of providing employment to armies of jobless individuals while at the same time transforming the United States in ways that would define it for the rest of the century and beyond. Robert D. Leighninger Jr., in his excellent book on the legacy of the New Deal, which he titled *Long-Range Public Investment*, noted that even historians have tended to underestimate just how much was built by FDR's public works agencies and how much is still in use. "They produced thousands of enduring contributions to community life," Leighninger wrote. "Schools and university buildings, courthouses and prisons, hospitals and clinics, waterworks and incinerators, parks and zoos, golf courses and tennis courts, stadiums and auditoriums, botanical gardens and museums, fairgrounds and farmers' markets, city halls and fire stations appeared almost magically."

The Tennessee Valley Authority, which Roosevelt brought to

fruition, was a spectacularly bold experiment in government planning that substantially improved the quality of life in a region with nearly three million people who were desperately poor, even by Depression standards. Among many other things, the TVA provided flood control, reclaimed farmland that was being ruined by erosion, protected forests that, in Leighninger's words, "were being harvested to extinction," and generated stunning amounts of hydroelectric power that brought the wonders of electricity and economic development to a section of the country that had seemed hopelessly mired in the distant past.

Ultimately, the New Deal remade America. Its projects built or rebuilt bridges and causeways and hundreds of thousands of miles of streets and highways. They installed sanitary systems and laid tens of thousands of miles of drainage pipes. They built or refurbished housing, hospitals, and thousands of schools, all the while bringing a crucial paycheck and the dignity of work to millions in the midst of the nation's worst-ever economic crisis. To those who criticized the enormity of the public investment, Roosevelt replied, "Of course we spent money. It went to put needy men and women without jobs to work." Unlike many leaders today, he understood the essential links between employment, investments in the nation's built environment, and the long-term health of the economy.

So did Dwight Eisenhower.

When Eisenhower became president in 1953, he inherited detailed plans for an interstate highway system dating back to FDR's administration. It's well-known that Eisenhower had been impressed by the German autobahn network and viewed an American interstate system as an essential national defense initiative. Such a system would facilitate the movement of troops, equipment, and armaments in the event of a war or other national emergency. But as Earl Swift has pointed out in *The Big Roads*, a history of American superhighways, there were several other things about the benefits of highway construction that Eisenhower also understood. He knew, for example, "that building new highways would supply jobs to homecoming soldiers when the Korean conflict ended, and a ready source of employment and spending whenever the economy required it. That modern expressways could provide a long-lasting boost to interstate commerce, promote tourism, reduce the cost of goods and shipping. That they might put a dent in the automotive death toll. And that they would ease congestion, at a time when vehicles continued to multiply and the daily commute was lengthening for millions of Americans decamping from city to suburb."

Eisenhower made the interstate system a reality, and in the process his administration outpaced even Roosevelt's in spending on public works. Swift summed the matter up this way: "At nearly forty-seven thousand miles long and at least four lanes wide, the Dwight D. Eisenhower System of Interstate and Defense Highways, as it's formally known, is the greatest public works project in history, dwarfing Egypt's pyramids, the Panama Canal, and China's Great Wall."

Dwight Eisenhower was born in the nineteenth century, and his presidency ended more than half a century ago. Today, in the twenty-first century, America seems to have hit a wall when it comes to public works. We might once have been able to build a transcontinental railroad or Hoover Dam or a nationwide network of superhighways or send a man to the moon, but the vitality, vision, and commitment of those days seem to be long gone. The Obama administration and Congress did include increased infrastructure investments as part of the first stimulus package at the height of the Great Recession. But they were temporary and very modest in terms of the overall need. Subsequent efforts by President Obama and some Democrats in Congress to include relatively small amounts of infrastructure spending as part of a program to boost job creation were rebuffed by conservative legislators who insisted that they were unaffordable.

Lincoln could have said that investments in infrastructure were unaffordable in the midst of the Civil War. Roosevelt could certainly have said it during the Depression. Harry Truman and a Republican Congress could have said it about the Marshall Plan in the aftermath of World War II. They all chose to follow a different, more visionary path.

11 *Cashing In on Schools*

How do we use technology so that we
require fewer highly qualified teachers?

—JOHN KATZMAN, *education entrepreneur*

B ill Gates had an idea. He was passionate about it, absolutely
sure he had a winner. This was back in the early 2000s, and
Gates, through the Bill & Melinda Gates Foundation, was developing philanthropic initiatives. His idea? America's high schools were
too big.

When a multibillionaire gets an idea, just about everybody leans
in to listen. And when that idea has to do with matters of important public policy and the billionaire is willing to back it up with
hard cash, public officials tend to reach for the money with one
hand and their marching orders with the other. Gates backed his
small-schools initiative with enormous amounts of cash. So, without a great deal of thought, one school district after another signed
on to the notion that large public high schools should be broken up
and new, smaller schools should be created. This was an inherently
messy process. The smaller schools—proponents sometimes called
them academies—would often be shoehorned into the premises of
the larger schools, so you'd end up with two, three, or more schools
competing for space and resources in one building. That caused
all sorts of headaches. Which schools would get to use the science
labs, or the gyms? Which lavatories were for which students of

which schools? How would the cafeterias be utilized? And who was responsible for policing the brawls among students from rival schools?

Those were not Gates's concerns. He was on a mission to transform American education, and he would start with the high schools, which he saw as an embarrassment, almost a personal affront. They were "obsolete," he declared, and certainly no match for the wonders to be found overseas. "When I compare our high schools to what I see when I'm traveling abroad," he said, "I am terrified for our workforce of tomorrow."

There used to be a running joke in the sports world about breaking up the Yankees because they were so good. Gates felt obliged to break up America's high schools because they were so bad. The smaller schools were supposed to attack the problems of low student achievement and high dropout rates by placing students in a more personal, easier-to-manage environment. Classes wouldn't necessarily be smaller, but students, teachers, and administrators would be more familiar with one another because the schools themselves would be smaller. Better peer relationships and stronger support systems could be developed. Acts of violence and other criminal behavior would diminish as everybody got to know everybody else. Academic achievement would soar.

That was Bill Gates's grand idea. He spent $2 billion and disrupted 8 percent of the nation's public high schools before acknowledging that his experiment was a flop. The size of a high school proved to have little or no effect on the achievement of its students.

As Gates said in the fall of 2008, "In the first four years of our work with new, small schools, most of the schools had achievement scores below district averages on reading and math assessments. In one set of schools we supported, graduation rates were no better than the statewide average, and reading and math scores were consistently below the average. The percentage of students attending college the year after graduating high school was up only 2.5 percentage points after five years. Simply breaking up existing schools into smaller units often did not generate the gains we were hoping for."

There were other problems. The small schools were unable to

offer as many electives as the large schools they replaced. Fewer students made it more difficult to field athletic teams. Extracurricular activities withered. And many of the students in the original schools were somehow left out of the attempted upgrade. Referring to the New York City school district, which was by far the largest and most aggressive system to sign on to the Gates small-schools agenda, Diane Ravitch wrote,

> What happened to the missing students? Invariably, they were the lowest-performing, least motivated students, who were somehow passed over by the new schools, who did not want kids like them to depress the school's all-important scores. These troublesome students were relegated to another large high school, where their enrollment instigated a spiral of failure, dissolution, and closing. The [New York City Department of Education] set into motion a process that acted like a computer virus in the large high schools. As each one closed, its least desirable students were shunted off into yet another large high school, starting a death watch for the receiving school.

There was very little media coverage of this experiment gone terribly wrong. A billionaire had had an idea. Many thousands had danced to his tune. It hadn't worked out. *C'est la vie.*

But Bill Gates was by no means finished. He and his foundation quickly turned to the task of trying to fix the nation's teachers. They were determined, one way or another, to powerfully influence American public education. *Bloomberg Business Week* described the Gates Foundation as a "behemoth" and said, "It has since shifted its considerable weight behind an emerging consensus—shared by U.S. Education Secretary and Gates ally Arne Duncan—that quality of teaching affects student performance and that increasing achievement is as simple as removing bad teachers, identifying good ones, and rewarding them with more money."

I've covered Gates, and his desire to improve the quality of education in America seemed sincere. But his outsized influence on school policy has, to say the least, not always been helpful. While he and his foundation were committed to the idea of putting a great teacher into every classroom, Gates himself acknowledged that there was not much of a road map for doing that. "Unfortunately," he said, "it seems that the field doesn't have a clear view on the characteristics of great teaching. Is it using one curriculum over another? Is it extra time after school? We don't really know . . . I'm personally very intrigued by this question, and over the next few years I want to get deeply engaged in understanding this better."

This hit-or-miss attitude—let's try this, let's try that—has been a hallmark of school reform efforts in recent years. The experiments trotted out by the big-money crowd have been all over the map. But if there is one broad approach (in addition to the importance of testing) that the corporate-style reformers and privatization advocates have united around, it's the efficacy of charter schools. Charter schools were supposed to prove beyond a doubt that poverty didn't matter, that all you had to do was free up schools from the rigidities of the traditional public system and the kids would flourish, no matter how poor they were or how chaotic their home environments. The enormously successful documentary *Waiting for "Superman"* presented charters as the ultimate cure-all, just the thing to vanquish what many reformers saw as the outright villainy of teachers and their unions. President Obama praised charter schools as "incubators of innovation" and made their expansion a central component of his Race to the Top initiative. States that did not make it easier to increase their stock of charter schools could not share in the Race to the Top billions.

Corporate leaders, hedge fund managers, and foundations with fabulous sums of money at their disposal lined up in support of charter schools, and politicians were quick to follow. They argued that charters would not only boost test scores and close achievement gaps but also make headway on the vexing problem of racial isolation in schools.

None of it was true. Charters never came close to living up to the hype. After several years of experimentation and the expenditure of billions of dollars, charter schools and their teachers proved, on the whole, to be no more effective than traditional schools. In many cases, the charters produced worse outcomes. And the levels of racial segregation and isolation in charter schools were often scandalous.

The initial conception of charter schools was that they would, in fact, be laboratories of innovation, working closely—collaboratively—with traditional schools to improve the education of disadvantaged youngsters. Lost in the mists of time and the fog of propaganda was the original idea, first formulated in the late 1980s, that charter schools would be run within existing school districts by creative groups or teams of teachers seeking new ways to reach the youngsters who were having the most difficult time. Albert Shanker, president of the American Federation of Teachers, was one of the leading early proponents. The schools were to be experimental, closely monitored and rigorously evaluated as the teachers developed new and better strategies and techniques that could be expanded to school systems at large. The notion that classroom teachers were the villains in America's public schools would have been considered absurd.

That original conception was scrapped for the most part, and what has emerged is a system that ensures that the most disadvantaged youngsters will be left behind. In her book *Reign of Error*, Diane Ravitch wrote,

> Many studies show that charters enroll a disproportionately small share of students who are English-language learners or who have disabilities, as compared with their home district. A survey of expulsion rates in the District of Columbia found that the charters—which enroll nearly half the student population of the district—expel large numbers of children; the charters' expulsion rate is seventy-two times the expulsion rate in the public schools. The students who are kicked out of the charters return to the public schools. As the charters shun these students, the local district gets a disproportionately large number of the students who are most expensive and most challenging to educate; when public students leave for charters, the budget of the public schools shrinks, leaving them less able to provide a quality education to the vast major-

ity of students. In effect, a cycle of decline is set in motion: the charter school enrolls the most motivated students, avoids the students with high needs, and boasts of its higher scores; the test scores in the public school decline as some of its best students leave for the charter, and the proportion of needy students increases.

For all the attention that charter schools received, the truth was that they reached only a small percentage of American kids. Nationwide, more than 90 percent of students attend traditional public schools. When resources are lavished on charters at the same time that budgets are being cut and services drained from traditional schools, enormous numbers of students suffer the consequences.

While there undoubtedly were charter schools that performed exceptionally well (just as there have always been many first-rate traditional schools), the overall record of charters, especially considering the amount of financial and political support they have received, has not been impressive.

Bill Gates's experiments with the education of millions of children offered clear evidence of the powerful influence that big money in private hands could have on an enterprise as vast and important as the public schools. But few people would accuse Gates of acting out of greed. For other school reformers, however, a huge financial return has been the primary motivation. While schools and individual districts were being starved of resources, the system itself was viewed as a cash cow by so-called education entrepreneurs determined to make a killing. Even in the most trying economic times, hundreds of billions of taxpayer dollars, earmarked for the education of children from kindergarten through the twelfth grade, are appropriated each year. For corporate types, especially for private equity and venture capital firms, that kind of money can prove irresistible. And the steadily increasing influence of free-market ideology in recent years made public education fair game. Stephanie Simon, writing for Reuters in the summer of 2012, captured the excitement of investors eager to pounce: "The investors gathered in a tony private club in Manhattan were eager to hear about the next big thing, and education consultant Rob Lytle was happy to oblige. Think about the upcoming rollout of new national academic standards for public schools, he urged the crowd. If they're as rigorous as advertised, a huge number of schools will suddenly look really bad, their students testing way behind in reading and math. They'll want help, quick. And private, for-profit vendors selling lesson plans, educational software and student assessments will be right there to provide it."

The scene Simon described was a conference trumpeting the investment potential of for-profit education firms. (Lytle was a partner at the Parthenon Group, a Boston consulting firm.) Ordinary citizens may tend to view public education as, first and foremost, about teaching children. But for the high rollers it's an opportunity to harvest bountiful acres of taxpayer dollars.

As Simon wrote, "Speakers at the conference identified several promising arenas for privatization. Education entrepreneur John Katzman urged investors to look for companies developing software that can replace teachers for segments of the school day, driving down labor costs. 'How do we use technology so that we require fewer highly qualified teachers?' asked Katzman, who founded the Princeton Review test-prep company and now focuses on online learning."

Katzman's question, which once would have seemed outlandish, reminded me of Allen Sinai's assertion about the attitude of corporate executives toward employees. "You basically don't want workers," Sinai said. "You hire less and you try to find capital equipment to replace them."

With billions to be reaped from the schools by profiteers, teachers would find that they, too, were expendable. That was made abundantly clear as profit-obsessed proponents of online classes and entirely online charter schools—virtual schools—emerged as major players in public education.

The foothold established by for-profit virtual schools was extremely disturbing. Their most fervent advocates promoted these elusive entities as cheap online replacements for traditional public schools. They spoke in the most glowing terms about getting rid of buildings, classroom teachers, playgrounds, everything most people associate with going to school. All of those elements and their related expenses could happily vanish, like a program deleted with the click of a mouse. "Kids have been shackled to their brick-and-mortar school down the block for too long," said Ronald Packard, a former Goldman Sachs banker who was the CEO of K12 Incorporated, the nation's largest operator of online public schools. Packard was an operator, not an educator. When he founded K12 in 2000, one of his two primary financial backers was Michael Milken, the disgraced junk-bond king of the 1970s and 1980s. The other was Larry Ellison, the billionaire co-founder of Oracle and the fourth-richest person in America. The first chairman and chief proselytizer of K12 was William Bennett, who had served as education secretary under Ronald Reagan and drug czar under George H. W. Bush. There was something odd about Bennett's trumpeting the wonders of cyberschools. In his book *The Educated Child*, published just a year earlier, he had sounded less than enthralled about the potential of online schooling. "When you hear the next pitch about cyber-enriching your child's education," he wrote, "keep one thing in mind: so far, there is no good evidence that most uses of computers significantly improve learning."

He was, nevertheless, the energetic public face of K12 until 2005, when he had to resign because of a controversy that erupted over a comment he'd made on his radio program. (In response to a caller, Bennett had offered what he described as a thought experiment, saying, "If you wanted to reduce crime . . . you could abort every black baby in the country, and your crime rate would go down." He added, "That would be an impossible, ridiculous, and morally reprehensible thing to do, but your crime rate would go down." The ensuing furor dictated that Bennett had to go.)

Virtual schools remained under the radar for several years before eventually becoming too big to ignore. There were close to a quarter of a million full-time students attending online charter schools in the United States in 2014, and that number was growing.

The schools were heavily advertised, and the companies running them spent tens of millions of dollars on political lobbying. Very few taxpayers were aware that some of the money they thought was paying for schools of the brick-and-mortar variety was actually being used for advertising and politics and to fatten the portfolios of virtual school proselytizers and promoters.

Even fewer knew how poorly virtual schools performed. The National Education Policy Center at the University of Colorado did extensive research on the academic outcomes of primary and secondary cyberschools, with a particular focus on K12, the largest and most aggressive outfit in the field. The results were grim. Math and reading scores were poor. Attrition rates were high and graduation rates were abysmally low. When the center looked at virtual schools in Colorado, it found that "half the online students wound up leaving within a year, and when they returned [to their traditional schools] they were often further behind academically than when they started."

Student achievement across the board was substantially worse in profit-seeking cyberschools than in traditional public schools or privately operated, nonprofit charter schools. Referring specifically to the K12 schools, in which nearly 100,000 students were enrolled, the policy center's researchers wrote, "All of the diverse measures we reviewed indicated a consistent pattern of weak performance."

When the researchers compared the average test scores of K12 students with the relevant statewide averages, the K12 kids were far behind—five to twelve points behind in reading and fourteen to thirty-five points behind in math.

The policy center also made an interesting observation on the relationship between the profit and the education imperatives at K12:

It is relevant to note that K12 Inc. shares positive news with investors about the profitability of the company and announced in May 2012 that it seeks to "increase profitability in fiscal year 2013" by implementing as much as $20 million in costs savings. K12 argues that these cuts can be made "without any adverse effects on student performance, employee retention, customer satisfaction, or our growth rate." Such statements by K12 suggest that it believes that weaknesses in performance

are not due to insufficient revenues or cannot be addressed
with additional resources. An alternative explanation is that
the company chooses not to address the weak performance of
its schools to protect profits.

Though cyberschools received large amounts of public money,
there was no way for outsiders to know what cyberpupils were
really doing in the privacy of their homes, often with minimal, or
no, adult oversight. The teachers were in remote locations, usually
their own homes, sometimes hundreds of miles away. They were
less well paid than traditional classroom teachers and were typically saddled with sky-high student-teacher ratios. The potential
for a wide variety of abuses, including cheating, was enormous.
And, of course, the socialization process that is normally an integral part of actually attending school can be hampered.

The evidence that cyberschools have done a dreadful job of educating children has steadily mounted. As early as the fall of 2011,
the *New York Times* reporter Stephanie Saul wrote a long investigative article on K12's operations in the U.S. She opened the piece
with an overview of the Agora Cyber Charter School in Pennsylvania. Nearly 9,000 students were enrolled in Agora, and in some
cases individual teachers were responsible for up to 270 boys and
girls at a time.

Saul wrote, "By almost every educational measure, the Agora
Cyber Charter School is failing. Nearly 60 percent of its students
are behind grade level in math. Nearly 50 percent trail in reading.
A third do not graduate on time. And hundreds of children, from
kindergartners to seniors, withdraw within months after they
enroll."

Ronald Packard did not seem at all dismayed by the performance
of the students in his company's schools. When I talked to him, he
had the prototypical upbeat air of the corporate pitchman. Everything K12 was doing was great. Test scores lagged, he said, because
the students drawn to virtual schools were, in many cases, already
behind their peers academically. As he explained it, "With virtual
schools you get an adverse selection bias. We had researchers look
at this. Somewhere between 50 and 75 percent of the kids com-

ing into the school are one or more years behind grade level." In Packard's view, K12 students were doing fine. "We're making good gains," he said.

He dismissed critics of online schools, saying, "There were critics of the automobile when it came out as well." And he made no apology about being in the field for the money: "K12 is for-profit in the same way that a textbook company would be for-profit, or a computer company."

Packard received $5 million in compensation in 2012 and $3 million the following year. When I asked if that presented a public relations problem, he seemed unperturbed. If you looked at the compensation of CEOs at public companies comparable to K12, he said, "I am paid right in the middle."

The more I learned about full-time online schooling for children, the more disturbing it seemed. There was something soulless about the very idea of cyberschools. They offered none of the joys or benefits that are derived from going to a school that is housed in a building filled with real people. There was no interaction with classmates and hardly any with teachers.

While full-time online learning can be appropriate, and perhaps even essential for some students—children who are ill, for example, or youngsters with serious behavioral issues, or some teenage mothers—it is clearly no substitute in any general sense for traditional public schools.

Ron Packard might have been a leader in the spread of full-time online schooling, but he and his academically challenged virtual schools were just a small part of the corporate stampede to cash in on the public education system. The biggest player of all, the corporate behemoth known as Pearson, pounced on the testing craze set off by No Child Left Behind. Pearson didn't just provide schools with tests, it offered entire standardized testing systems. It sold the tools to grade tests and the programs for analyzing test performance. It had remedial systems for students who did poorly. It sold textbooks, online courses, and data systems. For dropouts, there were

GED courses and the tests that inevitably followed. "Pearson has it all—and all of it has a price" was the way the *Texas Observer* characterized the company in a 2011 article. Pearson's influence in Texas, the birthplace of No Child Left Behind, was particularly powerful. Its contract with the state for the years 2010 to 2015 was worth close to half a billion dollars. According to the *Observer*, "Pearson pays six lobbyists to advocate for the company's legislative agenda at the Texas Capitol—often successfully. This legislative session, lawmakers cut an unprecedented $5 billion from public education, including funding for a variety of programs to help struggling students improve their performance on state tests. Despite the cuts, Pearson's funding streams remain largely intact. Bills that would have reduced the state's reliance on tests didn't pass."

The corporate tail was wagging the education dog. It was easy to lose sight of the best interests of children as corporations throughout the country did all they could to maximize profits from public education. Consider, for example, the Rupert Murdoch–Joel Klein connection. Murdoch, king of the News Corp media empire, moved aggressively into the increasingly contested territory of market-based education. Klein—who had previously run the New York City school system under Mayor Michael Bloomberg—was his point man. Murdoch and Klein tried hard to present themselves as reformers, but Murdoch found it difficult to hide his delight as he broached the subject of profit potential. Two weeks after hiring Klein, he spent $360 million to acquire 90 percent of a Brooklyn-based technology company called Wireless Generation. He said at the time, "When it comes to K through 12 education, we see a $500 billion sector in the U.S. alone that is waiting desperately to be transformed by big breakthroughs that extend the reach of great teaching."

The Murdoch-sponsored breakthroughs had to be put on hold a little more than six months after Klein signed on when News Corp became embroiled in a ferocious phone-hacking scandal at its *News of the World* tabloid in Great Britain. A political and media firestorm erupted with the disclosure that reporters at the tabloid had hacked into the cell phone of a thirteen-year-old girl who had been murdered. Klein, a politically savvy lawyer who had served as an assistant attorney general in the Clinton administration, dropped his education duties at News Corp to become one of Murdoch's most important strategists on the scandal. The episode was a dramatic example of the wildly different priorities of high-powered, bottom-line-oriented corporations and traditional educators charged with the delicate task of guiding children and teenagers through their formative years.

The former Florida governor Jeb Bush was another prominent figure in the front ranks of the corporate push for public education dollars. He hosted an education conference in San Francisco in the fall of 2011 at which Murdoch was the keynote speaker. In the audience were corporate executives, supporters of market-oriented education, and elected officials responsible for the laws and policies that regulate corporate access to public education dollars. Using his allies and contacts from his days in the Florida statehouse and his relationship with two former presidents, Bush (who once famously told the *Miami New Times*, "I want to be very wealthy") was tireless in his promotion of the corporate education agenda. With the former West Virginia governor Bob Wise, he started an organization called Digital Learning Now!, which took on the task of persuading state legislators to make it easier for companies to get public funding for virtual schools and for the installation of virtual classrooms in brick-and-mortar schools. In June 2010 he gave the commencement speech to graduates of a huge, for-profit virtual school in Columbus, Ohio, called the Electronic Classroom of Tomorrow. Bush used the occasion to extol the virtues of online learning, but in fact the Electronic Classroom of Tomorrow was a particularly poor example. In an investigative article detailing Bush's efforts as an education entrepreneur, *Mother Jones* magazine reported on his appearance at the school and examined its background: "With more than 10,000 kids, ECOT is bigger than some of Ohio's 609 school districts. But its test scores rank above those of just 14 other districts. In 2010, barely half of its third graders scored proficient or better on state reading tests, and only 49 percent scored proficient in math, compared with state averages of 80 percent and 82 percent, respectively. ECOT's graduation rate has never exceeded 40 percent."

More than a decade earlier, in 1996, Bush himself had stumbled badly when he co-founded Florida's first charter school in a poor black neighborhood of Miami. The Liberty City Charter School struggled academically and in 1999 received a grade of D on the A-to-F rating system set up by Bush after he was elected governor in 1998. The school had been unable to meet the state's minimum requirements for reading and math. Bush severed his ties with Liberty City Charter when he became governor. He also appointed his partner in the ill-fated school venture—T. Willard Fair of the Greater Miami Urban League—to the Florida State Board of Education. Liberty City Charter was never able to get its act together. Poorly managed and buried in a mountain of debt, the school was finally shut down by the state in 2008.

Joel Klein—first Bloomberg's right-hand man, then Murdoch's— also encountered problems. From the perspective of market-oriented school reformers, Bloomberg and Klein had been riding high for a few years. The state legislature had given Bloomberg almost total control of the New York City school system. He and Klein quickly imposed their vision of corporate-style governance, which included extensive testing, an intense commitment to charter schools, and, more than anywhere else, the adoption of Bill Gates's notion that breaking up large high schools into smaller, often specialized schools was a key to improving education outcomes.

The Bloomberg-Klein reforms seemed promising at first, and kudos from around the nation and even around the world rolled in. Student achievement appeared to be rising significantly, and the black-white achievement gap seemed to be narrowing. But it was mostly smoke. Rigorous analyses showed that much of the progress had been illusory. The apparent gains in reading in 2009, for example, were the result of a test score bubble. The tests had been dumbed down. As the *New York Times* put it in August of the following year, "When the results from the 2010 tests, which state officials said presented a more accurate portrayal of students' abilities, were released last month, they came as a blow to the legacy of the mayor and the chancellor, as passing rates dropped by more than 25 percentage points on most tests. But the most painful part might well have been the evaporation of one of their signature accomplishments: the closing of the racial achievement gap."

Just as there had been no Texas miracle in education achievement under Governor George W. Bush in the 1990s, no miracle had occurred in New York City, either. But worse was to come. With the test score gains disappearing like morning fog, city residents looked on in a state of wonder as New York's already troubled school scene degenerated into outright farce. It started with Klein's announcement in November 2010 that he was quitting as chancellor to move into the much higher-paying precincts of the Murdoch operation. Bloomberg's choice to replace him was bizarre. Cathleen Black—or Cathie, as she preferred to be called—was a longtime media executive. Her most recent positions had been president and then chairwoman of the Hearst magazine empire. Her social world was similar to that of Bloomberg—the glitzy, moneyed playgrounds of the corporate and media elite. She and the mayor had crossed paths many times, at cocktail parties and dinners on the Upper East Side and at high-powered corporate conferences and retreats. But there wasn't any obvious, logical reason for Bloomberg to put her in charge of the schools. Political observers, and even some of the mayor's closest associates, scratched their heads. The pick seemed to come out of the blue. It wasn't the result of any wide or systematic search. Even Klein had been kept in the dark. He didn't know until the announcement was about to be made that Black would be his successor. Local activists, already at odds with Bloomberg and Klein, scoffed at the appointment. Said one, "She's a Park Avenue socialite. When she leaves Manhattan it's to go to the Hamptons, not Brooklyn." The *New York Times* wrote that Bloomberg "appears to have taken the idea of the outsider-chancellor to a new level."

Black herself never saw the appointment coming. She told a *New York Post* gossip columnist, Cindy Adams, that Bloomberg called her one Monday morning and asked to see her. "I didn't know what he wanted," Black said. When she showed up the following morning, she was offered the job of running the nation's largest school system, a behemoth of an operation with a multibillion-dollar budget, 135,000 employees, and 1.1 million students.

Black had had no previous experiences with the public schools.

She hadn't attended them (as Joel Klein had). She hadn't taught in them. She hadn't sent her children to them. In one of her first public appearances after the appointment, she said, "What I ask for is your patience as I get up to speed on the issues facing K–12 education."

Bloomberg insisted that Black would be great. He was wrong. She was hapless in the job. Less than two weeks after taking over from Klein, she caused a furor with an offensive quip to parents concerned about school overcrowding. Trying to be funny, Black said, "Could we just have some birth control for a while? It would really help us."

She apologized, but her troubles were only beginning. With her lack of knowledge about the system at a time when severe budget cuts were looming and schools were being closed, Black was a target of hisses and boos at a number of neighborhood appearances. At one meeting, when Black complained about the din coming from the audience, the crowd mockingly cried out, "Awww!" Black responded in kind, making a face and mocking the audience in return: "Awww!" Politically savvy aides winced.

The public relations problems were an outward manifestation of the struggles Black was enduring inside the city's Department of Education. It was clear even to her own aides that she didn't know what she was doing. According to the *Times,* she had come to be seen as a "feeble figure within the department," sitting quietly, or silently, at high-level meetings and deferring to the people she was supposed to be supervising. She had trouble mastering the system's maddeningly complex budget processes and was inept in her preparations for television interviews. Aides finally decided to just keep her off TV.

The sharpest blow was a devastating series of resignations submitted by top officials of the department. "You can't really say she lost control of the department," a Bloomberg ally told me. "She never had control. It was painful to watch."

Black lasted in the job just ninety-five days. Bloomberg pulled the plug suddenly on a Thursday morning in April 2011. Black hadn't seen that coming, either. The mayor called her into his office and told her she was done. By that afternoon she was gone. She would tell reporters that she had used her unexpected free time to buy a new pair of sneakers. Later, reflecting on her brief tenure, she expressed irritation at what she felt were unflattering photos of her that had appeared in the press. "The worst pictures!" she complained in an interview with *Fortune* magazine.

The Cathie Black debacle, Bill Gates's small-schools initiative, and the Packard-Milken-Ellison virtual schools venture were vivid examples of the dangers inherent in a school reform movement driven by millionaires and billionaires with no real knowledge or understanding of public education.

Above all, the Bloomberg-Black fiasco put a spotlight on America's class divide and the damage that members of the elite, with their money and their power and their often misguided but unshakable belief in their talents and their virtue, are inflicting on the less financially fortunate.

The Pittsburgh activist Jessie Ramey, like so many others I spoke with, used a David and Goliath reference to describe what it was like for grassroots groups trying to push back against the outsized influence of the well-heeled. "You can barely get your voice heard," she said. "The wealthy individuals, the foundations, the corporations—they're able to command attention, and they get nearly all of it." She paused for a long moment, then went on:

It's complicated. There are astonishing amounts of money in play, and some of those deep-pocket types are in it for personal gain, for sure. But the motives and the aims vary. It's not just about profits. It's not simply a case of greedy people. For an awful lot of them it's ideological. They're playing this game of education reform not because they're educators, not because they know anything about education, necessarily, but because they have an agenda. It might be political, or corporate, or anti-union, or they have an excessive belief in the wonders of technology, or they don't believe government can or should be running the schools. They have something to prove, and at the moment they're trying to prove it through

education. They will all tell you that they genuinely care
about the students. But when you look at what they're pushing, it's not good for kids. None of this corporate reform stuff
has actually worked in practice and a lot of it is damaging,
particularly for poor children and children of color.

The amounts of money in play are breathtaking. In addition to
those cashing in directly on school reform—like K12, Murdoch's
News Corp, profit-making charter schools, and the entire corporate
testing apparatus—market-reform types have at their disposal the
geysers of cash coming from powerful foundations. These include,
most prominently, the Bill & Melinda Gates Foundation, the Eli
and Edythe Broad Foundation, and the Walton Family Foundation.
The often interlocking forces of foundations, corporations, and fabulously wealthy individuals have all but overwhelmed the discussion of public education issues.

Most Americans are unaware of the titanic influence of the Big
Three foundations when it comes to education policy. Gates, Walton, and Broad have been by far the biggest drivers of the corporate
reform movement that has gripped school systems nationwide and
especially in cash-strapped urban areas. The Walton Foundation
has unabashedly pushed a privatization agenda that, in addition
to strong support for privately run charter schools, would siphon
money from public schools by funneling tax dollars, in the form of
vouchers and other initiatives, to families that want to send their
children elsewhere.

The Broad (rhymes with "road") Foundation, the smallest of the
Big Three, has had a truly outsized impact on America's schools.
Broad established a pair of training programs to groom non-
traditional types—business executives, military officers, lawyers—
for appointments as public school superintendents or to other
high-level managerial positions. (Some educators are also included
in the programs, but the preference is for people without a strong
education background.) Once in the districts, the Broad graduates
begin putting the foundation's free-market and privatization policies into practice.

Broad has had amazing success getting its people into the top ranks of organizations and agencies that control America's schools. The Broad graduate Jean-Claude Brizard took over the Chicago school system as chief executive officer under Mayor Rahm Emanuel. Three successive superintendents of the Oakland school system were Broad alumni. The Los Angeles school system has at times looked like a Broad subsidiary. By 2013 the foundation was boasting that ninety-six superintendent positions had been filled by graduates of its programs. That represented an astounding level of influence for a private foundation. Schools in Dallas, Denver, and Philadelphia had all been headed by Broad graduates.

In Chicago, Brizard took over a system that had already endured the long-term shocks of Bill Gates's involvement. In 2004, Gates was one of the prime movers and the lead funder of a citywide initiative called Renaissance 2010, a program that was supposed to transform Chicago's public schools in just six years. Lousy teachers would be fired, failing schools would be closed, and charter schools would blossom. Chicago's business community and the mayor at the time, Richard Daley, could hardly have been more enthusiastic. They felt that turning the school system around would be one of the most effective ways of lifting the fortunes of the city. As the school system's CEO, Arne Duncan was responsible for designing and implementing the initiative, which was popularly known as Ren 10.

The enthusiasm was misplaced. Like Gates's "transformative" small high schools initiative, Ren 10 was a flop. On January 17, 2010, under the headline "Daley School Plan Fails to Make Grade," the *Chicago Tribune* wrote, "Six years after Mayor Richard Daley launched a bold initiative to close down and remake failing schools, Renaissance 2010 has done little to improve the educational performance of the city's school system, according to a Tribune analysis of 2009 state test data." Test scores from the elementary schools created under the program were found to be "nearly identical to the city average," while the test results from high schools that had been completely overhauled were "below the already abysmal city average." According to the *Tribune* analysis, "The moribund test

scores follow other less than enthusiastic findings about Renaissance 2010—that displaced students ended up mostly in other low
performing schools and that mass closings led to youth violence as
rival gang members ended up in the same classrooms." The article
noted, "The architect of Renaissance 2010, former schools CEO
Arne Duncan, is now the U.S. Secretary of Education—and he's
taking the Daley-Duncan model national as part of his Race to the
Top reform plan."

Renaissance 2010 never delivered the promised goods, but Duncan was not hurt by its failure, and neither was Gates. For the
schoolchildren in Chicago, however, it was another matter. The
obsession with Ren 10 drew attention and resources away from
other, more promising initiatives that were not the pet programs of
the free-market, privatization zealots.

When Emanuel became mayor in 2011, he and Brizard adopted
the same playbook that had guided Renaissance 2010 and Race
to the Top. (Brizard would not see the project to fruition. He was
shoved out as CEO by the hard-charging Emanuel after just seventeen months.) But Emanuel and Barbara Byrd-Bennett, Brizard's successor, continued lumbering along the same misguided
path, paying little or no attention to the evidence of past failures
all around them. They closed traditional public schools with a ven-
geance and showered their attention and the government's financial support on charter school operators and entrepreneurs. When
a huge cluster of school closings was made official in the spring of
2013, an appalled Ravitch wrote in her blog, "Never in U.S. history has a local school board—or any other board, appointed or
elected—chosen to close 49 public schools. Never. That's what the
Chicago Public Schools did yesterday. Thousands of parents, students, and teachers objected, but Mayor Rahm Emanuel and his
puppet board didn't care. Yesterday was a day of infamy in Chicago
and in the history of American education."

One morning, soon after the mass school closings, I called Rousemary Vega, a woman whose two children had gone to Lafayette
Elementary School in Chicago's Humboldt Park neighborhood. She
wept almost from the beginning of the conversation. "The people

closing these schools—all they see are numbers," she said. "They don't see the pain that they're causing. Our kids are not numbers, they're human beings. But they're being scattered and displaced to other schools like they were pieces on a chessboard or in a Monopoly game. They're not Monopoly pieces. When all you see are numbers, when all you care about is data, then you won't understand that every child has different needs, speeds, and challenges. And you won't understand the importance of a school to a neighborhood and to the families in that neighborhood. It's just a building to you. You won't understand how we're anchored to these schools.

"It's cruel, you know. They like to tell people that they're offering us choice, but they're actually giving us ultimatums."

When I googled the Web site of Lafayette Elementary, the following notice appeared: "Thank you for visiting. This website is no longer in service. The 2012–2013 school year is now complete and our school has closed for good."

For some Chicago residents, the most recent round of school closures sparked feelings of déjà vu. Dozens of Chicago schools had already been shut down—and dozens of charter schools created—during Arne Duncan's tenure as CEO. That churning process and the disruption of the lives of tens of thousands of students and their families were being renewed under Emanuel despite overwhelming evidence that the prior changes had not improved academic performance. The vast majority of Chicago's student population was economically disadvantaged, and most of the students were black. Those groups, the ones that were supposed to be helped most by the reforms, made almost no progress at all, according to an analysis of school reform efforts in the city by nonpartisan researchers at the University of Chicago.

Those who are genuinely interested in improving the quality of education for all American youngsters are faced with two fundamental questions: First, how long can school systems continue to pursue market-based reforms that have failed year after demoralizing year to improve the education of the nation's most disadvantaged children? And second, why should a small group of America's richest individuals, families, and foundations be allowed to exercise such overwhelming—and often such toxic — influence over the ways in which public school students are taught?

There is no reason why plutocratic school systems should be any more acceptable to a majority of Americans than plutocratic government in general.

12 *Mistreating the Troops*

This war, like all wars, must end.

—BARACK OBAMA

On a muggy afternoon in June 2013, Dan Berschinski strapped on his legs, hoisted a backpack into place, picked up a cane, and then reached for his sleek new racing wheelchair. With his cane in his left hand, he grabbed the front wheel of the chair with his right and walked out of the door of his apartment. Pulling the chair behind him, he walked about seventy-five yards to the elevator, which he rode to the basement garage. Then he walked another hundred yards or so to his car. He tossed the wheelchair into the trunk, climbed into the car, and drove to a nearby air force base that had a track that he used to practice racing the wheelchair. He was building up his strength and endurance for a triathlon event.

Dan, who had moved several months earlier from suburban Silver Spring, Maryland, to downtown Washington, D.C., had exceeded every expectation of the medical experts.

He grinned. "My walking is getting very good," he said. "I usually walk with two canes out in the real world and one cane when I'm here at home. I can pretty much walk anywhere I want. I only rely on the second cane a little bit, just a fraction. But there is something about when you take it away—it changes the way I walk. My goal now is to always walk with one cane."

I'd seldom seen anyone work harder to achieve a personal goal than Dan. In tremendous pain, indoors and out, in cold weather and hot, at times with strangers staring at him with misplaced pity, he'd struggled and fought for every hard-won step. The struggle had gone on day after day, month after month for nearly four years. Even with all the progress he'd made, when the weather was warm and the humidity high, as it often was in Washington, walking could leave him drenched in sweat. The effort to walk was never less than a strain. But nothing curbed Dan's epic determination. He would not complain, and he would not let anything stop him.

"I can walk anywhere I want," he told me. "I no longer do any official physical therapy but I still go to Walter Reed about once every two weeks. They check me out and sometimes I'll practice specific skills, like walking up and down stairs or down steep hills."

He did not try to hide the pride he felt in his accomplishment. "Without a doubt," he said, "I'm the first military guy to come through Walter Reed with my injuries to ever walk on a daily basis. Unfortunately, more guys have been injured just like me. But because of what the prosthetists and I have figured out at Walter Reed, other guys who are newer, who are coming in with the same kinds of injuries, they're also starting to walk, just like me."

At twenty-eight, Dan was retired with the rank of captain and had put together a life that was remarkably full by any measure. He'd started a business. A retired army officer who met Dan at a Washington Nationals baseball game introduced him to a business-man named Nick Reinhart, who was the president of a small plas-tic injection molding company in central Ohio. As Dan explained, "They make those plastic items you typically find in your home— plastic storage bins, that sort of thing. You can buy them at Home Depot, Costco, all over."

Dan and Reinhart hit it off, and Dan came up with the idea of forming a partnership to sell Reinhart's products on military bases. They reached an agreement and the new company was named Two-Six Industries after Dan's call sign when he was wounded in Afghanistan: Bravo Two-Six. "The buyers liked our idea," said Dan, "and we've already got six or seven products that are going into production. We'll sell them on the post exchanges under my label. Our other focus, which will take longer but I think will be bigger, will be for us to make plastic products to sell directly to the Department of Defense. Nothing fancy. Just little plastic grab handles inside of trucks or fuselage components for airplanes and small boats. Things like that. It's been fun, and it's certainly been a learning opportunity."

Dan told me he felt fortunate that he was living what he described as "a very good life." Early in 2013 he and his girlfriend, Rebecca Taber, had both been accepted into the MBA program at Stanford. Taber took a leave from her job as education adviser to Governor Jack Markell of Delaware. Dan planned to continue running his business from the West Coast. In a few weeks they would pack their things and move across the country to a two-bedroom apartment on the sprawling campus in Palo Alto. "We're pretty excited," Dan said. "It's a whole new adventure."

In one of our last conversations, I asked Dan how he felt about the war in Afghanistan, now that so much had happened and so much time had passed. "It's winding down," he said, "thank God. That war needed to be over yesterday. My opinion hasn't really changed. I'm all for killing terrorists and disrupting their networks, but in my opinion that is best done through a combination of intelligence, international cooperation, special operations, and targeted drone strikes—almost like police work, just like we treat organized crime."

His views were all but indistinguishable from Matthew Hoh's. As Dan put it, "My guys and I, a brigade of regular army infantrymen, all we were doing over there was pissing off the locals and occupying a foreign country."

On a Thursday afternoon in May 2013, President Obama made the short trip from the White House to venerable Fort Lesley J. McNair at the southwestern edge of Washington to deliver a speech at the National Defense University. It was a long speech, and he was interrupted three times by the antiwar activist Medea Benjamin before Benjamin was finally ejected. The president was tolerant of the interruptions, saying to Benjamin at one point that free speech entailed "you being able to speak, but also you listening and me being able to speak." When Benjamin was finally dragged from the room while crying out, "I love my country, I love the rule of law," Obama said, "The voice of that woman is worth paying attention to."

Obama's speech was viewed by the political, military, and media establishment as one of the most important of his presidency. He seemed to be saying that the so-called war on terror that had turned American life upside down in the long years since the attacks of September 11, 2001, would be brought to a conclusion. "This war, like all wars, must end," he said. "That's what history advises. It's what our democracy demands."

The president was not specific about how the war would end. He promised to rein in the use of drones, take another stab at closing the prison at Guantánamo Bay, Cuba, and develop new civil liberties protections. At the time of the speech, there were still 166 prisoners at Guantánamo, and the president noted the absurdity of spending nearly $1 million per inmate per year to keep them there. "Imagine a future," Obama said, "ten years from now or twenty years from now, when the United States of America is still holding people who have been charged with no crime on a piece of land that is not part of our country."

The speech did not generate much reaction from the general public. It was a one-day story. Most ordinary Americans had long since shoved the painful topic of warfare into the deeper recesses of consciousness. They did not want to dwell, or even think about, the myriad horrors that so many service men and women had endured. They didn't want to hear about torture and rendition and Guantánamo, about civilians slaughtered and contractors behaving badly and wartime expenditures streaking out of sight. Matthew Farwell, an army veteran who spent sixteen months in Afghanistan, told NBC News, "All the 'support the troops' stuff is bumper sticker deep."

The tragic irony was that the absence of any real interest in the military was the prerequisite that made near-perpetual war possible. Less than 0.5 percent of Americans served in the military, and the distance between them and their fellow citizens in civilian life could hardly have been greater. The consequences of that yawning gap were profound. Craig Bryan, associate director of the

National Center for Veterans Studies at the University of Utah, told me during an interview, "It's amazing how frequently, when you ask people if they know someone in the military, the answer is no. They won't have a family member in the service. They won't have a friend. What I and others have been arguing is that we now have a warrior caste system in the United States. We have this group of men and women who have a very different way of thinking about the world. They follow different rules. They have very different experiences, and whether or not they have been deployed, they don't necessarily feel like they fit in or belong to the larger American society."

Bryan, a former member of the air force, served in Iraq in 2009. "I was over there when Michael Jackson died," he said. "I remember being in the recreation center with soldiers, airmen, a couple of sailors. We're sitting around this big TV and all you could see was this wall-to-wall coverage of Michael Jackson. And then on this little news feed that scrolls along the bottom of the screen, there was the information that nine soldiers had been killed in Afghanistan during a suicide bombing. And I just remember this one soldier getting up and going on a tirade. He's like, 'Everyone in the U.S., all they're talking about is some stupid singer, and nine of our brothers have just died and we're just relegated to a few words at the bottom of the news feed.'

"It was a huge morale letdown for those of us who were basically in harm's way. It really kind of felt like nobody really cared about what we were doing."

Bryan and his colleagues at the center were studying the grim and steadily growing problem of military suicides, which had reached a record 350 in 2012. Nearly one a day. Suicides had doubled in annual frequency since the years before the wars in Afghanistan and Iraq. By 2013, more active-duty service members were killing themselves than were being killed in Afghanistan, and most experts believed the official numbers were an undercount. No one had solid answers as to why the toll kept rising. Speaking in June 2012, the then defense secretary, Leon Panetta, said, "This issue, suicides, is perhaps the most frustrating challenge that I've come across since becoming Secretary of Defense last year. Despite the increased efforts, the increased attention, the trends continue to move in a troubling and tragic direction."

Military veterans were also killing themselves at a stunning rate. The data available were not definitive, but best estimates put the number at somewhere between eighteen and twenty-two every day. Many were young people who had returned from Iraq or Afghanistan. Their stories, inevitably, were heartbreaking. I remember a telephone conversation I had back in 2007 with the parents of Jeffrey Lucey. Kevin and Joyce Lucey of Belchertown, Massachusetts, took turns talking about Jeff, a member of the Marine Corps Reserve who had turned twenty-two on the day before the Iraq war began in March 2003. They wept as they talked. Jeff's unit had been activated, and he was part of the first wave of troops to pour into the combat zone. Like so many others, he came home with memories that slashed at the psyche like a razor, tales that he felt were too gruesome to tell to civilians leading ordinary lives, heading out to ball games or the movies.

Jeff was in bad shape, his dad told me. He drank furiously. He wrecked the family car. On a Christmas Eve he hurled his dog tags at his sister Debra and denounced himself as a murderer. His parents tried desperately to help, but to no avail. As I wrote in the *New York Times*:

> On the evening of June 22, 2004, Kevin Lucey came home and called out to Jeffrey. There was no answer. He noticed that the door leading to the basement was open and that the light in the basement was on. He did not see the two notes that Jeffrey had left on the first floor for his parents: "It's 4:35 p.m. and I am near completing my death." "Dad, please don't look. Mom, just call the police—Love, Jeff."
>
> The first thing Mr. Lucey saw as he walked down to the basement was that Jeff had set up an arrangement of photos. There was a picture of his platoon, and photos of his sisters, Debra and Kelly, his parents, the family dog and himself. "Then I could see, through the corner of my eye, Jeff," said Mr. Lucey. "And he was, I thought, standing there. Then I noticed the hose around his neck."

When Joyce Lucey took the phone, she told me, "We see him everywhere. Every little dark-haired boy you see, it looks like Jeff. If we see a parent reprimanding a child, it's like you want to go up and say, 'Oh, don't do that, because you don't know how long you're going to have him.' "

This is what America's nonstop twenty-first century warfare has wrought—hundreds of thousands of lives destroyed or crippled through physical or psychological wounds. It's unconscionable that a tragedy so vast could occur while most Americans were barely paying attention.

An army report on the epidemic of suicides noted in 2010 that more than seventeen hundred soldiers had attempted to kill themselves the previous year but had not succeeded. Scores of thousands required medication for their daily fight against physical pain and psychological distress. According to the report, "Approximately 106,000 soldiers are prescribed some form of pain, depression or anxiety medications." The potential for abuse was "obvious," the report said. Soldiers struggling with depression, post-traumatic stress disorder, rampant anxiety, and chronic pain were being given a range of psychiatric drugs and narcotic painkillers. Many were taking multiple medications. Not infrequently the mixtures and subsequent overdoses proved fatal. Some of those deaths undoubtedly were suicides, but without evidence to prove that the soldiers had deliberately killed themselves, the deaths would be ruled accidental.

The army offered a bleak portrait of the lives of those soldiers who were drawn to self-destruction. "For some," the report said, "the rigors of service, repeated deployments, injuries and separations from family resulted in a sense of isolation, hopelessness and life fatigue." I was struck by that last term. The idea of "life fatigue" setting in on someone twenty-one or twenty-two years old was one of the saddest things I could imagine.

Craig Bryan, at the National Center for Veterans Studies, said it was important to view the military suicides in a broad social context. Not only were soldiers and veterans dealing with combat and other stresses of military life; they also had to cope with the often disorienting sense of estrangement from the larger society. "We have research now showing that the absence of that sense of belongingness and that sense of being able to connect with others, especially after deployment, is a super-important driver of suicide risk," he said. "That sort of demonstrates most clearly this separation of the warrior caste from the rest of our society. I almost always get asked, 'What is the military going to do about this?' My response is, 'What is society going to do about this?' This is *our* problem."

About a half hour after midnight on a Sunday in early May 2013, a man who appeared to be drunk approached a woman in a parking lot in Crystal City, Virginia, not far from the Pentagon. According to the police, the man grabbed the woman and, despite her furious struggle, began fondling her sexually. When the woman finally managed to fight the attacker off, she summoned the police, and he was arrested. To the military's great embarrassment, the man was identified as Lieutenant Colonel Jeffrey Krusinski, the officer in charge of the air force's sexual assault prevention program. Krusinski's face, as it appeared in his widely distributed mug shot, was a mass of scratches and bruises. His arrest and his downcast eyes and miserable expression seemed a perfect reflection of the country's miserable response to yet another harrowing problem: a culture of sexual assault and rape that had ruined countless lives and debased the military for decades.

Krusinski's arrest came just as the Department of Defense was disclosing that its own analysis, based on a confidential survey, estimated that twenty-six thousand service members, most of them women, had been assaulted sexually in 2012. Officials believed the true number was far higher. Many victims remained silent. The U.S. military, along with its many other problems, was coming face-to-face with the ugly fact that it offered a hellish environment to many of the women it was supposed to be welcoming into its ranks. Around the same time that Krusinski was arrested, a sergeant on the staff of the U.S. Military Academy at West Point was accused of videotaping unsuspecting female cadets in the bathroom or shower. (He would later plead guilty and be dismissed from the army.) Those cases came on the heels of a long-running scandal at Lackland Air Force Base in Texas in which dozens of female trainees had been raped or otherwise violated by instructors.

For years the public and the press had been reluctant to criticize the military, preferring instead to reflexively characterize it as heroic and almost miraculously competent. Now, after several decades of being covered up, the sordid facts related to sexual assault were emerging. What was happening to women in the military was beyond scandalous. According to the Department of Defense, about a third of all women serving in uniform are sexually assaulted during their enlistment.

In May 2013, Secretary of Defense Chuck Hagel acknowledged that sexual assault, which he denounced as "a despicable crime," was one of the most serious challenges facing the Department of Defense. "This department," he said, "may be nearing a stage where the frequency of this crime and the perception that there is tolerance of it could very well undermine our ability to effectively carry out the mission and to recruit and retain the good people we need."

On the day after President Obama's major speech on America's anti-terror policies, he felt compelled to speak out about sexual assaults during his commencement address at the U.S. Naval Academy. "Those who commit sexual assault are not only committing a crime, they threaten the trust and discipline that makes our military strong," he said. He urged the graduates, leaders of the newest generation of sailors and marines, to find the moral strength to resist abusive behavior. He asked them to rely on "that inner compass that guides you," and added, "Even more than physical courage, we need your moral courage—the strength to do what's right, especially when it's unpopular."

The brutal treatment and systematic humiliation of women by members of the armed forces had hardly been a secret in recent decades. The 1991 convention of the Tailhook Association in Las Vegas generated widespread publicity after it was learned that scores of women and a few men had been sexually assaulted. The convention was an annual gathering of elite navy fliers who rev-

eled in an anything-goes atmosphere in which the brass either participated in sexual assaults or looked the other way. The result was
a nightmare of debauchery. T-shirts at the convention proclaimed,
"Women Are Property." Fired up by endless drinking, servicemen
lowered their trousers to moon people and engaged in an activity
called "ballwalking" in which they strutted around with their testicles hanging out. The most notorious disclosure was the so-called
gauntlet. Scores of laughing, jeering men would line up on either
side of a corridor and sexually maul any woman who tried to get
through.

One of the women snared in the gauntlet described her ordeal in
the documentary *The Invisible War,* a deeply moving film about the
epidemic of rape and sexual assault in the military. "I got off the
elevator on the third floor," she said.

> You could see maybe two hundred men. It was just a few steps
> into the hallway before they closed ranks around me. And
> then it happened very quickly that from both sides and from
> behind, men . . . started reaching in my shirt. I was getting
> pushed down to the floor and someone was reaching under
> my skirt, pulling my underwear off. And it was about maybe
> about thirty or forty feet of two hundred guys trying to pull
> my clothes off—like I was a high-value target . . .
>
> The next morning I met with my boss for breakfast and I
> said, you know, "What happened here?" And he said, "That's
> what you get for walking down a hallway full of drunk avia-
> tors."

Heads rolled when news stories broke about the 1991 convention. High-ranking officers, including admirals, were forced out
of the service. The secretary of the navy, H. Lawrence Garrett III,
who had attended the convention, resigned. The navy insisted that
attitudes would change. But while career opportunities for women
in the military have expanded tremendously since the 1990s, the
treatment of women is still, very often, reprehensible.

In an op-ed article for the *Los Angeles Times* in March 2008, Representative Jane Harman, at the time the chairwoman of the House Homeland Security subcommittee on intelligence, said the horrifying scale of the problem had been driven home to her during a visit with female veterans and their doctors at a VA health center in Los Angeles. She recalled being stunned "when the doctors told me that 41 percent of female veterans seen at the clinic say they were victims of sexual assault while in the military, and 29 percent report being raped during their military service."

There has always been a brutal contrast between the military's public posture of "zero tolerance" for sexual violence and the reality that women throughout the armed forces experienced on a daily basis. As early as February 2004, Secretary of Defense Donald Rumsfeld was writing to his undersecretary for personnel and readiness, "I am concerned about recent reports regarding allegations of sexual assaults on service members deployed to Iraq and Kuwait. Sexual assault will not be tolerated in the Department of Defense. Commanders at every level have a duty to take appropriate steps to prevent sexual assaults, protect victims, and hold those who commit offenses accountable."

Rumsfeld's directive had no more impact than a puff of smoke in a gust of wind. Seven years later more than two dozen women and three men who said they were raped or otherwise sexually assaulted filed a federal lawsuit against the Department of Defense, specifically naming Rumsfeld and his successor, Robert Gates, as defendants. Several of the plaintiffs were profiled in *The Invisible War*. The suit charged that the Pentagon failed to protect the plaintiffs against a system-wide chain of abuses that included not just rape and sexual assault but also the deliberate refusal to properly investigate complaints and prosecute offenders. Victims who complained said they were routinely subjected to harsh retaliation. One of the plaintiffs, Sergeant Rebekah Havrilla of South Carolina, who served in the army from 2004 until 2009, said that when she sought counsel with the chaplain in her unit, he told her the rape "must have been God's will." Another plaintiff, Panayiota Bertzikis, who was in the Coast Guard from 2005 to 2007, said she was beaten and raped by a shipmate while stationed in Burlington, Vermont. She was told, according to the suit, that she and her attacker "should work out their differences." Bertzikis went on to found the Military Rape Crisis Center, which has provided services to thousands of women who were raped and assaulted by servicemen.

The plaintiffs had hoped that by filing a lawsuit, they could get the courts to intervene and order changes in a system that was relentlessly degrading to women. But that did not happen. A judge dismissed the suit in December 2011. He said the case was "troubling" but ruled that the injuries suffered by the plaintiffs were related to their service in the military and that civilian courts were not authorized to intrude in such matters.

Victims' advocates thought that the flurry of scandals in 2013—especially the arrest of the officer in charge of the air force's sexual assault prevention program—might spark real reform. But that never happened, either. The spotlight on the mistreatment of women in the military soon faded.

The Eisenhower Study Group at Brown University's Watson Institute for International Studies published an important analysis in 2013 called *The Costs of War Since 2001: Iraq, Afghanistan, and Pakistan.* Its authors asked, "What have the wars that the U.S. has undertaken since September 2001 cost in blood and treasure, lives reduced to bareness and grief, opportunities lost and possibilities foreclosed? How has the local and political landscape of Afghanistan, Iraq and Pakistan been altered? What are the ongoing consequences for the people who fought them, for bystanders, for democracy, human rights, and civil liberties, for the American economy, budget, and the deficit? What do we know about the likely future costs of the wars?"

The report estimated, conservatively, that 330,000 people had died by 2013 as a direct result of the wars, with "several times that number" wounded and injured. In addition to members of the ordinary noncombatant civilian population, the dead included, at that time, more than 6,700 U.S. military personnel and at least

3,000 American contractors. The deaths of contractors had gotten very little attention in the press. The dead also included members of the Iraqi and Afghan security forces, other allied troops, journalists and their crews, humanitarian aid workers, and—based on very rough estimates—between 75,000 and 87,000 enemy insurgents or militants.

Life in a war zone can be tough to imagine for those who have never experienced it. Many of those killed or badly wounded in Iraq and Afghanistan were children. A 2011 study of three hundred children in Kabul by the British humanitarian aid group Tearfund described youngsters traumatized to the extent that they believed it was highly likely that they would die in war. Eighty percent said they were "frightened, sad and unable to cope."

Many other studies showed evidence of an Afghan population, children and adults, in the grip of extreme emotional and psychological distress. It could hardly have been otherwise. The long years of war that followed the U.S. invasion of 2001 were piled atop the years of war and terror brought to the country by the Soviet Union, whose troops invaded Afghanistan in December 1979, and the brutal civil war (culminating in rule by the Taliban) that followed the Soviet exit in 1989. The result of so much killing and terror, as Terry J. Allen wrote in an article for *In These Times,* was an Afghan population severely traumatized "by invading armies, mercenaries, women-hating Taliban and warlords." He noted that the World Health Organization found that some 60 percent of Afghans suffered from mental illnesses or severe emotional distress, including depression and post-traumatic stress disorder. The Dutch organization HealthNet estimated that more than half of all Afghan women were depressed and nearly 80 percent suffered some form of anxiety disorder. Suicide was a chronic problem.

Americans have not generally expressed any sense of responsibility for even the smallest portion of that suffering. Very few Americans have even the slightest awareness of the extent of the carnage that has resulted from wars supposedly fought to benefit the population of the United States.

In Iraq, as in Afghanistan, the population had endured many

long years of brutal conflict and suffering before the American invasion in 2003. There had been the war with neighboring Iran from
1980 to 1988, the first Gulf War of 1991, and then years of devastating economic sanctions, ostensibly aimed at Saddam, which cost
the lives of more than half a million Iraqi children. Such a loss in
the United States would have been considered a stupendous tragedy. In 1996, Lesley Stahl of *60 Minutes* asked Madeleine Albright,
who was then the U.S. ambassador to the United Nations, if she
was concerned about the deaths of so many children. "We have
heard," said Stahl, "that a half million children have died. I mean,
that's more than died in Hiroshima. And, you know, is the price
worth it?"

"I think this is a very hard choice," Albright replied. "But the
price—we think the price is worth it."

In the spring of 2012, the *New York Times* asked Gian P. Gentile, the director of West Point's military history program, what the
United States had gained from the wars in Iraq and Afghanistan.
His reply was blunt: "Not much." A highly regarded colonel who
had led a combat battalion in Iraq in 2006, Gentile was the author
of *Wrong Turn: America's Deadly Embrace of Counterinsurgency.* In that
book and other writings he warned against the belief, widespread
among American policy makers, that military invasions were an
effective way of stabilizing and reforming troubled nations. That
notion, he said, was a dangerous historical fiction.

Just how dangerous was made tragically clear in the spring and
summer of 2014, two-and-a-half years after the last American
combat troops had left Iraq. When fierce fighters from a radical
Sunni group that few Americans had ever heard of, the Islamic
State of Iraq and Syria, stormed into northern Iraq and captured a
number of important cities and towns, the country descended into
the agony of chaos and outright civil war. The death toll of soldiers
and civilians was appalling. Many were summarily executed.

There could no longer be any doubt that the war launched by the
United States in Iraq had been an absolute and utter catastrophe.
The loss of so many American and Iraqi lives, and the expenditure
of vast sums of U.S. taxpayer dollars, had not resulted in the Bush
administration's dream of a free and democratic Iraq capable of

defending itself against violent enemies. What was left instead was the very real possibility that the nation-state of Iraq had been irrevocably shattered.

Near the end of his State of the Union address in 2014, President Obama delivered a tribute to Sergeant First Class Cory Remsburg, a thirty-year-old Army Ranger whom the president had met at Omaha Beach in 2009 on the sixty-fifth anniversary of D-day. Remsburg listened from a seat next to First Lady Michelle Obama as the president said, "Along with some of his fellow rangers, he walked me through the program—a strong, impressive young man with an easy manner, sharp as a tack. We joked around and took pictures, and I told him to stay in touch."

A few months later, in October 2009, Sergeant Remsburg was gravely wounded by a roadside bomb in Afghanistan. President Obama told the audience, "His comrades found him in a canal, face down, underwater, shrapnel in his brain. For months he lay in a coma. The next time I met him, in the hospital, he couldn't speak. He could barely move. Over the years he's endured dozens of surgeries and procedures, and hours of grueling rehab every day. Even now, Cory is still blind in one eye. He still struggles on his left side. But slowly, steadily . . . he's learned to speak again and stand again and walk again. And he's working toward the day when he can serve his country again."

The audience, including members of both houses of Congress, the president's cabinet, and the Supreme Court, gave Remsburg a long and heartfelt standing ovation.

Two things struck me as I watched. The first was how similar his story was to Dan Berschinski's. Remsburg had been wounded just two months after Dan, and the ovation at the State of the Union address seemed to echo the one Dan had received when he walked to the podium in Peachtree City, Georgia.

I was also struck by the fact that Remsburg had been wounded on his *tenth* deployment to the war zones of Iraq and Afghanistan. Ten times he was sent into harm's way. That's what happens when a country is in a nonstop state of war and the overwhelming majority of its population is unwilling to serve. The United States had been at war for nearly all of the twenty-first century. Many of the children who had been in first grade at the time of the attacks on the World Trade Center and the Pentagon were in college when the president threw a national spotlight on Sergeant Remsburg's ordeal. In all those years no thought was given to spreading the wartime sacrifice around. Cory Remsburg was summoned for combat duty an astonishing ten times, and ten times, without hesitation, he answered the call. If he hadn't by sheer chance crossed paths with the president, the nation would never have noticed.

Epilogue: Looking Ahead

The time for action is always now.

—MARSHALL GANZ

The United States needs to be reimagined. What it has been doing for the past several decades has not worked for the majority of its people. A huge and growing segment of the American population has been left out of full participation in the society as a result of joblessness, underemployment, inadequate education, and political and economic inequality. Opportunities of all kinds have been constrained. The great promise of America, which had always viewed itself as a vibrant, upwardly mobile, fair, and just society, has been undermined by the self-inflicted wounds of near-perpetual warfare, irresponsible and grotesquely exploitive economic behavior, and political dysfunction. There was no reason this had to happen. There was nothing inevitable about it. The powers that be sold ordinary Americans a bill of goods. Tall tales were spun about the wonders of globalization and the magic of markets that would work infallibly if only they were left alone. We were told that everyone would benefit from trade liberalization, from industrial and financial deregulation, from tax cuts for the very wealthy, from an unwavering faith in the savvy of corporate leaders, and from the wanton use of America's military might overseas.

Americans drank the Kool-Aid and crashed into the worst conditions since the Great Depression.

Not everyone suffered. Market failures threw millions out of work and millions more into poverty, but most of the banks and megacorporations that caused the economic collapse emerged from the debacle just fine, bigger and more prosperous than ever. The wars have taken a heartbreaking toll on the men and women who served, and on their families, but for the wartime profiteers—the weapons and equipment manufacturers and contractors of every sort—Afghanistan and Iraq were, above all else, extraordinary opportunities to bolster the bottom line.

At the midpoint of the century's second decade there were signs everywhere that the United States had completely lost its way.

On the afternoon of February 1, 1960, four students from the all-black North Carolina A&T College walked into an F. W. Woolworth department store in downtown Greensboro. No one knew it at the time, but they were part of the first wave of a titanic change in American life. The four neatly dressed students, all of them male, all of them freshmen, quietly slid into seats at the lunch counter, which had a strict policy of serving only white customers. When they were refused service, they remained at the counter until management ordered the store closed. The next day nearly two dozen more students showed up to join the sit-in. "By the fourth day," as the historian James T. Patterson wrote, "white women from the local University of North Carolina Women's College joined them. By then protesters, mostly black students, were starting to sit in at lunch counters elsewhere in the state."

A fire had been lit, and it spread with great quickness and energy. Later that same February, the future congressman John Lewis and two other students from Fisk University in Nashville, Tennessee, kicked off a series of sit-ins at segregated lunch counters in the heart of Nashville's business district. Diane Nash, a key student leader of the effort, reflected on the sit-ins in the documentary *Eyes on the Prize*: "The first sit-in we had was really funny because the waitresses were nervous and they must have dropped $2,000 worth of dishes that day. Literally, it was like a cartoon. We were sitting there trying not to laugh because we thought laughing would be insulting . . . At the same time, we were scared to death."

After a few days, the police began arresting the protesters, but always there was a new contingent that immediately took the seats vacated by those who were carted off to jail. "No matter what they did and how many they arrested," said Nash, "there was still a lunch counter full of students there."

Within months, the sit-ins spread to dozens of American cities. Many of the protesters were beaten and thousands were arrested, but they would not give in. Some cities desegregated their lunch counters; others resisted. But by the mid-1960s the civil rights movement, with its marches and demonstrations, its freedom rides, court fights, and other initiatives, had achieved a critical mass. The era of legal segregation in America was brought to a close.

What had happened was astonishing. Ordinary citizens far from the traditional centers of power had profoundly changed American society. Through sustained, thoughtful, and courageous efforts they had shifted the nation onto a better path.

A comparable effort by ordinary citizens is needed today if the United States is to regain its great promise of fairness and opportunity for all. It's essential that ordinary, everyday Americans intervene, because the changes that are required to get the country moving in a more equitable and economically sustainable direction will never be initiated by the banking and corporate elite or the politicians in their thrall. The uncomfortable and mostly unspoken reality of power politics in the United States is that the interests of the very wealthy and those of the middle class and the poor are not the same. That fact was never more clearly articulated than in a 1974 *Business Week* editorial, which expressed the corporate community's desire for a much larger slice of the American pie. The magazine unabashedly proclaimed, "It will be a hard pill for many Americans to swallow—the idea of doing with less so that big business can have more. Nothing that this nation, or any other nation, has done in modern economic history compares in difficulty with the selling job that must now be done to make people accept the new reality."

That editorial was part of a deliberate long-term campaign to

siphon more and more of the nation's income and wealth from the
bottom and the middle to the top. The campaign, which kicked
into high gear during the Reagan administration, proved wildly
successful. Over the past three to four decades, the riches at the
apex of society expanded beyond anything most 1970s executives
could have imagined. Between 2010 and 2012 the top 1 percent of
American households took in nearly *all* of the income growth—95
percent. And they had 43 percent of the nation's wealth. The bottom half of the population was left with a pittance—just 1.1 percent of the wealth—to divide up. It became nearly impossible in
that environment for ordinary individuals and families to make
any significant headway.

If today's poor and middle-class Americans are to have a fair shot
at establishing and maintaining decent standards of living, that
extreme imbalance of resources will have to be corrected. Wider
circles of prosperity and opportunity will have to be created. And
America's increasingly stratified education, civic, and social hier-
archies will have to be modified. The great imperative of our time
is to imagine what that newer, fairer version of America would be
like and then to begin the very difficult work of creating it.

A step into the future is often helped by a glance back at the past.
Lyndon Johnson's legacy might have been forever undermined
by the war in Vietnam, but he did a first-rate job of reimagining
America way back in 1964, when the United States still seemed
young and the broad outlines of its great promise were still intact.
More than eighty thousand people gathered in the football stadium
at the University of Michigan in Ann Arbor on the morning of
May 22 to hear Johnson deliver the commencement address. The
weather was warm and sunny, and the crowd was unusually atten-
tive. The country was still trying to get back to normal after the
trauma of John Kennedy's assassination six months earlier. Johnson's speech was only twenty minutes long, but that was enough
time for him to lay out what amounted to a sense of national purpose—an explicit statement of what the United States, the wealthiest and most powerful nation on earth, should be about.

"For a century," said Johnson, "we labored to settle and subdue
a continent. For half a century, we called upon unbounded inven-

tion and untiring industry to create an order of plenty for all of our people. The challenge of the next half century is whether we have the wisdom to use that wealth to enrich and elevate our national life, and to advance the quality of our American civilization."

Johnson called upon Americans to build a society that was much more than just rich and powerful. He wanted one in which the people were more concerned "with the quality of their goals than the quantity of their goods." He imagined an enormous effort in which Americans would pull together and with hard work and the support of the federal government would fashion a new era. The nation's physical plant would be rebuilt, poverty would be annihilated, a quality education would be made available to all children, and the United States would present itself to the world as the foremost purveyor of peace.

The fact that nothing remotely like that occurred does not mean that it should be left to the realm of fantasy. Johnson made a formidable beginning with his war on poverty, passage of the Civil Rights and Voting Rights acts, the creation of Medicare and Medicaid, and many other initiatives. But less than three months after his speech in Ann Arbor, the Gulf of Tonkin Resolution was passed, and the war in Vietnam soon began laying waste to Johnson's dream of the Great Society.

Half a century has passed since that speech, but Johnson's vision remains a good starting point for a reimagined America. Johnson saw himself as the heir to Franklin Roosevelt, and like Roosevelt he wanted the United States to be a country in which no one was left behind. It was a reading of America that was the polar opposite of the unabashedly selfish, terminally competitive, winner-take-all philosophy that has steered U.S. policy for most of the past forty years. That greed-based philosophy has driven America into a monumental ditch. It has left us with rampant joblessness, poverty, hunger, homelessness, and a shrinking middle class. Roosevelt and Johnson would have been staggered by the notion of soup kitchens, food pantries, and homeless shelters in the United States in the second decade of the twenty-first century.

The drastic four-decade shift that turned the United States from a reasonably egalitarian society to one in which the gaps between the rich and everyone else reached historic extremes was the result of a monumental effort. Dramatic changes in tax, trade, and regulatory policies and a decades-long war on labor unions undermined the interests of the middle class and the poor. Think tanks and media outlets devoted solely to corporate interests and free-market pros-elytizing were created. And astonishing sums of money were spent on lobbying and the financing of campaigns. The very wealthy consolidated their political power to such a degree that hardly any-one else could be heard. Members of Congress and occupants of the White House responded far more favorably to their wealthiest constituents, no matter which party was in power. Researchers at Demos put the matter well: "As private interests have come to wield more influence over public policy, with ever larger sums of money shaping elections and the policymaking process, our political sys-tem has become less responsive to those looking for a fair shot to improve their lives and move upward."

The big money and the heightened influence were self-reinforcing. The rich used their wealth to acquire political clout and then used that clout to add to their wealth.

Ordinary Americans have been all but politically helpless in the face of that onslaught. The political scientists Martin Gilens of Princeton and Benjamin I. Page of Northwestern wrote ominously in 2014, "The central point that emerges from our research is that economic elites and organized groups representing business inter-ests have substantial independent impacts on U.S. government policy, while mass-based interest groups and average citizens have little or no independent influence."

An analysis of the policy preferences of wealthy Americans, sponsored in 2013 by the Russell Sage Foundation, was instructive. Its authors wrote,

> Our evidence indicates that the wealthy are much more concerned than other Americans about budget deficits. The wealthy are much more favorable toward cutting social wel-fare programs, especially Social Security and health care. They are considerably less supportive of several jobs and income programs, including an above-poverty-level minimum wage,

a "decent" standard of living for the unemployed, increasing the Earned Income Tax Credit, and having the federal government "see to"—or actually provide—jobs for those who cannot find them in the private sector.

Judging by our evidence, wealthy Americans are much less willing than others to provide broad educational opportunities, by "spend[ing] whatever is necessary to ensure that all children have really good public schools they can go to" or "mak[ing] sure that everyone who wants to go to college can do so." They are less willing to pay more taxes in order to provide health coverage for everyone, and they are much less supportive of tax-financed national health insurance. The wealthy tend to favor lower estate tax rates and to be less eager to increase income taxes on higher-income people. They express concern about economic inequality and favor somewhat more egalitarian wages than they perceive as presently existing, but—to a much greater extent than the general public—the wealthy oppose government action to redistribute income or wealth.

In 2010 the already extreme imbalance in political power was further heightened when the Supreme Court, in its *Citizens United* ruling, opened the floodgates to unlimited campaign spending by corporations. Joseph Stiglitz called the ruling "a milestone in the disempowerment of ordinary Americans." Bill Moyers said, "Rarely have so few imposed such damage on so many. When five conservative members of the Supreme Court handed for-profit corporations the right to secretly flood political campaigns with tidal waves of cash on the eve of an election, they moved America closer to outright plutocracy, where political power derived from wealth is devoted to the protection of wealth."

The real-world impact of the power imbalance and maldistribution of wealth was manifest in the conditions that prevailed in the difficult years that followed the end of the Great Recession. The cruel squeezing of the middle class continued and poverty remained rampant, while, conversely, stock markets soared to record heights and corporate profits boomed. The *New York Times* headlined an article in March 2013 "Recovery in U.S. Is Lifting Profits, but Not Adding Jobs." By the fall, the columnist William A. Galston was writing in the *Wall Street Journal*, "Participation in the workforce is falling, the pace of job creation is anemic, and long-term unemployment remains stubbornly high. Many newly created jobs pay less than those that disappeared during the Great Recession, so real wages are stagnating and median household income is no higher than it was a quarter of a century ago."

To those at the top of the wealth and income pyramid, things were as they should be. The rich were getting a first-class return on their investment in politics. For ordinary Americans, excluded for the most part from the wealth of the nation and from any meaningful participation in policy making, new avenues to a better life would have to be found. Voting would not be enough. How else could ordinary people get their voices heard?

The short answer is direct action. The legendary organizer Saul Alinsky taught that there were two main sources of power: money and people. As virtually all of the money is currently on the side of entrenched power, the only viable option for ordinary Americans is the creative use of their own energy, intelligence, and superior numbers. Democracy might have taken a beating in the United States in recent years, but it is not dead. A tremendous amount of power still resides with the people. And history has shown again and again that direct action, when properly organized and sustained, can be remarkably effective. The abolitionists, civil rights activists, labor organizers, and feminists all understood that democracy was not meant to be a sporting event, a pastime for interested onlookers. Taking responsibility for one's individual circumstances *and* the well-being of the country has always required much more than merely casting a ballot. If ordinary Americans truly want better lives for themselves and their children, they will have to step forward, roll up their sleeves, and make it clear by their actions that the current unfair status quo will no longer be tolerated. Without that kind of increased citizen involvement no real change for the better can be expected.

If a dramatic new surge of citizen action were to develop, what would be its focus? With so much that desperately needs to be done, almost any attempt at change can seem overwhelming. The challenges are enormous. America needs to rein in its raging inequality. In an era of global warming, it needs creative new approaches to safeguarding the environment. Workers need protection from the tyranny of employers. Students need easier, more affordable access to higher education. The nation's physical plant needs to be rebuilt, the economy revived, and the banking system reformed. And the overwhelming influence of big money in politics needs to be drastically curtailed.

Where to start?

In fact, the raw materials of a vast and vigorous citizens' movement are surprisingly close at hand. There has been a high level of exasperation in the recent attitude of many Americans. Former students have been fed up with their often futile hunt for decent employment. Low-wage workers have expressed growing dissatisfaction with their wages and working conditions. And the population at large, as reflected in poll after poll, has been fed up with the craven, often incompetent behavior of their representatives in government.

Citizens' groups have been rising up across the country and are already hard at work on a wide range of issues. Low-wage workers and their allies have engaged in a series of strikes, protests, and acts of civil disobedience in a sustained fight for higher pay and better working conditions. In November 2013 more than a hundred people were arrested on Black Friday, the busiest shopping day of the year, as coordinated protests were staged in cities across the country against Walmart and other big-box retailers. Less than a week later fast-food workers in dozens of cities participated in a one-day strike in their campaign for a pay increase to $15 an hour.

Individuals and organizations have mounted efforts to reverse the effects of the *Citizens United* ruling and to push back against the Supreme Court's weakening of the Voting Rights Act. The Occupy movement was a loud expression of dissatisfaction with the status quo. And in Wisconsin, Indiana, and Ohio, tens of thousands of ordinary citizens turned out to protest drastic curbs on the collective bargaining rights of public employee unions.

In Pittsburgh, Jessie Ramey and her colleagues have enjoyed significant success in their fight to reclaim the public schools from corporate-style reformers. Their efforts resulted in a shift in control of the city's school board in 2013, with the new board "far more favorable," as Ramey put it, "to the grass roots." Pittsburgh residents also elected a new mayor, William Peduto, who sought Ramey's counsel in developing his education policies and invited her to serve on his transition team. The parents who organized around education issues in Pennsylvania were among many thousands across the country who have fought back against the test zealots, privatization advocates, and others who have wrung much of the richness and joy out of public education. "When you're fighting the power structure, victories can at times seem few and far between," Ramey told me. "But they're important. They sustain you. They keep you in the fight."

While there has been no shortage of citizen action in recent years, what has been missing is leadership capable of pulling the many various strands together to form a broader movement—one that is strong enough to bring about fundamental societal change. But as more and more people become civically engaged, the opportunities for that kind of inspired leadership to emerge increase. Dr. Martin Luther King Jr. did not become an important leader of the Montgomery bus boycott until after the boycott was under way. The right kind of leadership—men and women of great passion, vision, commitment, and extraordinary organizational skills—can heighten awareness of critically important issues and attract more participants to the cause. It can mobilize vastly diverse individuals and organizations into a force that recognizes common interests and is capable of mapping more effective political strategies. It is when that type of leadership comes to the fore that a popular movement can take off and big changes begin to unfold.

If a bold new wave of citizen action were to emerge in the United States, a logical issue for it to focus on would be employment. It's the issue that hovers above all else. When joblessness is high in America, the nation's spirits inevitably are low. When Americans are working, they have the money to power the economy, which creates more jobs. They pay taxes, which provide government with the revenues required for public services and investments in a more secure future. Not surprisingly, nearly nine in ten respondents to a Pew Research Center survey said that having a decent job was the single most important requirement for being middle-class, far more important than homeownership, one's level of education, or any other factor. For an overwhelming majority of Americans, secure, gainful employment is the only real route to upward mobility.

When Americans are decently employed, it is easier for them to focus on society's other challenges, from education to the environment and everything in between. The idea that nearly two and a half centuries after its founding the United States still cannot offer employment to all who want and need to work is a tragic absurdity. There is more than enough work that needs to be done. What's required is an all-but-obsessive focus on how to link the nation's workers to the profound needs and best interests of a truly egalitarian society. No one understood the importance of work in a free and democratic society better than Franklin Roosevelt. "Democracy has disappeared in several other great nations," Roosevelt said, "not because the people of those nations disliked democracy, but because they had grown tired of unemployment and insecurity, of seeing their children hungry while they sat helpless in the face of government confusion and government weakness."

The dynamics now are much different than they were in the 1930s, but the imperative of finding employment for an anxious and often bewildered population is the same. The thought that widespread joblessness might somehow be accepted as a normal aspect of American life is both dangerous and repellent. The crucial impact of employment on virtually every facet of American society is the reason activists with widely different agendas might be induced to rally around a sustained campaign to wipe out joblessness and underemployment. If America cannot get its act together on the jobs front, its many other serious wounds will not heal.

There is a single day that stands out as a shining precedent for the idea of a national campaign geared toward employment: August 28, 1963. A. Philip Randolph, the legendary founder and president of the Brotherhood of Sleeping Car Porters, was the driving force behind that day's March on Washington, which drew an astonishing quarter of a million people to the heart of the nation's capital.

At the time it was the largest political gathering in U.S. history. The march has been remembered primarily for Dr. King's "I Have a Dream" speech. But that mass gathering was not just a demand for racial equality. Formally billed as a "March for Jobs and Freedom," it embodied Randolph's passionate belief that racial discrimination was inextricably bound up with the broader issues of joblessness and the political impotence that accompanied economic deprivation. Those were hardly issues limited to black Americans, and in fact the march attracted supporters who had been engaged in a vast array of social justice efforts.

When Walter Reuther, the president of the United Automobile Workers, addressed the crowd, he pointedly referred to the phenomenal increase in production and employment that had resulted from World War II, which had ended just eighteen years earlier. "If we can have full employment and full production for the negative ends of war," he said, "then why can't we have a job for every American in the pursuit of peace?"

A twenty-year-old college student named Joseph Stiglitz, the future Nobel laureate, was among the vast throngs at the march. Stiglitz had originally planned to be a theoretical physicist. But he was unable to ignore the pain and suffering caused by joblessness, racial discrimination, and the widespread unfairness in the ways that the nation's wealth and income were distributed. Those issues pushed him into the study of economics. "I wanted to contribute in a way that would somehow alleviate the suffering," he told me. "It was a very hopeful time. I'd have to say that I never thought the problems would persist to the degree that they have."

The odds against a new citizens' movement emerging and ultimately changing America's cultural and economic landscape are no more unrealistic than the original odds against the civil rights movement or the women's movement or the labor movement of old. None of those movements were taken seriously in the beginning. And yet they endured and ultimately prevailed. If our nation is to be changed for the better, ordinary citizens will have to intervene aggressively in their own fate. The tremendous power in the hands of the moneyed interests will not be relinquished voluntarily.

ACKNOWLEDGMENTS

This book would never have happened if not for Phyllis Grann, the legendary publisher and editor who conceived of the project and saw it through from beginning to end. I will be forever grateful. Kathy Robbins, my agent (I've called her K-Rob for so long that her real name sounds strange to me), provided a foundation of support, sharply intelligent advice, and encouragement that proved absolutely essential. A fierce advocate but also a wise and upbeat sounding board, she became a true friend. And the professional staff at Doubleday was unfailingly first-rate as they guided the book to publication. I'd like especially to thank Bill Thomas, Kris Puopolo, Suzanne Herz, John Pitts, and Todd Doughty.

I'd also like to thank three former assistants of mine at *The New York Times* whose help was invaluable. All have flourished professionally in their own right: J. Courtney Sullivan, Alisha Gorder, and Johanna Jainchill. They were crackerjack smart and I miss the daily give and take, the wisecracks, and the laughter of the time we worked together.

My colleagues at Demos, an organization that is doing extremely important work on the progressive issues so close to my heart, have been unstinting in their willingness to help in whatever ways I've asked. Their research and rigorous policy analyses have helped shape my thinking in any number of ways. I would especially like to thank Miles Rapoport, Demos's former president, who is now the president of Common Cause; Heather McGhee, the current president; Tamara Draut, the vice president of policy and research; and Rich Benjamin, the director of the Fellows Program.

And, finally, a very special thanks to Bill Moyers, a good friend who offered crucial intellectual and practical support with a warmth and quiet smile that belied his legendary status as a giant of American journalism and one of the most important thinkers of our era.

NOTES

Author's Note

2   By 2012 the net worth: Jesse Bricker, Arthur B. Kennickell, Kevin B. Moore, and John Sabelhaus, "Changes in U.S. Family Finances from 2007 to 2010: Evidence from the Survey of Consumer Finances," *Federal Reserve Bulletin* 98, no. 2 (2012), http://www.federalreserve.gov/Pubs/Bulletin/2012/PDF/scf12.pdf.

3   The head of Goldman Sachs: Susanne Craig, "Goldman Sachs Gives Blankfein a Big Raise," *DealBook* (blog), *New York Times,* Jan. 28, 2011, http://dealbook.nytimes.com/2011/01/28/blankfein-gets-13-2-million-for-2010/?_php=true&_type=blogs&_r=0.

3   "I pray to God": Bernie Sanders, in discussion with the author.

4   "the high noon of American capitalism": Nelson Lichtenstein, *Walter Reuther: The Most Dangerous Man in Detroit* (New York: Basic Books, 1995), 396.

4   "steadily increasing affluence": Doris Kearns Goodwin, *Lyndon Johnson and the American Dream* (New York: Harper & Row, 1976), 211.

4   "There's plenty of work": The Temptations, "Since I Lost My Baby," by Smokey Robinson and Pete Moore, in *The Temptin' Temptations,* Gordy, 1965, album.

1. Falling Apart

9   "I wasn't in any hurry": Mercedes Gorden Rudh, in interviews with the author.

16   "She was so upset": Paula Coulter, in interviews with the author.

17   "was a man-made debacle": Douglas Brinkley, *The Great Deluge: Hurricane Katrina, New Orleans, and the Mississippi Gulf Coast* (New York: HarperCollins, 2006), 426.

17   An estimated ten thousand people: American Society of Civil Engineers,

"2013 Report Card for America's Infrastructure: Roads," http://www
.infrastructurereportcard.org/a/#p/roads/conditions-and-capacity.

17   "I was with a colleague": Peter Kim, in discussion with the author.

18   "It's just hard to imagine": Ed Rendell, in discussion with the author.

18   On a quiet Thursday evening: Adam Nagourney and Malia Wollan, "Inquiry Sifting Cause of Blast in the Bay Area," *New York Times*, Sept. 10, 2010.

18   An enormous fireball: Marisa Lagos, Kevin Fagan, Michael Cabanatuan, and Justin Berton, ". . . San Bruno Fire Levels Neighborhood—Gas Explosion," *San Francisco Chronicle*, Sept. 10, 2010, http://www.sfgate .com/bayarea/article/San-Bruno-fire-levels-neighborhood-gas -explosion-3175334.php#page-1.

18   Cars, trucks, and station wagons: Carolyn Lochhead, "Scrutiny Vowed for Safeguards; San Bruno Blast," *San Francisco Chronicle*, Sept. 29, 2010.

18   "I thought a 747 had landed on us": "San Bruno Fire Chief Puts Explosion Death Toll at 6," *L.A. Now* (blog), *Los Angeles Times,* Sept. 10, 2010, http://latimesblogs.latimes.com/lanow/2010/09/san-bruno-fire -chief-puts-explosion-death-toll-at-6.html.

18   The pipeline that erupted: John Hoeffel, Rich Connell, and Marc Lifsher, "The San Bruno Explosion: Older Tests Were Used on Gas Line," *Los Angeles Times*, Sept. 14, 2010, http://articles.latimes.com/2010/sep/14/ local/la-me-san-bruno-inspections-20100914.

18   Hundreds of natural gas pipelines: Andrew W. Lehren, "Gas Blasts Spur Questions on Oversight," *New York Times*, Sept. 24, 2010.

18   "You just heard this big bang": Katharine Q. Seelye, "Investigation Begins in Neighborhood Where Blast Killed 5," *New York Times*, Feb. 11, 2011, http://www.nytimes.com/2011/02/12/us/12allentown.html.

18   "We were like, 'There goes Bea's house' ": Ibid.

19   Bea was seventy-four-year-old: Ibid.

19   On a cold morning: Rocco Parascandola, Mark Morales, and Bill Hutchinson, "Eight Who Died in East Harlem Explosion Burned, Crushed to Death: Medical Examiner," *New York Daily News*, March 17, 2014.

19   An analysis of federal data: Charles Duhigg, "Saving U.S. Water and Sewer Systems Would Be Costly," *New York Times*, March 14, 2010.

19   The Gerald Desmond Bridge: Ronald D. White, "Plan to Replace Bridge at Port of Long Beach Progresses," *Los Angeles Times,* Feb. 5, 2010.

2. *Falling Apart II*

21   Most people viewing the ruins: Details on the I-35 bridge collapse came from multiple news sources including the *New York Times* and

voluminous coverage by the *Minneapolis StarTribune* (print, digital, and video); online accounts by survivors and their families; the report of the National Transportation Safety Board; extensive interviews with several survivors, especially Mercedes Gorden Rudh, Paula Coulter, and Garrett Ebling; Ebling's book, *Collapsed: A Survivor's Climb from the Wreckage of the Interstate 35W Bridge* (Minneapolis: Two Harbors Press, 2011); my own personal visits and on-site interviews in Minneapolis; and extensive interviews with infrastructure experts and public officials.

23 "While accepting federal funding": Barry B. LePatner, *Too Big to Fall: America's Failing Infrastructure and the Way Forward* (New York: Foster, 2010), 9.

24 "was a tentative plan": Ibid., 21–22; Barry B. LePatner, in discussion with the author, March 7, 2013.

24 The board isolated a single factor: National Transportation Safety Board, *Highway Accident Report: Collapse of the I-35W Highway Bridge, Minneapolis, Minnesota, August 1, 2007,* www.ntsb.gov (Nov. 2008).

24 "A bridge in America": Emily Kaiser, "Our Bridges: To Do Nothing Will Cost More," *Minneapolis StarTribune*, July 31, 2008.

25 On December 15, 1967: Chris LeRose, "The Collapse of the Silver Bridge," *West Virginia Historical Society Quarterly* 15, no. 4 (2001).

25 The Mianus River Bridge: Susan Chira, "Mianus Bridge Collapse Scrutinized at Hearings," *New York Times*, Sept. 23, 1983; Carl White, "The Mianus River Bridge Collapse," *Historically Speaking* (blog), March 24, 2011, http://www.greenwichlibrary.org/blog/historically_speaking/2011/03/the-mianus-river-bridge-collapse.html.

25 The Schoharie Creek Bridge: Robert O. Boorstin, "Bridge Collapses on the Thruway, Trapping Vehicles," *New York Times*, April 6, 1987; Tim O'Brien, "25 Years Ago, 'the Bridge Was Gone,' " timesunion.com, April 4, 2012; "A Timeline of the Events Surrounding the 1987 Thruway Bridge Collapse," *Amsterdam (N.Y.) Recorder*, April 5, 2012, http://www.recordernews.com/news/04052012_bridgetimeline.

26 "A West Virginia court": LePatner, *Too Big to Fall*, 6.

26 "The bridge is believed": Elizabeth Kolbert, "Construction Shortcuts Caused Fatal Bridge Collapse, Panel Says," *New York Times*, Dec. 4, 1987.

26 Today nearly a quarter: American Society of Civil Engineers, "2013 Report Card for America's Infrastructure: Bridges," http://www.infrastructurereportcard.org/a/#p/bridges/overview.

27 "According to the FHWA": National Transportation Safety Board, *Highway Accident Report: Collapse of the I-35W Highway Bridge, Minneapolis, Minnesota, August 1, 2007,* 48.

28   "I think they are": Randi Kaye and Katherine Wojtecki, "Nation's Bridges, Roads, Still 'Structurally Deficient,'" CNN.com, Aug. 1, 2008, http://www.cnn.com/2008/US/08/01/kaye.crumbling.infrastructure/index.html?iref=nextin.

28   Most were expected to last: American Association of State Highway and Transportation Officials, *Bridging the Gap: Restoring and Rebuilding the Nation's Bridges* (July 2008), 2.

29   "We never seem to learn": Samuel I. Schwartz, in discussion with the author, Nov. 20, 2013.

29   "The health of our nation's bridges": American Society of Civil Engineers, "2013 Report Card for America's Infrastructure: Bridges," http://www.infrastructurereportcard.org/a/#p/bridges/conditions-and-capacity.

29   Badly congested roads: The information on America's dilapidated physical plant is taken from a myriad of sources, which are all cited in this Notes section.

30   "No one was killed": Dan McNichol, *The Roads That Built America: The Incredible Story of the U.S. Interstate System* (New York: Sterling, 2006), 85–93.

30   We've fallen so far: American Society of Civil Engineers, "2013 Report Card for America's Infrastructure: Bridges."

31   "somehow, as a nation, we've come": Stephen E. Flynn, in discussion with the author.

31   "At age eight": Stephen E. Flynn, at the Infrastructure: A Pathway to Prosperity conference, Iona College, Feb. 19, 2008.

32   "It is estimated that every $1 billion": Daniel Alpert, Robert Hockett, and Nouriel Roubini, "The Way Forward: Moving from the Post-bubble, Post-bust Economy to Renewed Growth and Competitiveness," New America Foundation (Oct. 2011), 16.

3. Jobs and the Middle Class

35   "My life was always about": Lamar Hayes, in discussion with the author.

38   According to official government: Catherine Rampell, "Getting Back to Even," *Economix* (blog), *New York Times*, Dec. 6, 2013, http://economix.blogs.nytimes.com/2013/12/06/getting-back-to-even/?_php=true&_type=blogs&_r=0.

38   "Today, the share of the nation's": Harold Meyerson, "The Forty-Year Slump," *American Prospect*, Oct. 2013, 24.

39   "Americans are awash": Jackson Lears, "The American Way of Debt," *New York Times*, June 11, 2006.

39   From 2000 to 2012: Janet Boguslaw, Hannah Thomas, Laura Sullivan, Tatjana Meschede, Sara Chaganti, and Thomas Shapiro, *Hard Choices: Navigating the Economic Shock of Unemployment*, Pew Charitable Trusts (2013), http://www.pewstates.org/research/reports/hard-choices-navigating -the-economic-shock-of-unemployment-85899465040.

40   A 2011 McKinsey & Company survey: James Manyika, Susan Lund, Byron Auguste, Lenny Mendonca, Tim Welsh, and Sreenivas Ramaswamy, *An Economy That Works: Job Creation and America's Future*, McKinsey Global Institute (2011), http://www.mckinsey.com/insights employment _and_growth/an_economy_that_works_for_us_job_creation.

40   In New York City in 2012: Patrick McGeehan, "Blacks Miss Out as Jobs Rebound in New York City," *New York Times*, June 20, 2012.

40   "In 1965, only one": Lawrence Summers, "Three Ways to Combat Rising Inequality," *Washington Post*, Nov. 20, 2011.

40   An analysis by the Pew: Pew Research Center, *The Lost Decade of the Middle Class: Fewer, Poorer, Gloomier* (2012), http://www.pewsocialtrends .org/files/2012/08/pew-social-trends-lost-decade-of-the-middle-class .pdf.

41   "The notion that we": Rebecca Trounson, "Eroding Middle Class Falls to 51%, Survey Finds," *Los Angeles Times*, Aug. 23, 2012.

41   "Sometimes people will come": Frank Bass and Elise Young, "NJ's Richest County Leads Rise in Food Stamp Recipients," *Bloomberg News*, Dec. 15, 2011, http://www.bloomberg.com/news/2011-12-15/new -jersey-s-wealthiest-county-leads-rise-in-residents-using-food-stamps .html.

41   "Definitely yes," he said: Mark Swann (executive director, Preble Street social service agency), in discussion with the author, Feb. 2014.

42   Fifty-eight percent of Roswell: Author interviews in Roswell of discussion group participants.

42   Social service agencies: City of Roswell Mayor's Office.

43   "We were sort of a solid": Jere Wood, in discussion with the author, Feb. 2012.

44   Soon after President Obama: Christina Romer and Jared Bernstein, *The Job Impact of the American Recovery and Reinvestment Plan* (Jan. 9, 2009), http://www.thompson.com/images/thompson/nclb/ openresources/obamaeconplanjan9.pdf.

44   "The earnings of the great": Robert Reich, "Why the Economy Can't Get Out of First Gear," RobertReich.org, June 12, 2012, http://robertreich .org/post/24974761785.

45   "I rigged up a generator": Richard and Susan Crane, in discussion with the author.

45 "We were up against it": Rahn Harper, in discussion with the author.

46 "Those jobs aren't coming": Charles Duhigg and Keith Bradsher, "The iEconomy, Part 1: An Empire Built Abroad," *New York Times*, Jan. 21, 2012.

46 Three years into the recovery: Sudeep Reddy, "Millions of Long-Term Unemployed Risk Losing Benefits in 2013," *Real Time Economics* (blog), *Wall Street Journal*, Dec. 7, 2012, http://blogs.wsj.com/economics/2012/12/07/millions-of-long-term-unemployed-risk-losing-benefits-in-2013/.

46 "I'll tell you the truth": Matt Diersen, in discussion with the author.

47 According to the federal government: Cheryl K. Chumley, "Cheaper Labor: 77 Percent of 2013 Jobs Were Part-Time Positions," *Washington Times*, Aug. 2, 2013.

48 "had been slower in the 1980s": Richard Parker, *John Kenneth Galbraith: His Life, His Politics, His Economics* (New York: Farrar, Straus and Giroux, 2005), 592.

48 "From Franklin Roosevelt's presidency": Ibid.

49 "The net job growth": Ibid.

49 Its retail stores at the time: David Segal, "The iEconomy, Part 4: Apple's Retail Army, Long on Loyalty but Short on Pay," *New York Times*, June 23, 2012.

50 "American business is about": Peter S. Goodman, "Despite Signs of Recovery, Chronic Joblessness Rises," *New York Times*, Feb. 20, 2010.

50 "What these companies have": Bob Herbert, "In America; Firing Their Customers," *New York Times*, Dec. 29, 1995.

51 "counted at least 30 million": Louis Uchitelle, *The Disposable American: Layoffs and Their Consequences* (New York: Vintage Books, 2007), 5.

51 Welch sacked more than: Steven Greenhouse, *The Big Squeeze: Tough Times for the American Worker* (New York: Anchor Books, 2009), 84.

52 "A staggering number of the unemployed": Carl E. Van Horn, *Working Scared (or Not at All): The Lost Decade, Great Recession, and Restoring the Shattered American Dream* (Lanham, Md.: Rowman & Littlefield, 2013), 72.

52 "Being unemployed is frustrating": Ibid., 71, 74.

52 "It's heartbreaking," said Nadya: Nadya Fouad, in discussion with the author, July 2013.

52 "It's over," he told me: Discussion with the author. Interviewee asked to remain anonymous.

53 "You're in a high state": Russ Meyer, in discussion with the author.

53 "It's a crucial source": David Blustein, in discussion with the author, July 2013.

54 A study at the University of California: Michael Luo, "Job Woes Exacting a Toll on Family Life," *New York Times*, Nov. 12, 2009.

54   "A range of studies": Peter Orszag, "OMB Director Focuses on 'Rescue, Recovery, and Reining in the Deficit' at NYU" (speech at New York University, Nov. 3, 2009), http://www.whitehouse.gov/omb/news_110309_nyu.

55   "Our estimates," von Wachter: Daniel Sullivan and Till von Wachter, "Job Displacement and Mortality: An Analysis Using Administrative Data," *Quarterly Journal of Economics* 124, no. 3 (2009): 1265–306.

55   "We knew that those men": Till von Wachter, in discussion with the author, Oct. 2011.

56   Rates were already rising: Tara Parker-Pope, "Suicide Rates Rise Sharply in U.S.," *New York Times*, May 2, 2013.

56   The British medical journal: Aaron Reeves, David Stuckler, Martin McKee, David Gunnell, Shu-Sen Chang, and Sanjay Basu, "Increase in State Suicide Rates in the USA During Economic Recession," *Lancet* 380, no. 9856 (2012).

56   "We prayed a lot": Geoff Wiggins, in discussion with the author.

57   "A lot of people are not": Jay Litton, in discussion with the author.

58   "I thought I would get": Steve Swindell, in discussions with the author.

58   Between 2007 and 2010: Bricker, Kennickell, Moore, and Sabelhaus, "Changes in U.S. Family Finances from 2007 to 2010."

60   "We realized after a while": Lynda and Steve Swindell, in discussions with the author.

62   "Fewer Americans now than at any": Paul Taylor, Rich Morin, D'Vera Cohn, Richard Fry, Rakesh Kochhar, and April Clark, *Inside the Middle Class: Bad Times Hit the Good Life*, Pew Research Center (2008), http://www.pewsocialtrends.org/files/2010/10/MC-Middle-class-report1.pdf.

62   "fallen backward in income": Pew Research Center, *The Lost Decade of the Middle Class*.

62   "the American dream may be": Jon Meacham, "Making of America: Keeping the Dream Alive," *Time*, June 21, 2012, http://content.time.com/time/specials/packages/article/0,28804,2117662_2117682_2117680,00.html.

63   "Step by step and debate": Jacob Hacker and Paul Pierson, *Winner-Take-All Politics: How Washington Made the Rich Richer—And Turned Its Back on the Middle Class* (New York: Simon & Schuster, 2010), 6.

65   "It didn't matter how bad": Guntars Lakis, in discussion with the author.

4. War and Its Aftermath

67   "Water consumption was a big problem": Dan Berschinski, in discussion with the author.

67   "It is serious": *State of the Union with John King,* CNN, Aug. 23, 2009.

72   The secretary of defense: John Esterbrook, "Rumsfeld: It Would Be a Short War," CBSnews.com, Nov. 15, 2002, http://www.cbsnews.com/news/rumsfeld-it-would-be-a-short-war/.

73   "The costs have been much higher": Linda J. Bilmes, in discussion with the author, Dec. 2010.

73   "more than half of the 1.56 million": Linda J. Bilmes, "The Financial Legacy of Iraq and Afghanistan: How Wartime Spending Decisions Will Constrain Future National Security Budgets," Faculty Research Working Paper Series, Harvard Kennedy School (2013).

73   "I have no memory": Luis Rosa-Valentin, in discussion with the author.

74   "By supporting and signing": Robert D. Hormats, *The Price of Liberty* (New York: Times Books, 2007), xix.

74   "If I left the woman": Goodwin, *Lyndon Johnson and the American Dream,* 251.

75   "Nothing is more important": James Surowiecki, "A Cut Too Far," *New Yorker,* April 21, 2003.

75   "I wasn't even sure it was a legitimate": Bob and Susan Berschinski, in discussion with the author.

5. Understating the Costs of War

83   "I remember at first I couldn't": Dan Berschinski, in discussions with the author.

84   "Everybody was taken aback": Tony Perry, "U.S. Troops in Afghanistan Suffer More Catastrophic Injuries," *Los Angeles Times,* April 6, 2011.

84   A special report prepared: *Dismounted Complex Blast Injury,* prepared by the Dismounted Complex Blast Injury Task Force for the army surgeon general (June 18, 2011), http://www.google.com/url?sa=t&rct=j&q=&esrc=s&source=web&cd=4&cad=rja&uact=8&ved=0CDgQFjAD&url=http%3A%2F%2Fwww.dtic.mil%2Fcgi-bin%2FGetTRDoc%3FAD%3DADA550676&ei=Fp0bU7bsIcO0rgHT-4CIAQ&usg=AFQjCNHC7Xe6MAThKXcvhyzpMAbqdYgvuQ&sig2=riTO1XZTARA9qAalfVhrkg.

84   By late 2010: David Brown, "Report Reveals Steep Increase in War Amputations Last Fall," *Washington Post,* March 9, 2011.

85   "The increased rate of double": *Dismounted Complex Blast Injury.*

85   "Six months after the blast": Jeremy Schwartz, "Catastrophic Amputations Rise in Afghanistan War's Final Years: Military Looks for Ways to Protect Troops from IEDs," statesman.com, Feb. 18, 2012,

http://www.statesman.com/news/news/special-reports/catastrophic
-amputations-rise-in-afghanistan-war-1/nRkbq/.

86 "Only a handful of prosthetists": Dan Berschinski, unpublished op-ed article shared with the author.

86 More than a hundred GIs: *Dismounted Complex Blast Injury.*

88 "The Iraq and Afghanistan conflicts": Linda J. Bilmes, "Testimony in Support of a National Veterans' Trust Fund," Veterans Affairs Committee, U.S. House of Representatives, Sept. 18, 2013; Linda J. Bilmes, and Joseph E. Stiglitz, Testimony before the House Committee on Veterans' Affairs, U.S. House of Representatives, Sept. 30, 2010.

89 James Hackemer would become: James Hackemer, interviews at Walter Reed Army Medical Center in Washington and various news accounts, including Ben Dobbin, "James Hackemer, Army Amputee Dies in Theme Park Accident," Associated Press/*Huffington Post*, July 9, 2011.

90 "It was the worst thing I ever saw": *Baghdad ER*, directed by Jon Alpert and Matthew O'Neill (New York Home Box Office, 2006), DVD.

91 I remember writing about Marla: Bob Herbert, "For Marla, No Sacrifice Too Great," *New York Times*, April 21, 2005.

91 "Even the dying is being outsourced": Rod Nordland, "Risks of Afghan War Shift from Soldiers to Contractors," *New York Times*, Feb. 11, 2012.

91 "One of the most remarkable aspects": John Tirman, *The Deaths of Others: The Fate of Civilians in America's Wars* (New York: Oxford University Press, 2011), 12.

92 "It hurt so bad I couldn't cry": Eugene Simpson Jr., in discussion with the author, Oct. 2004.

6. Poverty and Inequality

96 "I don't think I'm going to make it": Jessica Gallardo, in discussions with the author.

98 In the years since Bill Clinton: Unless otherwise noted, poverty statistics were taken from U.S. Census Bureau data.

99 "It is celebrated in speeches": Michael Harrington, *The Other America: Poverty in the United States* (New York: Touchstone, 1997), 1–2.

99 "Mike's book was a *cri de coeur*": Irving Howe, introduction to ibid., xiv.

99 "Indeed," he wrote: Ibid., xv.

100 "I have a job," he said: Anthony Fernandez, in discussion with the author, Dec. 2013.

101 "Often we have families with children": Father Glenn Chalmers, in discussion with the author, Dec. 2013.

102 "We can't help everyone": Susan St. Amour, in discussion with the author, Jan. 2014.

102 In New York, where nearly two million: Gail Quets, Astrid Spota, Triada Stampas, and Zemen Kidane, *Hunger's New Normal: Redefining Emergency in Post-recession New York City*, Food Bank for New York City (Oct. 30, 2013), http://help.foodbanknyc.org/site/DocServer/FINAL FINADRAFTHSNParticipantrptNoEmb.pdf; Theresa Agovino, "After Feds Cut Food Stamps, City Pantries Went Empty," *Crain's New York Business*, Jan. 23, 2014, http://www.crainsnewyork.com/article/20140122/NONPROFITS/140129951/after-feds-cut-food-stamps-city-pantries-went-empty.

102 "People said they felt desperate": Kim Severson and Winnie Hu, "Cut in Food Stamps Forces Hard Choices on Poor," *New York Times*, Nov. 8, 2013.

103 "When I came to New York City": Denis Hamill, "Fighting Hunger in a City of Glitz," *New York Daily News*, Nov. 28, 2013.

103 "I hear them in bed sometimes": *American Winter*, directed by Harry Gantz and Joe Gantz (View Film, 2013), DVD.

104 "Too poor to participate": Sasha Abramsky, *The American Way of Poverty: How the Other Half Still Lives* (New York: Nation Books, 2013), 4.

105 "We've abandoned these kids": Andrew Sum, in discussion with the author.

105 "I can't take it anymore": Angjell Brackins, in discussion with the author.

106 "Forty years ago a teenager": *Youth and Work: Restoring Teen and Young Adult Connections to Opportunity*, Annie E. Casey Foundation (2012), http://www.aecf.org/~/media/Pubs/Initiatives/KIDS%20COUNT/Y/youthandworkpolicyreport/kidscountyouthandwork.pdf.

106 "These young adults are the new face": Susan Saulny, "After Recession, More Young Adults Are Living on Street," *New York Times*, Dec. 18, 2012.

107 Five years after the end: Catherine Ruetschlin and Tamara Draut, *Stuck: Young America's Persistent Jobs Crisis*, Demos (2013), http://www.demos.org/sites/default/files/publications/Stuck(uploaded)_3.pdf.

107 "These aren't college labor": Andrew Sum, in discussion with the author.

108 "I've applied so often": Dean LeNoir, in discussion with the author.

108 "I was pretty idealistic": Bailey Jensen, in discussion with the author.

109 "It's been difficult," she told me: Liz Charpentier, in discussion with the author.

111 For a family of four: Laudan Aron, Wendy Jacobson, and Margery Austin Turner, *Addressing Deep and Persistent Poverty: A Framework for*

Philanthropic Planning and Investment, Urban Institute (2013), http://www.urban.org/UploadedPDF/412983-addressing-deep-poverty.pdf.

111   "These are folks who never": Mariana Chilton, in discussion with the author.

112   "to run uphill throughout": Sasha Abramsky, in discussion with the author.

112   "I wanted to see her": Anonymous, in discussion with the author.

113   With nearly half the city's: Sam Roberts, "City Report Shows More Were Near Poverty in 2011," *New York Times,* April 21, 2013.

113   The city's shelters: Ian Frazier, "Hidden City," *The New Yorker,* Oct. 28, 2013.

114   It was "commonplace": Margaret Sullivan, "Too Little for So Many, Even in the Times," *New York Times,* June 1, 2013.

114   "taken to living underground": Frazier, "Hidden City."

114   The fabulously wealthy Bloomberg: Tina A. Moore, "Mayor Bloomberg: Shelter Population Is Surging Because Even People Who Fly in Private Jets and Use Limos Are Entitled to Beds," *New York Daily News,* March 8, 2013.

114   "The income gap in Manhattan": Sam Roberts, "Income Data Shows Widening Gap in New York City's Richest and Poorest," *New York Times,* Sept. 20, 2012.

115   "The figures are so startling": Robert Reich, "Inequality for All," interview by Bill Moyers, *Moyers & Company,* Sept. 20, 2013, http://billmoyers.com/episode/full-show-inequality-for-all/.

116   The top *1* percent: Annie Lowrey, "The Rich Get Richer Through the Recovery," *New York Times,* Sept. 10, 2013.

116   "Imagine a giant vacuum": Andrew Hacker, "We're More Unequal Than You Think," *New York Review of Books,* Feb. 23, 2012, http://www.nybooks.com/articles/archives/2012/feb/23/were-more-unequal-you-think/.

116   The typical president: Jordan Weissmann, "CEOs Now Earn 273 Times the Average Worker's Pay—Should You Be Mad?," *The Atlantic,* June 2013.

117   The prevailing belief: Michael I. Norton and Dan Ariely, "Building a Better America—One Wealth Quintile at a Time," *Perspectives on Psychological Science* 6, no. 9 (2011): 9.

117   Thinking of a big number: Hacker and Pierson, *Winner-Take-All Politics,* 154.

117   Bloomberg, according to: "Forbes Announces Its 32nd Annual Forbes 400 Ranking of the Richest Americans," Forbes.com, Sept. 16, 2013, http://www.forbes.com/sites/forbespr/2013/09/16/forbes-announces-its-32nd-annual-forbes-400-ranking-of-the-richest-americans/.

118   These counselors, she said: Missy Sullivan, "The (Wealth) Doctor Is In," *Wall Street Journal*, Dec. 13, 2013.

119   "The lower people's income": Testimony of Steven Woolf, U.S. Senate Committee on Health, Education, Labor, and Pensions, Subcommittee on Primary Health and Aging, Nov. 20, 2013, http://www.help.senate .gov/imo/media/doc/Woolf.pdf.

119   "Where you stand in the social": Michael Marmot, *The Status Syndrome: How Social Standing Affects Our Health and Longevity* (New York: Henry Holt, 2004), 4.

119   "Instead of accepting each other": Richard Wilkinson and Kate Pickett, *The Spirit Level: Why Greater Equality Makes Societies Stronger* (New York: Bloomsbury Press, 2009), 43–44.

120   "In New Orleans, a person": Steven H. Woolf, Emily Zimmerman, and Sarah Simon, "The Inextricable Link Between Neighborhoods and Health," Virginia Commonwealth University, Center on Society and Health, Nov. 2013, http://www.societyhealth.vcu.edu/Landing .aspx?nav=312.

120   They noted that since 1980: Steven H. Woolf and Paula Braveman, "Where Health Disparities Begin: The Role of Social and Economic Determinants—and Why Current Policies May Make Matters Worse," *Health Affairs* 30, no. 10 (2011): 1852–59.

120   By 2013 it had slipped: OECD, *Health at a Glance 2013: OECD Indicators*, OECD Publishing (2013), http://dx.doi.org/10.1787/health_glance -2013-en.

121   "No one would argue": Joseph Stiglitz, in discussion with the author.

122   By 2013 student loan: Chris Denhart, "How the $1.2 Trillion College Debt Crisis Is Crippling Students, Parents, and the Economy," Forbes .com, Aug. 7, 2013, http://www.forbes.com/sites/specialfeatures/ 2013/08/07/how-the-college-debt-is-crippling-students-parents-and -the-economy/.

122   "The American dream": Joseph Stiglitz, in discussion with the author.

122   "The workload was too heavy": Jessica Gallardo, in discussion with the author.

122   "I met with him": Andy Martier, in discussion with the author.

7. The Public Schools

124   "You won't believe it": Jessie Ramey and Kathy Newman, in discussions with the author.

125   According to the Pennsylvania: Mary Niederberger, "Report Shows Sharp Cuts in Pennsylvania School Programs due to Funding Shortfalls," *Pittsburgh Post-Gazette*, June 5, 2013.

126 "The worst part was": David Mekeel, "Reading Teacher Layoffs Cut to the Quick," *Reading (Pa.) Eagle*, June 9, 2012.

128 "Just look at the increased": Jessie B. Ramey, "Cuts Have Consequences," *Yinzercation* (blog), Oct. 8, 2012, http://yinzercation.wordpress.com/ 2012/10/08/cuts-have-consequences/.

130 Nationwide, public schools: U.S. Bureau of Labor Statistics, Occupational Employment Statistics Surveys, 2010–2012.

131 "At least 23 states": Phil Oliff and Michael Leachman, "New School Year Brings Steep Cuts in State Funding for Schools," Center on Budget and Policy Priorities, last modified Oct. 7, 2011, http://www.cbpp .org/files/9-1-11sfp.pdf.

131 "It's like a long, slow bleed": Nicholas D. Kristof, "Our Broken Escalator," *New York Times*, July 15, 2011.

131 "A core American value": Laura D'Andrea Tyson, "Income Inequality and Educational Opportunity," *Economix* (blog), *New York Times*, Sept. 21, 2012.

133 "Sadly, this is no urban": Jessie B. Ramey, "Corbett Blames . . . Us," *Yinzercation* (blog), Feb. 15, 2012, http://yinzercation.wordpress .com/2012/02/15/corbett-blames-us/.

134 "Believe it or not": Jessie B. Ramey, "Arts Education an Operatic Tragedy," *Yinzercation* (blog), May 7, 2012, http://yinzercation.wordpress .com/2012/05/07/arts-education-an-operatic-tragedy/.

135 "The lifetime achievement award": Pamela Haag, "Let Them Eat Opera: Pennsylvania Governor Corbett Gets Honored for Supporting the Arts While Slashing the Arts," *Huffington Post*, May 10, 2012, http://www.huffingtonpost.com/pamela-haag-phd/let-them-eat -opera-pennsy_b_1506441.html.

137 "Yes, there is a crisis": Diane Ravitch, interview with the author.

140 "the gains we have made": Joel Klein, "The Failure of American Schools," *Atlantic*, June 2011, http://www.theatlantic.com/magazine/ archive/2011/06/the-failure-of-american-schools/308497/.

140 "When results from the 2010 tests": Sharon Otterman and Robert Gebeloff, "Triumph Fades on Racial Gap in City Schools," *New York Times*, Aug. 15, 2010.

142 "The scores tell us nothing": Diane Ravitch, "No Student Left Untested," *NYR Blog* (blog), *New York Review of Books*, Feb. 21, 2012, http://www .nybooks.com/blogs/nyrblog/2012/feb/21/no-student-left-untested/.

142 "The school has a sizable": Michael Winerip, "On Education; Superior School Fails a Crucial Federal Test," *New York Times*, Nov. 19, 2003.

142 "I eat, drink and sleep": Abby Goodnough, "No Child Left Behind; On the F List," *New York Times*, Nov. 10, 2002.

143   In Atlanta, two years: Michael J. Bowers, Robert E. Wilson, and Rich-
       ard L. Hyde, "Special Investigation into Test Tampering in Atlanta's
       School System," Office of the Governor, Special Investigators: State
       of Georgia, June 30, 2011, https://archive.org/stream/215252-special
       -investigation-into-test-tampering-in/215252-special-investigation
       -into-test-tampering-in_djvu.txt; Kim Severson, "Systematic Cheat-
       ing Is Found in Atlanta's School System," *New York Times*, July 5, 2011.

144   In 2011 more than 70 percent: Mark Hayward, "Official: Tests, Not
       Schools, Are Failing," *New Hampshire Union Leader*, April 3, 2012.

144   "This year," Winerip wrote: Michael Winerip, "In a Standardized Era,
       a Creative School Is Forced to Be More So," *New York Times*, Oct. 30,
       2011.

8. Poverty and Public Education

146   "Are you going to make": Deonne Arrington, in discussions with the
       author.

147   "We will sometimes talk": N. R. Kleinfield, "A System Divided: 'Why
       Don't We Have Any White Kids?,' " *New York Times*, May 11, 2012.

151   Despite what Duncan routinely: Joy Resmovits, "International
       Tests Show East Asian Students Outperform World as U.S. Holds
       Steady," *Huffington Post*, Dec. 11, 2012, http://www.huffingtonpost
       .com/2012/12/11/international-tests-show-_n_2273134.html.

151   "were poorly prepared to compete": Arne Duncan, "Secretary Arne
       Duncan's Remarks at OECD's Release of the Program for Inter-
       national Student Assessment (PISA) 2009 Results," ED.gov, U.S.
       Department of Education, Dec. 7, 2010, http://www.ed.gov/news/
       speeches/secretary-arne-duncans-remarks-oecds-release-program
       -international-student-assessment-.

151   "The past year was a sobering": Michelle Rhee, "Keep All the Top
       Teachers," *New York Times*, Jan. 22, 2011.

152   "The relative decline of American": Evan Thomas, "Why We Must
       Fire Bad Teachers," *Newsweek*, March 5, 2010.

152   From his lofty perch: Bill Gates, speech at the National Education Sum-
       mit on High Schools, Bill & Melinda Gates Foundation, Feb. 26, 2005,
       http://www.gatesfoundation.org/media-center/speeches/2005/02/
       bill-gates-2005-national-education-summit.

152   "Our schools should get five": This Bill Bennett quotation is widely
       accessible on a number of Web sites, including successstories.com,
       inspirationalstories.com, and brainyquote.com.

152   "The educational foundations": National Commission on Excellence
       in Education, *A Nation at Risk: The Imperative for Educational Reform*

(April 1983), http://datacenter.spps.org/uploads/SOTW_A_Nation _at_Risk_1983.pdf.

153   He demonstrated, in a devastating: Richard Rothstein, " 'A Nation at Risk' Twenty-Five Years Later," *Cato Unbound: A Journal of Debate*, April 7, 2008, http://www.cato-unbound.org/2008/04/07/richard -rothstein/nation-risk-twenty-five-years-later.

155   Among its findings: Martin Carnoy and Richard Rothstein, *What Do International Tests Really Show About U.S. Performance?* Economic Policy Institute (Jan. 28, 2013), 3–4.

156   Finland has a first-rate: Peter Adamson, *Child Well-Being in Rich Countries: A Comparative Overview*, UNICEF Office of Research, Innocenti Report Card 11 (2013), 7, http://www.unicef-irc.org/publications/ pdf/rc11_eng.pdf.

156   "From such tests": Carnoy and Rothstein, *What Do International Tests Really Show About U.S. Performance?*, 7.

157   Another former secretary of state: Julia Levy, *U.S. Education Reform and National Security: Independent Task Force Report No. 68*, Council on Foreign Relations (March 2012), 4, http://www.cfr.org/united-states/ uzsz-education-reform-national-security/p27618.

158   "Let's end the myth": Bill Gates, speech at the National Urban League, Bill & Melinda Gates Foundation, July 27, 2011, http://www .gatesfoundation.org/media-center/speeches/2011/07/bill-gates -national-urban-league.

158   "It's easy to blame external": Gary Fields, "D.C. Schools Chief Scores Gains, Ruffles Feathers," *Wall Street Journal*, Nov. 11, 2008.

159   In a *Frontline* documentary: "The Education of Michelle Rhee," *Frontline*, PBS, Jan. 8, 2013, correspondent John Merrow, producer Michael Joseloff.

161   "Twelve percent of sophomores": Bill Turque, "Rhee Assertive Right to the End," *Washington Post*, Oct. 29, 2010.

161   "One thing I never want": Anthony Cody, "Obama Blasts His Own Education Policies," *Education Week* (blog), March 29, 2011, http:// blogs.edweek.org/teachers/living-in-dialogue/2011/03/obamas _radical_critique_of_tes.html.

162   "Is President Obama aware": Ibid.

163   In a 2011 interview: Alix Spiegel, "Closing the Achievement Gap with Baby Talk," NPR, Jan. 10, 2011.

163   A 2011 article by researchers: Gary W. Evans, Jeanne Brooks-Gunn, and Pamela Kato Klebanov, "Stressing Out the Poor: Chronic Physiological Stress and the Income-Achievement Gap," *Community Investments* 23, no. 2 (2011): 22, 27.

163   "the group with the greater socioeconomic": Richard Rothstein,

"Whose Problem Is Poverty?," *Educational Leadership* 65, no. 7 (Economic Policy Institute, 2008): 8–13.

9. War's Madness Runs Deep

166   "You have got to see this": Dan Berschinski and his father, Bob Berschinski, in discussions with the author.

170   On the afternoon of November 2: Sources included original newspaper coverage, especially the *New York Times* and the *Washington Post*; Paul Hendrickson, *The Living and the Dead: Robert McNamara and Five Lives of a Lost War* (New York: Vintage Books, 1996); Robert S. McNamara, *In Retrospect: The Tragedy and Lessons of Vietnam*, with Brian VanDeMark (New York: Vintage Books, 1996).

172   "an outcry against the killing": McNamara, *In Retrospect*, 216.

172   "When we marched into": Philip Caputo, *A Rumor of War* (New York: Henry Holt, 1977), xiv.

172   "Time and again, members": Andrew J. Bacevich, introduction to *The Long War: A New History of U.S. National Security Policy Since World War II*, ed. Andrew J. Bacevich (New York: Columbia University Press, 2007), xiii.

173   "The truth," he said: McNamara, *In Retrospect*, 26.

173   "News stories were full of predictions": James T. Patterson, *Grand Expectations: The United States, 1945–1974* (New York: Oxford University Press, 1996), 494.

174   "one of the most disastrous military": Ibid., 492.

174   "I've got two problems": David Halberstam, *The Best and the Brightest* (New York: Modern Library, 2001), 86.

175   "I will not be the first": Patterson, *Grand Expectations*, 750.

175   "Fuck Saddam," he said: Gary Kamiya, "The Road to Hell," *Salon*, Oct. 7, 2005, http://www.salon.com/2005/10/07/packer_3/.

176   "That," he would tell me: Matthew Hoh, in discussion with the author.

180   And he joined with: *Restrepo*, directed by Sebastian Junger and Tim Hetherington (Outpost Films in association with National Geographic, 2010), DVD.

181   "Most Korengalis have never": Sebastian Junger, *War* (New York: Twelve, 2010), 47.

182   "You could see it in his face": *Restrepo*.

182   "If you got sick": Junger, *War*, 60.

183   "In 2010, a new set of commanders": Greg Jaffe, "U.S. Retreat from Afghan Valley Marks Recognition of Blunder," *Washington Post*, April 15, 2010.

185 "We took his letter very seriously": Karen DeYoung, "U.S. Official Resigns over Afghan War," *Washington Post*, Oct. 27, 2009.

185 "the conflict between the good": Halberstam, *The Best and the Brightest*, 250.

185 "The autumn of 2009": Jonathan Alter, *The Promise: President Obama, Year One* (New York: Simon & Schuster, 2010), 363.

185 "This is not a war of choice": Barack Obama, "Remarks by the President at the Veterans of Foreign Wars Convention," White House: Office of the Press Secretary, Aug. 17, 2009, http://www.whitehouse .gov/the_press_office/Remarks-by-the-President-at-the-Veterans-of -Foreign-Wars-convention.

186 "Those who attacked America": Ibid.

10. Hurricane Sandy and Other Disasters

188 "I don't fit into": Mercedes Gorden Rudh, and her husband, Jake Rudh, in discussion with the author.

192 "It shouldn't take a tragedy": Dirk Jonson, "A New Bridge Helps a City Heal Some Old Wounds," *New York Times*, Sept. 17, 2008.

192 The city's levees: Mark Schleifstein, "Upgraded Metro New Orleans Levees Will Greatly Reduce Flooding, Even in 500-Year Storms," *Times-Picayune*, Aug. 16, 2013, http://www.nola.com/hurricane/index .ssf/2013/08/upgrated_metro_new_orleans_lev.html.

192 "the best reactors in the world": "Investing in America's Infrastructure: From Bridges to Broadband," Brookings Institution, July 25, 2008, http://www.brookings.edu/~/media/events/2008/7/25%20infra structure/0725_infrastructure_transcript.pdf.

192 "It was a little bit scary": Rico and Frankie Blancaflor, in discussions with the author.

193 "We could be fishing": James Barron, "Storm Barrels Through Region, Leaving Destructive Path," *New York Times*, Oct. 29, 2012.

194 When the lights went out: J. David Goodman and Colin Moynihan, "Patients Evacuated from City Medical Center After Power Failure," *New York Times*, Oct. 30, 2012.

194 The Breezy Point fires: N. R. Kleinfield, "Battered Seaside Haven Recalls Its Trial by Fire," *New York Times*, Dec. 24, 2012.

196 "In apartment 8F": Eric Lipton and Michael Moss, "Housing Agency's Flaws Revealed by Storm," *New York Times*, Dec. 9, 2012.

197 "Mr. Anderson," the *Times* wrote: Sheri Fink, "A Queens High Rise Where Fear, Death, and Myth Collided," *New York Times*, Dec. 19, 2012.

197 State officials in New York: *Shaping the Future of Energy: 2014 Draft, New*

York State Energy Plan, New York State Energy Planning Board (2014), 1:12, http://energyplan.ny.gov/Plans/2014.aspx.

198   "We are a major superpower": David Firestone and Richard Pérez-Peña, "The Blackout of 2003: The Context; Failure Reveals Creaky System, Experts Believe," *New York Times,* Aug. 15, 2003.

199   A joint study by the former: J. Bradford DeLong and Lawrence H. Summers, "Fiscal Policy in a Depressed Economy," Brookings Papers on Economic Activity, March 20, 2012, http://www.brookings.edu/~/media/Projects/BPEA/Spring%202012/2012a_DeLong.pdf.

200   She noted that the Congressional: Laura D'Andrea Tyson, "The Infrastructure Twofer: Jobs Now and Future Growth," *New York Times,* Oct. 21, 2011.

200   "These investment dollars": Josh Bivens, Ethan Pollack, and John Irons, *Transportation Investments and the Labor Market: How Many Jobs Could Be Generated and What Type?,* Economic Policy Institute, no. 252 (2009), 2.

201   A study sponsored by: Emily Gordon, Jeremy Hays, Ethan Pollack, Daniel Sanchez, and Jason Walsh, *Water Works: Rebuilding Infrastructure, Creating Jobs, Greening the Environment,* Green for All, (2011): 24, http://www.pacinst.org/wp-content/uploads/sites/21/2013/02/water_works3.pdf.

201   "We don't have a lot of time": Ed Rendell, in discussion with the author.

201   "Every year," according to: Gordon, et al., *Water Works,* 2.

202   On a frigid December morning: Dan Morse and Katherine Shaver, "Water Main Break Forces Dramatic Rescue of Nine," *Washington Post,* Dec. 24, 2008.

202   Just four months later: Ben Greene, "Baltimore Water Main Breaks, Floods Downtown," *Huffington Post,* April 28, 2009, http://www.huffingtonpost.com/2009/04/28/baltimore-water-main-brea_n_192393.html.

202   A water main break on a spring: *Akron Beacon Journal* staff report, "Boil Alert Issued After Water Main Break in Akron's West Hill Neighborhood Submerges Cars, Floods Basements, and Collapses Foundations," Ohio.com, April 11, 2013.

202   Two weeks earlier, Hoboken: "Hoboken Water Main Repairs Complete, Boil Water Advisory Lifted," *WABC Eyewitness News,* ABC, March 30, 2013, http://abclocal.go.com/wabc/story?section=news/local/new_jersey&id=9044035.

202   "A cold snap," he wrote: Duhigg, "Saving U.S. Water and Sewer Systems Would Be Costly."

202 Seven billion gallons: "ITT Value of Water Survey: Americans on the U.S. Water Crisis," itt.com, Oct. 27, 2010.

203 "Public works in American": Jeanne VanBriesen, "The Nation's Big Water Repair Bill: Build Smarter Systems," *Room for Debate* (blog), *New York Times*, April 11, 2010, http://roomfordebate.blogs.nytimes .com/2010/04/11/the-nations-big-water-repair-bill/.

203 Deepwater ports no longer: American Society of Civil Engineers, "2013 Report Card for America's Infrastructure," http://www.infra structurereportcard.org/a/#p/grade-sheet/gpa.

204 "They produced thousands": Robert D. Leighninger Jr., *Long-Range Public Investment: The Forgotten Legacy of the New Deal* (Columbia: University of South Carolina Press, 2007), xv.

205 "Of course we spent money": H. W. Brands, *Traitor to His Class: The Privileged Life and Radical Presidency of Franklin Delano Roosevelt* (New York: Anchor Books, 2009), 453.

205 "that building new highways": Earl Swift, *The Big Roads: The Untold Story of the Engineers, Visionaries, and Trailblazers Who Created the American Superhighways* (New York: Houghton Mifflin Harcourt, 2011), 158.

206 "At nearly forty-seven thousand": Ibid., 5.

11. Cashing In on Schools

208 "When I compare our high schools": Bill Gates, speech at the National Education Summit on High Schools.

208 He spent $2 billion: Valerie Strauss, "Bill Gates: 'It Would Be Great if Our Education Stuff Worked But . . . ,' " *The Answer Sheet* (blog), *Washington Post*, Sept. 27, 2013, http://www.washingtonpost.com/ blogs/answer-sheet/wp/2013/09/27/bill-gates-it-would-be-great-if -our-education-stuff-worked-but/.

208 "In the first four years": Bill Gates, speech at A Forum on Education in America, Bill & Melinda Gates Foundation, Nov. 11, 2008, http:// www.gatesfoundation.org/media-center/speeches/2008/11/bill -gates-forum-on-education-in-america.

209 "What happened to the missing": Diane Ravitch, *The Death and Life of the Great American School System: How Testing and Choice Are Undermining Education* (New York: Basic Books, 2010), 84.

209 "It has since shifted": "Bill Gates' School Crusade," *Bloomberg Businessweek*, July 15, 2010.

210 "Unfortunately," he said: Gates, speech at A Forum on Education in America.

210   The enormously successful: *Waiting for Superman*, directed by Davis
      Guggenheim (Participant Media, 2010), DVD.

210   President Obama praised: Barack Obama, "Presidential Proclama-
      tion—National Charter Schools Week, 2012," White House: Office
      of the Press Secretary, May 7, 2012, http://www.whitehouse.gov/the
      -press-office/2012/05/07/presidential-proclamation-national-charter
      -schools-week-2012.

210   After several years: Jim Horn, "Charter Schools Are No Better Than
      Public Schools, and Don't Expect Them to Change," *Common Dreams*,
      Jan. 31, 2013, https://www.commondreams.org/view/2013/01/31-9.

210   And the levels of racial: Julie F. Mead and Preston C. Green III, *Char-
      tering Equity: Using Charter School Legislation and Policy to Advance Equal
      Educational Opportunity*, National Education Policy Center, Feb. 2012,
      http://nepc.colorado.edu/publication/chartering-equity.

211   Lost in the mists: Diane Ravitch, *Reign of Error: The Hoax of the Priva-
      tization Movement and the Danger to America's Public Schools* (New York:
      Alfred A. Knopf, 2013), 12.

211   "Many studies show": Ibid., 247–48.

213   "The investors gathered": Stephanie Simon, "Private Firms Eyeing
      Profits from U.S. Public Schools," Reuters, Aug. 2, 2012, http://in
      .reuters.com/article/2012/08/02/usa-education-investment-idINL2
      E8J15FR20120802.

213   "You basically don't want": Peter S. Goodman, "Despite Signs of
      Recovery, Chronic Joblessness Rises," *New York Times*, Feb. 20, 2010.

214   "Kids have been shackled": Stephanie Saul, "Profits and Questions at
      Online Charter Schools," *New York Times*, Dec. 12, 2011.

214   When he founded K12: John Hechinger, "Education According to
      Mike Milken," *Bloomberg Businessweek*, June 2, 2011.

214   "When you hear the next": Jacques Steinberg, "Skeptic Now Sees the
      Virtue in Teaching Children Online," *New York Times*, Dec. 28, 2000.

214   In response to a caller: David D. Kirkpatrick and Marek Fuchs, "White
      House Criticizes Bennett for Remarks," *New York Times*, Sept. 30, 2005.

214   There were close to a quarter: "Online Public Schools Gain Popu-
      larity, but Quality Questions Persist," *PBS NewsHour*, PBS, Feb. 23,
      2014, http://www.pbs.org/newshour/bb/education-jan-june12-cyber
      schools_02-23/.

215   The National Education Policy Center: Gary Miron and Jessica L.
      Urschel, *Understanding and Improving Full-Time Virtual Schools: A Study
      of Student Characteristics, School Finance, and School Performance in Schools
      Operated by K12 Inc.*, National Education Policy Center (2012), http://
      nepc.colorado.edu/publication/understanding-improving-virtual.

216   As early as the fall of 2011: Saul, "Profits and Questions at Online Charter Schools."

216   "With virtual schools you get": Ronald Packard, in discussion with the author, May 21, 2012.

218   "Pearson pays six lobbyists": Abby Rapoport, "Education Inc.: How Private Companies Are Profiting from Texas Public Schools," *Texas Observer*, Sept. 6, 2011, http://www.texasobserver.org/the-pearson-graduate/.

218   Two weeks after hiring: Valerie Strauss, "Murdoch Buys Education Technology Company," *The Answer Sheet* (blog), *Washington Post*, Nov. 23, 2010, http://voices.washingtonpost.com/answer-sheet/murdoch-buys-education-technol.html.

219   "I want to be very wealthy": Jefferson Morley, "Dirty Money," *Miami New Times*, Feb. 27, 1991.

219   "With more than 10,000 kids": Stephanie Mencimer, "Jeb Bush's Cyber Attack on Public Schools," *Mother Jones*, Nov./Dec. 2011.

220   The Liberty City: Ted B. Kissell, "Schoolhouse Knocks: Although the Liberty City Charter School Helped Make Jeb Bush Governor, Four Years on It's Barely Passing," *Miami New Times*, Aug. 24, 2000.

220   "When the results from the 2010": Sharon Otterman and Robert Gebeloff, "Triumph Fades on Racial Gap in City Schools," *New York Times*, Aug. 15, 2010.

221   "appears to have taken": Elissa Gootman and Jennifer Medina, "Mayor Takes Idea of Education Outsider to New Level," *New York Times*, Nov. 10, 2010.

221   "I didn't know what": Sharon Otterman, "For Black, a Cold Call from the Mayor, and a Job Offer," *New York Times*, Nov. 12, 2010.

222   "What I ask for": Sharon Otterman, "Big School Problems Await New Chancellor," *New York Times*, Nov. 11, 2010.

222   "Could we just have some birth": Rachel Monahan, "Parents Not Laughing at Schools Chancellor Cathie Black's 'Birth Control' Overcrowding Joke," *New York Daily News*, Jan. 14, 2011.

222   According to the *Times*: Michael Barbaro, Sharon Otterman, and Javier C. Hernandez, "After 3 Months, Mayor Replaces Schools Leader," *New York Times*, April 7, 2011.

222   Bloomberg pulled the plug: Barbaro, Otterman, and Hernandez, "After 3 Months, Mayor Replaces Schools Leader."

223   She would tell reporters: Julie Gerstein, "Cathie Black Is Totally Cool with Losing Her Job," *New York*, April 7, 2011.

223   "The worst pictures": Patricia Sellers, "Cathie Black Vows to Come Back: 'I'm a Warrior,' " *Postcards* (blog), *Fortune*, April 8, 2011, http://

postcards.blogs.fortune.cnn.com/2011/04/08/cathie-black-vows-to
-come-back-im-a-warrior/.

223   "You can barely get your voice": Jessie Ramey, in discussion with the
      author, May 1, 2013.

224   Broad established a pair: Joanne Barkan, "Got Dough? How Billion-
      aires Rule Our Schools," *Dissent* (Winter 2011), http://www.dissent
      magazine.org/article/got-dough-how-billionaires-rule-our-schools.

225   The Broad graduate Jean-Claude: Alain Jehlen, "Boot Camp for Edu-
      cation CEO's," *AlterNet*, Nov. 1, 2012, http://www.alternet.org/boot
      -camp-education-ceos.

225   By 2013 the foundation: "Academy Overview," Broad Superinten-
      dents Academy, http://www.broadcenter.org/academy/about/program
      -overview.

225   "Six years after Mayor": Stephanie Banchero, "Daley School Plan
      Fails to Make Grade," *Chicago Tribune*, Jan. 17, 2010.

226   "Never in U.S. history": Diane Ravitch, "Chicago School Closings: The
      Largest in US History," dianeravitch.net (blog), May 23, 2013, http://
      dianeravitch.net/2013/05/23/chicago-school-closings-the-largest-in
      -us-history/.

226   "The people closing these schools": Rousemary Vega, in discussion
      with the author, Oct. 30, 2013.

227   Those groups, the ones: Stuart Luppescu, Elaine M. Allensworth,
      Paul Moore, Marisa de la Torre, and James Murphy, with Sanja Jag-
      esic, *Trends in Chicago's Schools Across Three Eras of Reform*, University of
      Chicago Consortium on School Research (2011), http://ccsr.uchicago
      .edu/publications/trends-chicagos-schools-across-three-eras-reform
      -summary-report.

12. Mistreating the Troops

229   "My walking is getting": Dan Berschinski, in discussions with the
      author.

231   On a Thursday afternoon: Michael D. Shear, "Heckled by an Activist,
      but Getting the Last Word," *New York Times*, May 23, 2013.

232   Most ordinary Americans: " 'No One Really Cares': US Deaths in Afghan-
      istan Hit 2,000 in 'Forgotten' War," *NBC News*, Aug. 22, 2012, http://
      worldnews.nbcnews.com/_news/2012/08/22/13408945-no-one-really
      -cares-us-deaths-in-afghanistan-hit-2000-in-forgotten-war?lite.

232   Less than 0.5 percent: Karl W. Eikenberry and David M. Kennedy,
      "Americans and Their Military, Drifting Apart," *New York Times*, May
      26, 2013.

233 "It's amazing how frequently": Craig Bryan, in discussion with the author, May 22, 2013.

233 Bryan and his colleagues: James Dao and Andrew W. Lehren, "Baffling Rise in Suicides Plagues the U.S. Military," *New York Times*, May 15, 2013.

233 "This issue, suicides": Leon Panetta, speech at the Department of Defense/Veterans Administration Suicide Prevention Conference, U.S. Department of Defense Press Operations, June 22, 2012, http://www.defense.gov/speeches/speech.aspx?speechid=1686.

234 "On the evening of June 22": Bob Herbert, "Death of a Marine," *New York Times*, March 19, 2007.

235 An army report: General Peter W. Chiarelli, *ARMY: Health Promotion, Risk Reduction, Suicide Prevention, Report 2010*, Department of Defense (2010): ii, http://csf2.army.mil/downloads/HP-RR-SPReport2010.pdf.

235 "For some," the report: Ibid., i.

236 About a half hour after: Jena McGregor, "Leadership Failures on Sexual Assault in the Military," *On Leadership* (blog), *Washington Post*, May 7, 2013, http://www.washingtonpost.com/blogs/on-leadership/wp/2013/05/07/leadership-failures-on-sexual-assault-in-the-military/.

236 Krusinski's arrest came: Ibid.

236 Around the same time that Krusinski: Thom Shanker, "West Point Sergeant Pleads Guilty to Videotaping Female Cadets," *New York Times*, March 6, 2014.

237 According to the Department of Defense: James Risen, "Military Has Not Solved Problem of Sexual Assault, Women Say," *New York Times*, Nov. 2, 2012.

237 "a despicable crime": Chuck Hagel, news transcript at "Department of Defense Press Briefing with Secretary Hagel and Maj. Gen. Patton on the Department of Defense Sexual Assault Prevention and Response Strategy from the Pentagon," U.S. Department of Defense Press Operations, May 7, 2013, http://www.defense.gov/transcripts/transcript.aspx?transcriptid=5233.

237 "Those who commit sexual": Barack Obama, speech at the U.S. Naval Academy commencement, White House: Office of the Press Secretary, May 24, 2013, http://www.whitehouse.gov/the-press-office/2013/05/24/remarks-president-united-states-naval-academy-commencement.

237 The 1991 convention: Norman Kempster, "What Really Happened at Tailhook Convention: Scandal: The Pentagon Report Graphically Describes How Fraternity-Style Hi-Jinks Turned into a Hall of Horrors," *Los Angeles Times*, April 24, 1993.

238 "I got off the elevator": *The Invisible War*, directed by Kirby Dick (Chain Camera Pictures, 2012), DVD.

239 She recalled being stunned: Jane Harman, "Rapists in the Ranks," *Los Angeles Times*, March 31, 2008.

239 "I am concerned about recent": Donald Rumsfeld, "Memorandum for the Under Secretary of Defense (Personnel and Readiness), Subject: Department of Defense Care for Victims of Sexual Assaults," Feb. 5, 2004.

239 Seven years later more than: Ashley Parker, "Lawsuit Says the Military Is Rife with Sexual Abuse," *New York Times*, Feb. 16, 2011.

240 A judge dismissed the suit: Patricia Kime, "Troops' Sexual Assault Lawsuit Dismissed," *Army Times*, Dec. 13, 2011, http://www.armytimes.com/article/20111213/NEWS/112130326/Troops-sexual-assault-lawsuit-dismissed.

240 "What have the wars": *The Costs of War Since 2001: Iraq, Afghanistan, and Pakistan*, Watson Institute for International Studies, Brown University (2013), 3, http://costsofwar.org/sites/default/files/The%20Costs%20of%20War%20Since%202001%20Executive%20Summary%203.13.pdf.

240 The report estimated, conservatively: Ibid., 4.

241 A 2011 study of three hundred: "The Silent Illness Stalking Afghanistan," Tearfund.org, Nov. 23, 2011, http://www.tearfund.org/en/features/the_silent_illness_stalking_afghanistan/?d=1%3Fd%3D1%3Fd%3Fd%3Fd%3D1%3Fd%3D1%3Fd%3Fd.

241 The result of so much killing: Terry J. Allen, "Collateral Insanity in Afghanistan," *In These Times*, April 17, 2012, http://inthesetimes.com/article/13008/collateral_insanity_in_afghanistan.

242 In 1996, Lesley Stahl: "Punishing Saddam," *60 Minutes*, CBS, May 12, 1996.

242 His reply was blunt: Elisabeth Bumiller, "West Point Is Divided on a War Doctrine's Fate," *New York Times*, May 27, 2012.

Epilogue: Looking Ahead

246 "By the fourth day": Patterson, *Grand Expectations*, 431.

246 "The first sit-in": *Eyes on the Prize: America's Civil Rights Years, 1954–1965*, Henry Hampton, executive producer (Blackside, PBS, 1987), DVD.

247 "It will be a hard": Ken Silverstein, "Labor's Last Stand," *Harper's Magazine*, July 2009.

248 Between 2010 and 2012: Alan Dunn, "Average America vs. the One Percent," *Forbes*, March 21, 2012, http://www.forbes.com/sites/moneywisewomen/2012/03/21/average-america-vs-the-one-percent/.

248   The bottom half: Linda Levine, *An Analysis of the Distribution of Wealth Across Households, 1989–2010*, Congressional Research Service (2012), 4, http://www.fas.org/sgp/crs/misc/RL33433.pdf.

250   "As private interests have come": David Callahan and J. Mijin Cha, *Stacked Deck: How the Dominance of Politics by the Affluent and Business Undermines Economic Mobility in America*, Demos (2013), 1–2, http://www.demos.org/sites/default/files/publications/Demos-Stacked-Deck.pdf.

250   "The central point that emerges": Martin Gilens and Benjamin I. Page, "Testing Theories of American Politics: Elites, Interest Groups, and Average Citizens," *Perspectives on Politics* (forthcoming): 3, http://www.princeton.edu/~mgilens/Gilens%20homepage%20materials/Gilens%20and%20Page/Gilens%20and%20Page%202014-Testing%20Theories%203-7-14.pdf.

250   "Our evidence indicates": Benjamin I. Page, Larry M. Bartels, and Jason Seawright, "Democracy and the Policy Preferences of Wealthy Americans," *Perspectives on Politics* 11, no. 1 (2013): 67, doi: 10.1017/S153759271200360X.

254   Their efforts resulted in a shift: Jessie Ramey, in discussion with the author.

255   Not surprisingly, nearly nine: Wendy Wang, *Public Says a Secure Job Is the Ticket to the Middle Class*, Pew Social & Demographic Trends, Aug. 31, 2012, http://www.pewsocialtrends.org/2012/08/31/public-says-a-secure-job-is-the-ticket-to-the-middle-class/.

255   "Democracy has disappeared": H. W. Brands, *Traitor to His Class: The Privileged Life and Radical Presidency of Franklin Delano Roosevelt* (New York: Anchor Books, 2009), 494.

256   "If we can have full": Lichtenstein, *Walter Reuther*, 386.

A Note About the Author

Bob Herbert was an opinion columnist for the *New York Times* from 1993 to 2011. Before that he was a national correspondent for NBC News and a reporter and columnist for the New York *Daily News*. He has won numerous awards, including the American Society of News Editors award for distinguished newspaper writing and the Ridenhour Courage Prize for the "fearless articulation of unpopular truths." Currently a distinguished senior fellow at Demos, a public policy think tank in New York City, he also hosts *Bob Herbert's OP-ED.TV*, a weekly interview program on Time Warner Cable, and is producing a documentary on the black middle class for PBS.